The Parkslopian

This book is dedicated to my Mother. Without her these memories wouldn't be.

Table of Contents

1 - Memories of Brooklyn

- Boom Box

- Summer of '77 (Black out & Son of Sam)

- Suicide Hill

- Train Pit

- The Statue of Liberty

- The Twin Towers

2 -**Best of Our Memory**

- Best Magazines

- Best Ice Cream Truck

- Best Pastries

- Best Sicilian Pizza

3 -**Things We Ate And Candy**

- Bungalow Bar

- Cereal Box

- Cracker Jacks

- Chocolate Snaps

- Gold Nugget and Gums

- Good Humor

- Deli Meat Cakes

- Old Candy and Food

4 -**Games We Played**

- Atari

- Flipping cards
- Games
- Handball
- Old Games
- Rides
- Roller Skate
- Scooters-Go-Carts
- Skelzies
- Skitching
- Football-Baseball
- Stick Ball
- Wiffle Ball
- Whirly Corns and Noses

5-Hanging Out On the Stoop

- Hanging Out On the Stoop

6-Holidays in the Slope

- Easter
- 4th of July
- Halloween
- Christmas on 5th Ave
- Childhood Holiday Memories

7-New Park Slope

- Park Slopian
- Ugly Buildings
- Who Saved Park Slope
- More About Park Slope

8 -Places We Ate

- Bickford's
- Bonanza
- Chinese Restaurants
- Chinese Takeout
- Delis
- Fran's Pizza
- Gleason's Deli
- Heritage Diner
- Herzog's Deli
- Ice Cream Stores
- Lewnes
- Pizza Places
- Restaurants
- Santos Deli
- White Eagle Deli
- Polios Deli

9 -Places We Went

- Avon
- Bars

- Farrell's
- Timboo's
- Clubs
- Park Carousel
- Pool Halls
- Sanders
- YMCA
- Horse Stables
- Kate Wollman Rink
- Prospect Park

10 -<u>Places of Interest</u>

- Prospect Park
- Armory
- Prospect Park Bandshell
- Holy Family Church
- Kentile
- Methodist Hospital
- Monument Hill
- Museum
- Old Building
- Pink House
- St .Thomas Aquinas Church
- YMCA
- Botanical Garden
- The Williamsburgh Clock
- Prominent Places

11 -Schools We Went To

- Graduation Books
- John Jay
- Lunch Boxes
- IS 88
- PS 39
- PS 107
- PS 124
- PS 51
- School Book Covers
- Schools We Went To
- Slam Books
- St. Saviour Elementary
- St. Thomas Aquinas
- Crossing Guards
- Yearbooks

12 -Stores We Remember

- 5 & Dime
- Brooklyn Aquarium
- Butcher Stores
- Candy Stores
- Chinese Laundry
- Dixon's Bike Shop
- Funeral Homes

- Germain's
- Hardware Stores
- Ice Cream Parlors
- John's Bargain Store
- Kresge's
- Laundromat
- McCrory's, Woolworth's and Downtown
- Pat Kenny's
- OTB
- Pops & Al's
- Sam's Work Clothes And Stagenhaven
- S & H Stamps
- Soundtrack
- Sepe's
- Tony's Record Store
- Stores
- Shoes
- Sneaker Circus
- Places Left

13 -Things We Did

- Arcades
- Birthday Parties
- Ice Skating
- Johnny Pump
- Roller Skate
- Tar Beach

- TV Shows
- Paddle Boats
- Block Parties
- Water Balloon Fights

14 -Things We Wore

- Dungarees
- Jeans
- Earth Shoes and Stuff
- Sneakers
- Jewelry

15 -Toys We Played With

- Cap Rockets
- Bikes
- Bubble Straws
- Click Clacks
- Etch-A-Sketch
- Paddleball
- Pet Rock
- Spaldeen
- Toys
- Yo Yo
- Tops

16 –<u>Transportation</u>

- 7th and 4th Ave. Trains
- Penny Gum Machine
- Bus B77 B69 B63 B67
- First Cars

This book is dedicated to the people who were raised in Park Slope, Brooklyn, New York during the 60s and 70s. Park Slope was also known as South Brooklyn. The book is filled with so many of the memories of the parents and kids who made the life we shared together as kids while growing up in Park Slope. We lived in a time that will never be repeated again.

There has been quite a bit of controversy as to who created, who saved, or who made Park Slope what it was. Well, since this is my book, I will give my opinion: Having grown up there and having hung out and worked on practically every block at one time or another for 30 years, I believe that the hippies did! Along with the parents and their kids who were living out their lives and growing up. The hippies moved in and started their art studios, remodeled their houses, and infused the neighborhood with art, music, and culture, and eventually it took over. That was the revitalization and what created the atmosphere of Park Slope. That's what I grew up around. That is what influenced me, as well as thousands of other kids growing up there who were like me.

Once Upon a Time, the yuppies (no disrespect intended), who had priced themselves out of Manhattan, drove across the Brooklyn Bridge and found this amazing neighborhood called Park Slope. It was filled with beautiful architecture, music, art, and a smorgasbord of so many cultures. Over the years, the yuppies started to flock there and little by little they priced us out of our own neighborhood. Not only this, but they also replaced the family and neighborhood community values that we had worked to build over the past thirty years. After they stripped our neighborhood values, they began to strip all the oak baseboard moldings, the old doorknobs, and the vintage doors. It broke my heart to get rid of the stuff. I would try to find someone to take it, but by then the last of my generation was already grown and in their 30s. Kids were already being kept inside more and more by progress, computers and play dates. Children couldn't play out on the street because the cops would get called.

This started happening more in the late 80s and probably peaked in the 2000s. That is progress, but no matter what time did, they can't buy the memories we had in creating that neighborhood; they will never have the memories that are in this book. This is the closest they will get to growing up in The Real Park Slope, Brooklyn. We created the aura. We created the art. We did it while living and working there for about 30 years--from the 50s through the 80s, we made it an artsy community. We made it cultured. We made it chic; we made Park Slope what it is today. The yuppies just made it more expensive to live there.

When I started this book, I was talking to myself. Then some friends dropped by and then more friends dropped by. We all began to reminisce about the good old times we had while growing up in Park Slope, Brooklyn. These are not only my memories, but they are also the memories of many of the friends and of people I have met. They are also the memories of my brothers and sisters and their friends, and the memories of our parents. The common ground is that we all shared these memories at the same time and the same place. These were our memories, but they could be your memories, too.

If you grew up in Park Slope during this time, you probably also remember and have shared many of the same memories with your families and friends because you were a part of Park Slope, too. You probably went to the same stores and attended the same schools that we did. Being an adventurous little boy at the time, I got around the Slope and beyond. In this book, I have tried to include many of the iconic stores and landmarks that we would all remember, so that no matter who you are or where you grew up in the Slope, you will be able to remember at least half of these places or have done half of the things that are contained in this book.

The book is not only about the people who grew up in Park Slope, but it is more about the memories we made together as Park Slopians to make that neighborhood what it is today.

In putting this book together, I have combined stories, memories, and conversations that will not only bring you back to this wonderful place in time when we grew up, but it will also bring you back to a time and place where all the iconic things we remember are no longer around because they have disappeared from the fabric of time and now only live in pictures, collectibles, and memories.

In making this book, I had to come up with a formula, so it would flow through the years as if you were growing up along with us because you were there - from the doctors who delivered us to our first cars! I also had to separate the book into categories that would fit best. I hope you like the job I did. It was great writing this. It rebuilt much of my memory on growing up in Park Slope, Brooklyn, NY, as I am sure it will yours. And it's not so much about the place we grew up, it's also about a time in history, so that anyone can read this book and just put their names and neighborhoods into the story and relive their childhoods as well. We were all the last of a generation that participated and remembers most of this great stuff - from street games, some great fads, TV shows, candies, commercials and lots more; it's just that this book took place while growing up in Park Slope, Brooklyn.

Thank You,

ROCKMAN

1 - Memories of Brooklyn

- Growing Up in Park Slope
- Drs. Who Delivered Us
- Family and Community
- Sayings As a Kid
- Commercial Songs
- Favorite Memories
- Funny Songs We Sang
- Dentist
- Park Slope Memories
- The Milkman
- Movies Filmed in Park Slope
- Old TV
- Old Phone Numbers
- Playground
- Scariest Moments in Brooklyn
- Seltzer Guy
- Street Talk
- Things Parents Say
- Yankees and Mets
- First Jobs
- Clothes Lines
- 8 Track
- The Mail
- Boom Box
- Summer of 77 (Blackout Son of Sam)

- Suicide Hill

- Train Pit

- The Statue of Liberty

- The Twin Towers

Growing up in Park Slope

No matter what happened in our lives, we probably wouldn't trade anything for the memories we had growing up in Park Slope. Basically, that is what life is about, those 18 years or so where you live and learn; wherever you may have grown up these are the best years of your lives, and I had more than my share of bad times in my life but the good ones overshadowed the bad. I wouldn't and couldn't change any of it, 'cause that made me the person I am today.

So if you could have the chance to go back or relive the best part of "Growing up in Park Slope," go back for just 5 minutes...what would it be?

I would need five years. That being said, maybe a five minute game of touch football with all the guys I grew up with.

On the block in summer with the jonney pump on, holding a can in front of the water coming out of the jonney pump to make a waterfall, taking turns on who's gonna hold the can next while everybody else enjoys the spray! And seeing everybody from the past who I miss so very much!!!

The day we did a car wash on Second Street. The johnny pump, tin can sprayer and bucket of soap I dragged out from my house. Afterward we all went to Pinos and bought baby pizzas and ices with the money and chowed down on park side. I'll never forget that day.

Too many for 5-min. But it will be this: summertime, schools out, beautiful sunny day, just hangin' on the stoop with friends, music playing on the radio, a cool drink, watchin' all the activity on the street. 5-minutes just to breathe & soak it all in.

A stick ball in the middle of the street with all my friends watching all the girls who thought I was a dorky teenager ignore me LOL

Not sure how old I'd want to be - 5 and in the sprinklers in the 3rd St Playground - or 10 and on the BIG swings in the 9th St Playground...

And straight out of the johnny pump if it was open...

Empty appliance boxes were the best toys ever!

Chipping in for a beverage (lol) and listening to the radio!

Sitting on the stoop in the summer with my friends, listening to the best music on our boom box

Sitting on a stoop with my girl at my side thinking what the future would bring. What a long strange trip it's been!

Stick ball in John Jay school yard,

Coco-ring-a-leave-o, hanging out with all the wonderful people from those days, PPW, and so many other things that were fun, innocent and for the most part drug-free. We didn't really need it; it was just a kinder, sweeter era. I wouldn't trade 5 minutes of it, or the incredible memories.

5 minutes...just wouldn't be enough time. Sitting back remembering all the good times, the fun.

The school yard and the dungeon, the boys, stick ball games, Prospect Park, first loves, my first kiss, all the street games we played, learning to ride my bike and falling on concrete 20 times.

The music of the 60s, hanging out on the stoop, the johnny pump, the ice cream man, tar beach, having ten mothers all watching out for you, and just growing up very lucky to have had all these wonderful memories.

5 minutes isn't enough time; give me an hour and I'd walk around and say hey to everyone. It would have to be in the summer to get the best out of my hour.

Football Prospect Park mud!

It would be the last time my five best buds and I were sitting on the hill next to paddle Boat Lake (now bark beach) just laughing and talkin' shit. Death, distance and time can't erase those memories.

OH!! Just to daydream for awhile!!

Sneaking into Greenwood Cemetery at night.

In five minutes: climb the fence and run thru the street alley, walk the ledge and into the schoolyard, then hit a roofer and run the bases, then slide down the dungeon steps on an old door, toss a soda bottle on the grates and finish it off with a leak on the wall...ahh, it would be great to be 12 again.

I would sit on the stoop with my friends or play stick ball in the school yard.

You just spent the 5 minutes...sitting back and reading the above and remembering all the good times...time goes too fast...enjoy every minute and remember years from now...I'll be asking again in another 30 years...lol

Drs. Who Delivered Us

Well, I know none of us were around in the beginning, but in the end we made a cameo appearance on the greatest show on Earth...LIFE

If you were born in Park Slope, name the Doctor who delivered you. For me, it was Dr. Weller on 9th Street.

Dr. Mayes delivered me @ Methodist on his birthday (we shared the day...)

Dr. Lamb. I don't remember him, but apparently he made house calls.

Then we had Dr. Howard on 3rd St. I remember being miserable in his waiting room.

Dr. Bauersachs; that's all I recall.

Dr. Leschner from 3rd Street between 7th and 8th.

Dr. Leschner was our family doctor for many years, on 3rd Street. He was a great man.

My family doctor was on 13th St. just off 5th Ave. His name was Dr. Gillen; he even made house calls...

Yes, Dr. Weller was my pediatrician; he was a really nice man then. He retired and Dr. Withers became my GP.

She was great, wrote me excuses for gym all through high school!!!

She was the best doctor I've ever had. I cried for days when she died. You never think of a doctor *dying*, you know?

I remember she was even shorter than I was (LMAO), chain-smoked throughout the entire exam, wore these probably 6" platforms (and she was STILL shorter than me LOL), and that the exam took like two hours. She really took the Hippocratic Oath seriously. Not many like her anymore; I'm sad to say.

How could you not love Dr. Withers? She smoked, talked about all of her patients, and any time you went there, you hung out with other friends who were waiting to see her. I loved her, too!

Doctor Zarou

Dr. Areda on 8th Ave & President delivered us, but Dr. Leschner on 3rd St. was our family doctor.

She was between 8th & PPW on the right-hand side of the street. You entered through the basement. She had a receptionist who was so sweet, but I don't remember her name at all.

Dr. Butler

I heard Dr. Butler's nickname was DROPSY!! LMAO!! ;-)

Are you insinuating that Dr. Butler dropped me on my head as a baby and that's why I am this whacked out, lmao!!!

As usual, BAD ASSUMPTION! I never said he dropped you on your head, but it must be coming back to you!! Flashback, LOL!! Hope you're having a great day!!

Dr. Cunningham used to come to our house when we were sick. He was on 3rd St. between 7th Ave. and 8th Ave. Doctors do not do house calls anymore; those were the days.

Don't remember his name, but all of us had the same doc at Methodist; even my son was born at Methodist. Half my mom's friends worked there; we knew almost everyone there; those were the days.

My little sister and my son were delivered by the *best:* Dr. Baeursachs...I may have botched the spelling. He was on Carroll, above 8th Ave.

Bauersachs, I heard he was a great Dr. A lil' strange though, cause he had a FALLOUT shelter built in their backyard in the late 50's!!

Yes, they were both very proud of their German heritage.

Dr. Greenberg 8th Ave. & 8th Street around the corner from Methodist.

I, too, went to Dr. Withers for awhile. Weird lady; she creeped me out.

Dr. Horowitz & Nurse Hathaway on Park Circle by the Sanders Theater.

Dr. Seuss.

I went 2 him every time I was sick.

One cannot forget Dr. Weller's nurse, Penny.

Not a clue. But our paediatrician for years was Dr. Degennaro (sp?). I believe his office was on 9th St. as well.

Dr. Fescanero Methodist, yeah, I totally butchered that spelling!

Vetell Dan Drs. Howard, Fine and Howard...woo woo woo!

I was born in Bellevue Hospital. What's y'alls excuse?

Dr. Vinny Boom Bots.

Kings County Hospital.

Does anyone remember Dr. Epps and his wife, who was his nurse? (9th Street between 8th and 9th Avenue)

Dr. Degennaro was also my pediatrician.

He was my doctor through my teens. Then, when he realized I was "uncomfortable" with him, he referred me to Dr. Withers on (IIRC) 3rd St. Tiny little woman, more makeup than the Lancome counter, chain-smoked throughout the entire exam. And that exam took a minimum of two hours because she wanted to know EVERYTHING that was going on in your life. She did my GP & GYN work. I cried for days when she died.

Dr. Moterhaythe--probably butchered his name--he was on 7th Ave.

Dr. Brevetti delivered me and also delivered my daughters...Dr. Henning was our family Doctor on 9th St.

Dr. Mayes delivered me @ Methodist on his birthday (we shared the day...)

Family and Community

The biggest thing missing today is what made growing up in Park Slope so great: that is community. Can't have community without family. When we grew up, we had cousins, brothers, sisters, aunts and uncles that weren't even related to us, that's how close we all were--and we all knew we were all in the same melting pot. That was a tight-knit community; everyone knew who you were and watched out for you like you were their own. Today, it's more about *what* you own.

The one thing that I miss the most about growing up in Park Slope was that whole sense of "community & family." They sure don't make places or towns like that anymore, that's for sure...Park Slope was a one-of-a-kind neighborhood.

It was like our own "Pleasantville"...yes, Park Slope was a very special place, and we all were raised with respect and decorum...I am very very proud of my roots...xoxo

Did you know there was always at least one mom on a stoop keeping an eye out for us? I didn't, until years later. They must have had some grapevine!

That is exactly what I was referring to...

The funny thing is that we really didn't appreciate those "nosy neighbors" until we got older and realized that it was a really good thing that they were there most of the time.

Where I live now, well--there is no "community." It's a collection of sub-divisions. I'm blessed with good neighbors, but that's about it. I miss that sense of community & family (and everything *else* about Park Slope).

I feel sad that my children (grown) never experienced the real warm and secure feeling we did--from our neighbors. My parents knew everyone; we went to Coney Island, Palisades Amusement Park, and even upstate in the summer--with our neighbors. That's unheard of today. I don't know why people today are so disinterested, so detached. But I do know how lucky my sister and I were to have been lucky enough to grow up in the real Park Slope, not the newly gentrified one that exists today.

Yes, Park Slope was certainly a one-of-a-kind place! For those of us who grew up in P.S. from the late 60's through the mid-80s, we grew up in a special time and an *extra* special place! I lived for almost 29 years and never really wanted to leave P.S. I feel a tremendous emotional tie to this area and always will! The changes over the last 20 years have deeply saddened me, but unfortunately we have to accept what we cannot change!

I have the greatest childhood memories of growing up in Park Slope. I wouldn't change a thing, if I ever had the chance. People were people; friends were friends...just nothing but great memories.

Where else did everyone else's parents have the right (and were expected) to parent every kid in the neighborhood, including giving them beatings if they were warranted—I wouldn't change a thing!

There was the fact that you could just go outside to play, and there was always someone to play with. Kids nowadays have to make play dates, or sign up for arranged sports.

What the heck is a play date? Kids today don't know how to have fun at all. With the gadgets they have, they never have to leave the house. When I was punished, I got time out. It was cruel. Kids today? Go to your room! Okay, Ma, I'll just play with my Wii, TV, laptop...I wish I was punished like the kids today.

Whenever someone on the block hit hard times, be it work-related, a family tragedy or whatever, there was always a hat passed around. Everyone cared and looked out for each other.

How many Italians had uncles we weren't even related to, LOL?

Sayings as a Kid

In all the times we spent hanging out on the streets and playing games, you know we had to come up with some rules and terms In order to establish some form of hierarchy—or to explain what we meant—whether it was just playing games, or on a personal level. Sometimes funny, sometimes stupid, and sometimes said in a hurtful way, here are some of the sayings we said as kids.

Hindu was a do-over when your ball hit a crack and veered off-course while playing handball, slap ball, kings, stoop ball, and booty's up/off the wall.

Flat- leava!!...Of course!!

Later-for-you...

OK, no one in NJ knows what an area-way is, but I can't think of any other word for it!

Ya gotta spell it w/da Brooklyn accent -- its arreyway, lol.

Johnny pump!

Chips on the ball...

STOOP!!

I know you are but what am I...usually followed by sticking out one's tongue, LMAO.

OK, wait a minute. I still say and do that. Never mind.

Seat reserved!

I offer you out...

It's quits...

Take a picture; it may last a little bit longer...

I think it's showing I was a bully, lol

BOGART!! (And not the actor, lol)

I call "second" or "next"--when playing a two-person game

Don't "lip it either!!"

Wanna get on the nice train?

SKITCHIN'!

I don't think LMAO was around back then (LOL, and that wasn't either) !!

The oldest or youngest goes first...I think it depended on what it was for?

Not It!

Let me get a walk.

YOU SUCK.

No skeeves!

That's freaking great--how could we forget that one?

Kiss it up to God.

Good. I was trying to figure out what you said when you dropped something you didn't want to "give-up."

I SKEEV YOU!! SKEEVOTTZ!! EW I SKEEV HIM OR HER!! LOVE this one obviously!!

Cop a mope.

What you're delivering, Doc.

Go see where ya gotta go!

My favorite, "He thinks who he is!"

How's this one -- does everyone remember GO F
YOURSELF—LOL.

A "killer": in handball, when the ball hit the wall & ground at
the same time. A move that can't be beat.

We loved "He thinks who he is in this hood!!" LOL

"Kiss my ass, in Macy's window!"

Good one! The ladies should know this.

HIDE...DOYLE'S HERE!!

Right back at ya, Joe!!

Don't get all "hot & bothered"

An oldie but a goodie: "Cheese it; it's the cops!"

Right on!

"What you gonna do about it?"

Hey, rabbit! The cops!

Peace out.

Catch ya later.

How about "chickie the cops," or "chickie the bulls."

Solid!!

I was just about to say "Do me a solid," and you beat me to it!

That shit don't flush around here!

You don't know Jack!

Whatever you say bounced off me and back on to you!!

You're chucked!!

Whatta mook!

ABC (gum--Already Been Chewed).

Havsies.

You snooze; you lose

Let's burn one.

I gotta split. No, seriously, I gotta split; I'll catch up with you guys later!

I'm "rappin' here!!"

This is an A B conversation...C your way out!!

That's great; I forgot about that one, too.

Make like a banana and split.

Or make like a tree and leave.

Let's go buy a couple of "loosies."

Imagine that, you could buy a single cigarette for 5 cents--now they cost $13 a pack--those were the days, my friend!!

Don't get your freaking panties in a bunch.

All right...All right...I'm coming

Slap me five!

Are you for real?

No moochin'

Go ape shit! (What the hell did that mean?) LOL.

Easy there; you're over stimulated!! LOL. ;-0

Fuggedaboutit!

Get a grip!

I'm on a roll, Joe; I'm on a roll, lol !!!

Ur draggin' in the dirt!

Get off my case!

YOU'RE A SPAZ!

SIT ON IT!

OUTTA SIGHT!

How could we forget..."Who died and left you boss?"

Later for you!

There are too many to like. I remember them all...so funny

And lastly: "DYN-O-MITE!"

F@#k you and the horse you rode in on...

Your mother's a freaking HOO'ER (a.k.a. whore--I know that's bad, but it was a saying back then)...

No problemo!

Let's play hooky...something I never did, lol.

How's it hanging?

SHEEEETTTT—I'm not the only one on a roll!

Man! Like, ya know (every two or three words, followed by "ya know!").

Got it, Bro!

Low 'n towards da left (response)!!

Ya gotta be kiddin' me!

Lemme get a zip (sip). Had a friend who would ask, then slug back into bottle!! SKEEVOTZ!! Keep it, I would say!! He'd innocently look like he didn't know what he did!! LMAO!!

"I'll be at the gym or da otha joint!!"

Hey Casey! Snooky is a French Hoo'aw!

I'm tawkin' ova here!

Gonna rumble t'night. Cruisin' for a brusin'!

"What a maroon!" or "What a snook."

Oh...fuggedaboutit. That was Bugs Bunny who said that.

YO! Yo, Yo, Yo!!

Give me some skins...

How about "Yeee Beard?" Short-lived expression that meant someone was lying to you. Or what they were talking about was BS.

Your mudda wears combat boots!

That and 50 cents will get you on the subway.

If I had a nickel for every time someone said that to me...

You're all that and a bag of chips!

For all my John Jay friends: WALK OUT!!

How many people in here were Indian givers? Now it's an insult to say it. How the world has changed.

Haven't heard that in a long time...

Not I, but I used that expression often back in the day.

There was a song called "Indian Giver" as well.

Dibs on the ball and bat was an insurance policy, so if anything happened to your bat and ball it was the responsibility of everyone playing. If you didn't say it prior to playing, you were shit out of luck.

I think it was chips on the ball.

How about if you were sitting on the stoop and had to get up, and you said "set it" so you would have your seat back?

Those are a dime a dozen!

How about being a flat leaver?

Haven't heard that one in a few decades!! LOL

I'm pretty sure I said it to a friend a couple of years ago just to see her reaction. We both about fell on the floor laughing. :)

Leavers are bucktoothed b*stards, but not as bad as being conceited! Or an Indian giver.

What a pissa!

"I got dibs!"

"Thumbs down" if you came out of the house with something you didn't want anyone mooching off.

Wooow, flat leaver, that's so great—haven't heard or used that term in a long time!

What about putting your thumb to your forehead and yellin' "FUDGIES!" when someone stepped in dog poop!

What about "make like a tree and leave" lol.

How about as soon as you light up a cigarette, someone yells "saves" and someone else yells "kills," lol.

No backsies!

Owe me a coke!!

Punch Car!!

How about when you'd see a "Lucky Strikes" cigarette pack, and you would give a punch and say lucky strike, you're out!!

Or if you stepped on a crack, you'd break your mother's back...lol

If you saw a VW Bug, you would punch your friend and say punch BUGGY...

How about Jumper, when you would hang out with different kids?

"I touched black...no take-backs."

I'm rubber and you're glue; anything you say bounces off me and sticks on you!

Aerie Way!!! That's a phrase you can only use in Brooklyn!! Nobody else would know what you're taking about.

Remember Dugout?!

Ya owe me a coke--punch someone when you both say the same thing at the same time.

"Landing" and "Stoop." Not many people outside Brooklyn would understand this, LOL.

Aerie Way, I haven't heard that word in years...lol!

Commercial Songs

The two things that we lived with constantly were TV and radio, and our lives were filled with the non-stop bombardment of jingles to get us to bother our parents to buy us this or to buy us that. Even though there are so many more radio and TV stations today, I think the advertisements were at their best then, because of the nature of the times--and most of all, the creativity of the advertisers who created them was at its peak--so what say you? Who can remember the old time JINGLES of our youth?

OK, folks. Who remembers Choo choo Charlie? Once upon a time there was an engineer. Choo choo Charlie was his name, we hear. He had an engine and he sure had fun. He used Good n' Plenty candy, to make his train run. Charlie says, "Love my Good n' Plenty," Charlie says, "Really rings a bell." Ding ding, Charlie says, "Love my Good n' Plenty; don't know any other candy that I love so well." Good n' Plenty, Good n' Plenty. Classic.

And by the way, how many licks DOES it take to get to the chocolaty center of a Tootsie Pop?

"One...two...three...(crack). Three." LOL.

"Melts in your mouth, not in your hands." M&M's!

Me and my RC, me and my RC, 'cause what's good enough for other folks ain't good enough for me and my RC.

That's why it's B - O - N - O - M - O Bonomo - oh oh oh it's Bonomo! (Turkish Taffy)

Plop...plop...fizz...fizz: oh, what a relief It is!

Or "That's speecy, spicy meatball!"

"I can't believe I ate the whole thing...You ate it, Ralph!"

Ring Ding, Ring Ding, wish I had a Ring Ding...

I like to teach the world to sing.

You're gonna pay for that one...it will be in my head for HOURS LOL.

What's the story Jerry...?

Ancient Chinese secret. huh?

CALGON: "Take me away!"

La Chow makes Chinese food.

Country Kitchen: real egg noodles, pure egg noodles...

You show your union card, and you're in!

Schaefer is the one beer to have when you're having more than one.

My beer is Rheingold the dry beer...look for Rheingold wherever (whenever?) you buy beer...

To a smoker, it's a Kent!

Make a ring, and then another ring, and then another ring, and then you got 3 rings Ballentine!

GI Joe...GI Joe...fighting man from head to toe!

It doesn't taste greasy like fried?! It's Shake n' Bake and I helped!

Irish Spring: manly, yes, but I like it, too!

The quicker picker-upper.

Don't cook tonight, call Chicken Delight!

Everyone knows it's Slinky, everyone knows it's Slinky, It's Slinky It's Slinky--I can't remember what comes next. It's Slinky, It's Slinky! I still can't remember the rest. Ah crap, I can't get this out of my head now. Friggin' Slinky.

Wonderful, magical toy!

Ring around the collar!

Dr. Pepper. Wouldn't you like to be a Pepper too?

Whipple! Please don't squeeze the Charmin.

"It's The Real Thing! COKE!"

You can take it out of the country, BUT you can't take the country out of Salem!"

Where's the beef?

Time to make the donuts.

Meow meow meow meow? Meow mix! Tastes so good, cats ask for it by name...

I like Devil Dogs...more...than...Marsha.

I can't tell you how many times I have "quoted" these two!

Rosie the plumber! Wasn't she so "hot?"

Double mint gum...Double pleasure...

I'll walk a mile for a Camel...

Here comes the king; here comes the big number one. Budweiser beer, the king is second to none. Almost hear the Clydesdale's in the background.

The Teaberry Shuffle - Teaberry gum!

Wasn't it Josephine the plumber?

She was "hot," too! LMAO

Buster Brown Shoes.

Not exactly a particular commercial, but remember Mason Reese?

Mikey, and Life Cereal? It's in the last shot of the film *Network*. Along with an airline commercial.

Did anyone do airline jingles yet?

"Hi, I'm Linda; come on and fly me...through the friendly skies." National Airlines.

Also "I can't believe I ate the whole thing"....Alka Seltzer

CRAAAAZZZYY EDDDYYY'S!!!! His prices are insaaannee!

Silly rabbit, Trix are for kids!

I want my Maypo!

Anticipation...and it's making me wait.

Two all beef patties, special sauce, lettuce, cheese, pickles, onions on a sesame seed bun.

My bologna has a first name, its O-S-C-A-R! My bologna has a second name, its M-A-Y-E-R! Oh, I love to eat it every day and if you ask me why I'll say...'cause Oscar Mayer has a way with B-O-L-O-G-N-A.

Everything's better with Blue Bonnet on it.

I have a metal Slinky, still. Found it thrown away. One man's garbage was this girl's treasure. The plastic ones are just not the same.

Great. Yeah, the plastic Slinky sucked.

Butter...Parkay....Butter...Parkay...

CERTS: gives you two mints in one!

Maxwell House coffee commercials with the percolator!

Good to the last drop...

Nestles makes the very best...chocolate.

Fine Corinthian leather. Chrysler Cordova.

Palmolive dish detergent xxx "You're soaking in it...In dish washing liquid?! Relax it's Palmolive!" lol

Faberge Organic Shampoo and conditioner with wheat germ oil and honey...She told two friends, and so on and so on and so on...

Herbal Essence.

I think it's going to be another Aviance day!

Kind of young, kind of now, Charlie!

Take it off! Take it all off! (Shaving cream commercial)

The UN-Cola.

I like (It was a lemon-lime soda).

It was the 'UN-Cola Nut'...

In that deep, deep voice. Cola Nut! The UN-Cola Nut. Hah hah hah.

"Dr Pepper...so misunderstood"

Who wears short-shorts? Nair, for short-shorts.

Ho Ho Ho...Green Giant.

Lucky Strike. Strikes back. And I'd rather fight than switch.

Come up to the Kool taste...

Our L'eggs fit your legs; they hug you; they hold you; they never let you go.

Leggo my Eggo!

"We will sell no wine - before its time."

How do you handle a Hungry Man? The man handler! (TV Dinners)

I am stuck on Band Aid, and Band Aid's stuck on me!

Takes a licking, keeps on ticking. Timex.

The whole lyric of Dr. Pepper was: "Drink Dr. Pepper, the joy of every boy and girl. It's the most original soft drink ever in the whole wide world!"

"More Park Sausages, Mom, please!"

It's Kenner; it's fun - Squawk!!

No Baloney!

Candy-coated popcorn, peanuts and a prize! That's what you get in Cracker Jack!

Hai Karate...be careful how you use it!

Tum Ta-Tum Tum...Tums!

Chock Full O'Nuts is the heavenly coffee, heavenly coffee, heavenly coffee! Chock Full O'Nuts is the heavenly coffee. Better coffee a millionaire's money can't buy.

I remember that steamy cup of Chock Full O'Nuts in Times Square. Also the Lucky Strike cig.

How 'bout CHIFFON MARGARINE: "It's not nice to fool mother nature...if you think its butter...but it's not...it's Chiffon!

My dog's better than your dog; my dog's better than yours; my dog's better 'cause he gets Ken-L-Ration...my dog's better than yours! :)

You put the lime in the coconut and drink 'em both up? 7-Up!

We all tried a Big Mac, right?

Very old Big Mac 70's commercial.

I believe it's from the 70s.

2 all beef patties, special sauce, lettuce, cheese, on a sesame seed bun. We used to have contests on who could say it fastest.

Oh: pickle, onions on a sesame seed bun.

Never had one. Ever. Seriously. LOL.

What goes in must come out. Last time I had this and large fries, the cardboard tasted better!

I never liked the Big Mac myself. Wendy's or White Castle was better.

The Whopper Jr. was my favorite.

Never had one of those, either. :)

Mickey Dee's French fries are still addictive...

Remember the BK on 10th St. and 5th?

BK, my hang out...remember the short-lived yumbo sandwich-- eggs and ham? I used to work there and eat more than I made in a week...they had to fire me>HA!

Favorite Memories

We all have a favorite memory at several parts of our lives; some are recurring, like Christmas, and some are a moment in time. What is your best memory of growing up in park Slope?

Mine is walking up to Prospect Park and feeling safe there.

Mine is every year on Easter Sunday, taking pictures at the Monument on 9th Street & PPW with my mom, brother and sisters.

Sitting on the stoop on 8th St. with all the relatives. Priceless memories.

Having your family all on the same block. And, yes, having Prospect Park as a backyard was great--and still is. I would love one more night on the stoop, especially getting thrown off...ha ha

The annual stick ball games.

Playing stick ball and hanging out on the stoops with no care in the world.

Playing stick ball against the other blocks. Biggest rivals for 5th St. were 8th St. and 6th St.

Hit one off the wall in P.S. 39, had to be six sewers.

I was once playing fast pitch softball in 51 Park. Saw some kid hit 3 hrs dead center out on to the street.

I also remember going to the park and to the Sanders Movie Theater.

8th St. Labor Day stick ball games, finally being able to actually play was a rite of passage.

To be honest, there are so, so many best memories, so here is mine...my all time favorite>>>>playing Little League baseball on a traveling team in 1979 at the age of 10, for the 72nd Pct cub division. Best of the best memory for me while growing up in Park Slope.

Football...whether it was Prospect Park...the library yard...or just the street.

Lookin' back, how in the world were we able to play tackle football in the library yard and softball in the dungeon? The fields were so small.

We weren't all that big ourselves!

The mud was the draw.

On 5th St. between 7th and 8th Ave's, everyone on our block was like your extended family. It was the very definition of the word "neighborhood." There was respect, compassion, and loyalty to your neighbors.

Too many to count, but my friends I had in Brooklyn are my best friends now.

When the ice cream truck came down the street! Or the "rides"--didn't matter that the Carvel was on 5th Ave.

Ok, I have the ultimate memory...the guy on the truck selling watermelon and yelling..."waaaattterrmeellllloooon!"

Oh yeah, I remember that--he was like come pick your watermelon!!!!!!! lol

Everyone knew everybody...I still have many good friends from 45 years ago...

I loved growing up there as a kid.

Hitching rides on the back of the 63 bus on 5th, or on a skateboard or bike. The good ole days. Dangerous, but good. LOL

There used to be a bar on the corner of 9st and 2nd Ave. It was called Peewee's Bar.

I remember 10th St. Park; there was actually sand in the sandbox; the bathrooms worked; the swings, slides, the handball courts. Those were the days.

Yes, I do, and 10th St. Park was a lot of fun.

The 10th St. Park? Was that the one below the train tracks? I remember a big "Kentile Floors" sign that used to flash on and off. I learned to ride a bike there.

Kentile was between 2nd and that bridge we had to cross. Remember; it was made of wood and I used to cross it with my mom, and I remember that pieces used to be missing. I don't miss that, lol!

And yes, it was below the train tracks.

Yes, the big Kentile sign. 10th Street Park. I remember my brother playing "stick ball" there, and yes, handball courts. What fun memories.

Is Kentile still there? Or at least the sign?

I remember that the 11th St. Park was where the huge piles of rock salt used to be stored to treat the roads in winter. We used to swing from pile to pile from a rope somebody tied onto the overhead rafters. Just like Tarzan!

Standing at the corner of 23rd Street and 7th Ave., having a clear view of The Statue of Liberty--it was amazing, especially on July 4th.

What about the Statue of Liberty on the corner of 15th & 5th Ave. also?

How about the concerts in Prospect Park?

Playing handball down 10th St. Park?

We used to hang out on 5th Ave. and 7th St. by the pool room.

Sitting on the stoop - playing games in the street - sports in the park absolute favorite - winters spent up in Prospect Park at nite.

Terrorizing Danny in his candy store (Danny's), at the corner of Garfield & 7th AVE!! HEEEEEY BOOOOYYYY!!! In the mid 70's thru early 80's!! LMAO!!

Just hitting the streets on summer mornings and not coming back home 'till dark, always finding someone to play with or some kind of nonsense to get up to, knowing everyone's business, everyone knowing yours. Lol about Danny, although he terrorized us sometimes too! "Hey, kid, you're taking too long; get out!"

Not just the concerts at 9th St. Bandshell, but the Philharmonic in the sheep meadow was cool too!!

A summer vacation...all the parents used to sit outside, and, of course, the later they stayed out, the later we got to stay out; tag, coco-livio, relay races every night, then the good humor truck...

Shame on you for aggravating Danny so much! Lol. Hope he's smiling in heaven reading about our memories of him.

Summertime - going back outside to play and hang out with my friends after dinner. Hanging out on the stoop listening to music on a Sanyo box radio.

Those hot summer nights playing in the johnny pump, and later on we'd go up to Pinos Pizzeria up on 7th Ave. and everyone put in for a pie and soda.

I remember there always being people out along 6th Ave. Everyone knew each other; even as a kid u felt safe being out late. You always knew there'd be someone in front of Louie's on 7th St., on 39's or the library steps, and in front of the deli on 10th St. Me and my friends were the last of the kids from 8th St. to actually hang out on our corner.

Knowing everyone on the block!

Hanging out with all my friends on 3rd Street. We were quite a crew.

I loved the sand park playground at Prospect Park. Is it still there?

You didn't have to spend any money—or maybe a few dollars—to play a street game!

Just being outside, playing tag, freeze tag, red light/green light, hot peas & butter, skellie, handball, stick ball, punch ball, kickball!! And there was always something to do!!

Friends and neighbors were family.

Too many good times. Stick ball, stoop ball on the block. 4th of July fireworks - never had to go farther than the stoop.

Baseball, football in Prospect Park. Sprinklers and Sunset Park in summer. Sledding down Monument Hill in the winter.

The library (I was always a reader); both the 9th St. and 8th Ave. branches as well as the Grand Army Plaza.

It would have to be riding a snow sled down Monument Hill in Prospect Park. It was cold and wet, but we had a blast.

<u>Funny Songs We Sang</u>

Well, before we all grew into teens and got hooked on the radio, we sang songs together and made up a few ourselves: jumping rope, or clapping hands together (guys, I never did that) but these songs were like folklore handed down to us from the previous generation.

Miss Lucy had a baby...

Lincoln, Lincoln, I've been thinking. What the hell have you been drinking? Looks like water, tastes like wine, oh my God its turpentine.

Marijuana, Marijuana...LSD, LSD...Rockefeller makes it...Mayor Lindsay takes it.

Put five fingers in your mouth and say: "My father works in the shipyards cleaning up all the ashes."

Screw you, and the horse you rode in on...

Red Light, Green Light one, two, three!!

My mother and your mother were out hanging clothes; my mother punched your mother right in the nose! What color blood came out?

My name is Anna and my husband's name is Adam; we come from Alabama just to sell you apples. Haven't heard that one in a few decades!! LOL

Barnacle Bill the Sailor? No, I won't go in-depth... 8>)

What was the rest of Miss Lucy, was it "She named him Tiny Tim?" Forgot what came after that. Boggles my mind how this stuff just comes back to you.

Miss Lucy had a baby. She named him Tiny Tim. She put him in the bathtub to see if he could swim. There are other variations that I have to remember.

Something, something. Miss Lucy called the doctor. Miss Lucy called the nurse. Miss Lucy called the lady with the alligator purse.

Lol! Great memory!

We had those clapping games, and don't forget jumping rope and all the songs that went along with that. Boom, boom, boom go the marches calling _____ to my door. _____'s the one who's gonna have fun so we don't need _____ anymore (that was a jump rope game).

All in together, girls: how do you like the weather, girls? January, February, March (and everyone would jump in when they heard the month they were born).

Bluebell. Cockle shell. Evie Ivy over...

I remember these jump roping songs!

I played on many blocks, but mostly on 6th Street between 8th & PPW, and 5th Street between 7th & 8th. But always at school. I knew kids from almost every block in Park Slope.

Here comes the teacher with the big fat stick. What did I get in arithmetic? 1 and 1. 2! 2 and 2. 4! Now it's time for spell-ing. Spell cat. C-A-T. Spell rat. R-A-T. Now it's time for his-tor-y. George Washington never told a lie so he ran (jump out) around the cooooooooorrrrrnnnner (jump back in) and he stole a cherry pie. How many cherries were in that pie? Hahahah, I can't believe I remember all that!

That was great. What fun that all was back then. Innocent kids having the best time!

I see London I see France I see _____ ... what was the rest?

So and so's underpants.

I see someone without their pants?! LOL

That's it...I wasn't sure; I though it was something about underwear... lol

We're going to Kentucky; we're going to the fair, to see a senorita with flowers in her hair. Oh shake it, shake it, shake it, shake it all you dare, so all the boys around can see your underwear. Rumble to the bottom, rumble to the top, and turn around and turn around until you make a stop.

It so funny the things we did that kept us busy for the day...silly songs, jumping rope, roller skating, hop-scotch, bouncing the ball, lifting the leg to go over the ball and just having fun!

Permanent "wrinkles" on the brain!

I know; very simple stuff, uncomplicated toys, no bells and whistles. And we were never bored!

We used to play a game on the stoop, called Chinese School (sorry, not PC). Chinese school has just begun; no more laughing, no more fun. If you show your teeth or gum, you will get a penalty. (Then you would try to make them laugh).

There was a lot of stereotyping back then. What just came to my mind was the Ching Chow cartoon in the Daily News. I loved its pearls of wisdom. But it was getting extreme in its stereotyping and I think they eventually pulled it from the paper because of its political incorrectness.

This is another great Brooklyn expression.

Miss Lucy had a steamboat; the steamboat had a bell; Miss Lucy went to heaven and the steamboat went to hello operator, please give me number 9...

And if she doesn't answer it, you can show me your behind the refrigerator, there is a piece of glass...

And if you dare to touch it, it will blow up in your--ask me no more questions, please tell me no more lies...

Love this!

Oh, little playmate. Come out and play with me. And bring your dolly (something); climb up my apple tree. Slide down my rainbow. Open up my cellar door and we'll be jolly friends forever more. 1, 2, 3, 4. FREEZE!

Oh, little devil, I cannot play with you; my dolly has the flu, boo hoo hoo hoo hoo hoo!

Great green globs of greasy grimey gopher guts! Mutilated monkey's meat, chopped up little birdie's feet, French-fried eyeballs rolling down the dirty street...that's what we had for lunch!!

We used to sing the end: "And I don't have a spoon. But I have a straw...!"

Omg, crack me up to no end!! We were always accusing someone of doing that!

Engine, engine number nine, going down Chicago line. If the train falls off the track, do you want your money back? Y-E-S spells yes and you are not it...

One potato, two potato, three potato, four; five potato, six potato, seven potato more!!

Oom Pom pei cocka doodle cocka day, La fee la fay la oom pom pei.

Miss Mary Mac, Mac, Mac, all dressed in black, black, black with silver buttons, buttons, buttons all down her back, back, back!!!

I asked my mother, mother, mother, for fifteen cents, cents, cents...

And a sailor went to sea, sea, sea. To see what he could see, see, see. But all that he could see, see, see, was the blue sea, sea, sea.

I won't go to Macy's anymore more, more, more. There's a big fat policeman at the door, door, door. He grabbed me by the collar and made me pay a dollar. So I won't go to Macy's any more, more, more.

That's a great one! Never heard that one before.

Fuzzy Wuzzy was a bear; Fuzzy Wuzzy had no hair; Fuzzy Wuzzy wasn't fuzzy, wuzz he?

Choosing who goes first...eeny, meeny, miny, moe; catch a tiger by toe, if he hollers let him go...my mother told me to pick the very best one! And you are (it) (not It)...depended if you liked them; you could defer it by one or four.

Not because you're dirty, not because you're clean, not because you kissed a boy behind the magazine.

___ and ___ sitting in the tree...K-I-S-S-I-N-G! First came love, then came marriage, then came ___ with the baby carriage...

Dentist

Next to the hospital, where we usually wound up going in accidentally, the dentist was the most dreadful thing in our lives. Probably still holds true today—yes, we are paying through the teeth, literally *and* pun intended, 'cause of all that good candy we ate!

Does anyone remember the name of the dentist that practiced on the corner of 7th Ave. and 1st? Across from the Laundromat? It was on the 2nd floor. There were large blinds covering the outside window.

Remember the office, but ya finally got me with the name!! Was it Fischetti maybe?!

Dr. Vincent DiSimone.

Thanks. He filled many of my cavities. The huge dental chair and that drill sound! Agh!

What about the dentist on 9th Street between 5th and 6th? The Dr. of unsanitary tools that he used to stick in your mouth, with the assistant named Thelma?

Who went to the Williamsburg building for the dentist?

Mine was on the 15th floor.

Park Slope Memories

Memories are memories, 'cause that's what they are: a time in the past that can't be duplicated. And I do feel sorry for the youth of today, and am glad for the time I grew up in and for the people I grew up with. Everyone says, "Yeah, those were the good ole days; I wish I could go back, 'cause the candy was great, the games were great..." etc.

I did get to repeat it by raising my kids; I didn't let the way the world changed turn me into a machine that craved the materialistic things in life that would make me slave away and barely get to see my kids. I lived my life around them, and was there every snow to build the biggest snowman with them; I did things with them that money can't buy. Those are the real memories; those are like the ones we had.

Gosh I love this Ghostbusters (animal catcher) car! It's still on 15th St., right?

Boy, you're not kidding. Now everyone is looking to sue whomever they can. It was a wonderful time to grow up, especially in Brooklyn.

You're so right. Those were the days!

Brooklyn is not the same place as we knew it...

There was no place like it in the world...

Great memories, but very sad that the best times in life no longer exist.

As long as they exist in your heart, it will last forever...

I couldn't say it any better!!

I can sit down and talk about growing up in Brooklyn for hours...

It's gonna last even longer because I'm going back there to have a beer. Who wants to join me? Lol

My daughter's boyfriend was over at the house last night, and I asked him if he ever flipped baseball cards. He gave me a look as if I were nuts and said no. "How do you flip baseball cards?" Kids today have no clue...

It's very sad. Life was simple then, with the best quality. Nope, kids today have no clue.

I sit out front after dinner and I don't even see kids playing in the street. Hell, I had an army of kids to play with. We played outside all day.

I remember the days of having sooooo much fun playing stick ball, wiffle ball, handball, skelzie (spelling?), red light/green light, and soooo much more. We lived outside more than we did in our apartments!

We could go to the candy store and buy a 15-cent ball and play for hours. Stick Ball, Off the Point, Handball, Off the Wall, Punch Ball. The Game of War. All with a 15-cent ball, we made our own fun.

And the best thing was that Brooklyn was the safest place on earth.

I remember when I fell off the KK ride.

My dad said I couldn't go on until I was a little older.

Yeah!! It was a big thing back then. It scared the hell out of all of us.

I landed on my head and cracked my skull, and it didn't knock me out.

I still have nightmares about that ride and it was the 70's...

Wow! Brought back some great memories for me! KING-KONG & THE WHIP!

That was scary.

Me and my brothers had so much fun on this ride...

I use to love the whip!! Didn't like King Kong though.

King Kong, Mighty Joe Young, Whip Rides were great! Wow! 25 cents!

Yes, I remember...Omg, now it's an arm and a leg to get on a ride.

I remember the milk truck that used to come by. There was a Shepard in the truck and the truck was held together with duct tape...lol!

And the guy that sharpened knives, too...oh, OK...is the drug store still on 8th and 8th? I hung out up 8th Street back in the late 70s to 80s, I think...can't remember the years; it's a blur...LMFAO!

I remember that small little truck to sharpen knives & also, there was a White Rock soda truck that would deliver soda!!

Yes the drug store is still here, on 8th & 8th.

Who remembers the drug store on 6th Ave. and 9th St.? I do, was in there a lot--especially after I burnt my face on the 4th of July! I always had some mishap around then every year, never fail--I had to get some ointment put over my face and walk up to the Methodist Hospital in pain around 1975.

Who can remember the seltzer truck with all the bottles exposed in wooden crates on the side of the truck, but it also had soda, too?

When the seltzer came by, I knew we were having egg creams that day.

Here is how old I am. I remember those rides being a dime. Ugh.

Yes, I do! I also remember the whip ride, King Kong, and Mighty Joe Young rides as well!

King Kong, the owners name was Bill Blazer; I'll never forget since I was a kid. Used to love when he gave out jelly apples...LOL.

That knife sharpening truck guy's nephew comes out by me in LI. I still have my knives sharpened by him; I don't trust anyone else. His uncle did Brooklyn and parts of Queens; they still have the same truck.

How about the guy and his son who sold fruits and vegetables from horse and wagon, and would shout out "WATERMELON!"

The guy's name was Jumbo...The Best Watermelon...

That was the best ride; I loved sitting on the top. And also the Whip ride used to come around, also.

My mother used to get a lot of her prescriptions from Neergaards on 5th Ave.

What about the Avon AND RKO theaters on Ninth Street? I used to pay 30 cents and get two movies and a cartoon.

How about pay phone booths on every corner, and the row of them in Neegaard's? Played in those phone booths plenty of times...10 cents a call and an operator you could talk to...

They had those brown bubble walls and the small fans.

Loved the King Kong ride, always went to the top seats.

I loved that ride; the operator looked like a gorilla, and you always got a plastic whistle at the end. I also remember the whip ride.

Brought back some memories--some bittersweet, others good & great!! ;-)

Remembering and seeing pics of the subways is what gets me. Every car on every line was completely covered in graffiti - mostly - 99% ugly, but every once in a while it would be great!

Excellent portrayal of the way things were.

That was great. I could have sworn the 7th Ave. subway station was our Park Slope.

That is the 7th Ave. and 9th St. station. Same tiles are still missing, but it's better lit. Remember when the stations had those really weak bulbs (the ones that weren't smashed)?

Oh, I know that just made me remember the badly-lit stations which started getting the new lights in the 80's! Made the station look even worse.

Who heard this...your mother wears combat boots!

With all the women in the armed forces today there are a lot of mommy's wearing combat boots...lol

The more it changes, the more it stays the same. Less graffiti, and way fewer peep shows. My biggest gripe is that Beserkowitz is still breathing!

This was awesome, completely captured the 70's I remember, and yes, proud of where we came from. And have to say, grateful we survived it--not everyone did.

When I told my children that we used to hang out on the stoop with our friends, they said, "What's a Stoop?" While Facebook is useful, give me the old time--

"FACE TO FACE CONTACT!"

Right on!!

It's like when I say we would sunbathe on the roof...they look at me like I've lost my mind!

I wish Brooklyn was still the same; people don't know just how much fun it really was...

Brooklyn used to be a big family. Not so much now.

Tar Beach!!!

Who remembers the California Pie Factory next to the Daily News Garage, or the crayon factory on 4th Ave.? NO?! Damn, I'm old.

Used to love to get those broken pies.

I remember the Daily News Garage!

We--my mother and us--used to walk from 8th Street every week to get some broken pies.

You know, growing up there, then, was like living in a small town. You knew all the shop owners, the clergy, and everyone's parents on your "block!" Even the cops! Half of them lived on my block. Our neighborhood was the best. We had it all-- culture, architecture, libraries, a museum, botanical gardens, a zoo--all within our reach.

Do any of you remember the little place at Prospect Park that would turn on the water sprinklers in the summer time?

It was!! I guess our parents felt the same way we feel today. Life was simple when we were young; I remember looking at the news when I was a kid and saying that the news was only for adults; it didn't count for us kids!! Go figure, in a hundred years there'll be all new people.

I am proud to be "STOOPID!"

I'm w/u....face to face, outdoor activities, and exercise...xoxo

Happy to say I've been saying "stoop" to my children for so long, they don't even know it's odd.

Very *rarely* do ya see kids hangin' out on *STOOPS* these days!! Very sad!! But different times too, I guess!!

I am having a crisis on this one. I remember when I was young there was a show on TV named *Tommy Seven*. Does anyone else remember this TV show? Help me, please!

East side, west side, all around the town. The kids watch Tommy Seven; he's our favorite TV clown. He's got a nose that's magic, a push button loaded with fun. So let's watch Tommy Seven, for the show has just begun.

Finally, someone else that remembers that show. I've been singing that song since I'm a kid, and people think I'm crazy.

OMG, finally I KNOW THAT I'M NOT GOING CRAZY, LOL! TKU SO MUCH!

"Be Real Cool; Stay in School." Just something I remember seeing on the side of a milk carton, while in school. This is before we started putting pictures of missing kids on them.

Yes, Ethan Patz was the first missing kid on a milk carton back in 1979.

Got back from a weekend visit in Park Slope. Can't believe how much it's changed over the last couple of years...thank God for my wonderful memories growing up there!

NO MATTER WHAT TIME IT WAS, THERE WAS ALWAYS SOMEBODY HANGIN' OUT!

It was a "lifestyle," you just "hung out." Do it now and you might get cited for vagrancy? LOL

Something that comes to mind: when things were really good they were "boss," and if they were great they were "boss A;" just stirring the ashes.

They could even be "boose" (rhymes with loose). Very funny!

Forgot that one, must remember to stir the ashes again!

How about all of the jump rope songs?

How many of us had parlors and not living rooms?

We also had hassocks, not ottomans. And we held onto a banister, not a handrail.

Yes on the hassocks and banisters, but no on the parlor.

I remember them calling it a parlor.

We used to slide down the banisters in the hallway.

I remember making chains out of the soda can tabs. You would bend them and link them together 'till you had enough for a bracelet or chain.

I remember pulling the tabs off the can and putting them inside to dispose of it while drinking. That was until I saw an episode of "Emergency" where a guy did that and started choking!

And sat on plastic slip-covers on the furniture in the parlor...lol

Anyone remember the Carlton Theater on Flatbush Ave.? Back in the 60s, you would catch two movies on a Saturday morning/afternoon for $0.25.

When I was a kid, I didn't have a computer, internet, Nintendo DS, XBox, or Wii. I had a bike and a curfew. My toys were the outside world. If I didn't eat what my mom made me, I didn't eat. I didn't dare tell my parents "no," nor dare to talk back. Life wasn't hard, it was life…and I survived. And we drank water out of a hose.

And straight out of the johnny pump if it was open, too...

Empty appliance boxes were the best toys ever!

Remember the gas crisis of the 70s? What did most of us do? Most may have been too young, but still may have the memories of switching plates for the odd and even days, or waiting in line for hours with our parents.

The Milkman

According to everyone, this guy came a bit too early and woke us up, but there was nothing like fresh milk in the morning in your cup or bowl of cereal.

Do you remember when the milkman came to your door...?

We had glass bottle milk delivery way into the 60s. Geez, I'm old...

Who remembers RENKEN?! Those metal milk boxes were built like tanks!! LOL

I remember the milk boxes stank to high heaven. My friends and I would dare each other to take a whiff. And we did, like a**holes, and usually threw up. LOL

And who would get the cream off the top?

Even delivered a little into the 80's believe it or not...

Mom would bleach that box every week!

My oldest daughter was born in 1978, and we had the "milkman" bring fresh milk to us in our first apartment...wow...more flashbacks...thanks...

Miss those days!

My father was a milkman back in the early 60's.

And the old saying "you look like the milkman," lol!

We still had a milk man in the 80s.

My uncle was a milkman.

Milk never tasted better than it did in those glass bottles; I remember the clang of the milkman telling you morning would soon be upon us.

Rumor has it this guy did more than deliver milk...

Packages of JOY too!! LOL

Hey, you kinda look like the milkman...

Do you remember when they had to put locks on the boxes? Because the milk was being stolen.

My dad always told me & my bro, "Keep an eye on the milkman while I am on the road!" LOL ;-))

When the milkman, at Mom's request, started to deliver skim milk for my younger brother, Mom told him it was his "tiger energy" milk...

Yes...actually, if I was out early in the morn for whatever reason and saw the milkman, a fresh chocolate milk was good once in a while.

Milk from a glass bottle. Priceless.

Cream on top...foil lid, in a wooden box.

That's what the horse said.

The Famous Mister Ed!

I remember seeing the guys early in the morning sometimes. There were very few, mild deliveries in the 70s, but I guess enough to keep them in business.

We also used to sneak into people's driveways and take them out of the milk box and drink them. It was great milk; the chocolate was the best.

Now this I remember and the milk box outside our 3rd floor apt.

And we left ours outside, with the money in the bottle.

Our box was in the hallway where the bells were. And Mom would leave the money in there for him.

Movies Filmed in Park Slope

Growing up, we watched movies—and everyone wanted to be a star. A few people from the Slope made it out of Brooklyn to become stars back in the day, but when Hollywood came to the Slope we all gathered around. These were some of the films we saw being made in our 'hood, and I think a few got in the shots, too.

Does anyone remember *Next Stop, Greenwich Village* with Shelley Winters, filmed on 12th St. in 1973? I walked up to the director to ask if I could be in a crowd scene & he said, "Get outta here kid, you look too Irish." How I cried! My dad thought it was hysterical & mom was annoyed b/c I went to 12th St. w/out her knowing! Erin Go Bragh!

That was filmed in the Lyons family's house, on 12th St. off 5th Ave.

Who remembers the filming of *Dog Day Afternoon* on 9th Avenue & 17th Street?

Summer of '74, I believe, up by Bishop Ford.

I was in the 4th grade and our teacher took our class to see them filming the movie. It was a day trip; we walked from school on 8th Ave. and 14th Street to the set. I remember all the cameras and people.

I remember; I was in one of the shots.

Remember the scene where the pizza delivery guy comes out of the bank and yells, "I'm a f**king star?" From what I recall, that was unscripted, but they liked it and left it in. He worked at the pizza shop at 9th Ave.

I remember it was chilly out but it was supposed to be hot so we all had to hide our coats.

My cousin was in that film.

I remember that, and other movies, too: a short clip from the movie *On a Clear Day You Can See Forever* w/Barbra Streisand on 9th St. bet. 5th and 6th Ave. Also, the marriage scene from the movie *The Chosen* w/Robby Benson was filmed on Polhemus. Also, a couple of scenes from *The Godfather*, but I can't remember the details.

Yeah, I was there; I watched them film that scene.

Don't forget *For Pete's Sake* (Barbra Streisand & Michael Sarazin) on PPW between 7th & 8th Streets in that *big* apt. building (corner of 8th Street)!

They filmed the movie *Ragtime* on 8th Ave. and also in the Armory. I think it was the last film James Cagney made.

Attica! Attica!

Yeah, I always tell my kids I was in the crowd shots but I wasn't. I remember when Barbra Streisand was in the 'hood shooting *For Pete's Sake*; it has a great shot of 5th Ave. and 9th St. in the opening 5 mins. of the movie.

Who remembers the candy shop on the west side of 8th Avenue between 11th and 12th Streets, where *The Lords of Flatbush* was filmed? You could still buy rock candy from a wood and glass case.

That was Herman's, good home made ice cream and good memories.

I won tickets to *The Lords of Flatbush* on CBS FM 101 and went to the movie theater on Church Ave. near Flatbush.

Don't remember that, nor that scene, but I do remember the scene at the playing fields (by the Verrazano Bridge), because some friends and I were playing football there and we were "chased" off the field for the filming. What was funny was that we wanted to bust up those guys (small crew, low budget film). I mean (we didn't know then) who the heck were the likes of Stallone and Winkler? LOL!

Mr. Herman died on a cruise from the $$ he was paid to use his store. I remember going in there about 10 to 12 years ago and it was like walking back in time. Everything was the same.

I remember that candy store, and always thought the scene in the movie looked familiar.

Wasn't there a movie with Robert Redford where they were robbing some diamond from the Brooklyn museum?

The Hot Rock?

Just *Hot Rocks*.

Robert Redford & Streisand also made a movie in a building on Prospect Park West in '73. *The Way We Were*.

What about *Shamus*, filmed in Biff 's Pool Hall on 11th St. and 5th Ave. with Burt Reynolds?

The Old TV

Oh, the countless nights having to get up just to change the channel by hand! Even though there were only like 12...wow, that is a thing of the past, the knob itself. We did come up with a solution: yell as if something happened, or call a brother or sister and then say, "Could you change the channel?" I wonder if the person who invented the remote was one of those persons who often got tricked into being the human remote, like I did!

Remember the black and white TV with rabbit ears and no remote? We only had 6 channels; there was no cable with 300 plus channels or DVD players. On hot summer nights there was no air-conditioning, just a fan to cool you down.

Yes, I remember it like it was yesterday—and, right—a fan, no A/C and we survived!

Yeah, tell me about it. All was fine then. Even the TV stations signed off. The National Anthem, Air Force prayer, test pattern, etc. We didn't suffer from the "Crackberry syndrome."

That's right; the TV stations signed off at 1 a.m. and came back on at about 6 a.m. with *Modern Farmer*...

We used to sit on the fire escapes to cool off at nite...

Yeah, if you fell asleep watching TV, the "tone" would wake you up. LOL

And most kids didn't watch that much TV except on Sat. mornings, while we waited for each other to wake up so we could all go out and play. God forbid you woke up your friends' parents at 8 a.m. knocking on their door!

Either my brother or I, depending on who was closer, was "the remote." And of course there was the inevitable pair of pliers to change the channel because *both* my brother & I would twist that dial so fast (despite our parents' warnings).

And, lest we forget, the tinfoil on the rabbit ears for better tuning.

I'll never forget when we got an A/C. It was in the bedroom, but the three bedrooms were one right after the other (all connected), so one door sealed off the area. Before that, fans, fans, fans and more fans, LOL.

I feel like we lived in the same house. Lol!

One of our black & whites was sooooo old, it caught fire one day!! Effing hysterical!!

We only had one black and white TV, and it had to be shared between my mom, my dad, my two sisters and me.

Remember the big consoles? TV/ record player/ radio...all in one!

I remember when the tuner on the knob would get loose; we would fold up a matchbook cover and stick it behind it. Necessity, the mother of invention!

7 channels in my days as a kid: 2, 4, 5, 7, 9, 11, & PBS, 13. 13 was awesome: *Sesame Street, The Electric Company, ZOOM, Mr. Rogers & NOVA*. I loved *all* of my seven channels, but 11 & 13 the best!

Oh, but then we found the UHF channels.

UHF Channels...41, 47. 53. Spanish TV.

My favorite UHF station channel 68 with the great UNCLE FLOYD!

My parents' room had an air con—my brother and I slept on the floor listening to our AM radios all night.

Channel 11 was the best. Here come the Yankees; we're really proud of our Yankees! *Jungle Jim, Sky King, Lassie, The Alfred Hitchcock Hour, The Twilight Zone, Chiller Theater, Million Dollar Movie*, etc. Also, if a tube burned out, you just took it to the Pharmacy, tested them and bought a replacement. Very high tech. LOL, those old TV's lasted "forever."

I remember when Soupy Sales went color in the mid 60s. I still had a B&W (for a long long time after that, too) I swore (in my own little girl head) that I could tell which colors were what.

UNCLE FLOYD!! SNAP IT, PAL!

FLOYD, the absolute best!

Only three and eight TV channels...and that was when the weather was clear...

I remember the fire escape being the summer house...LOL!

I *was* my dad's remote, LOL!

Old Phone Numbers

Remember the old phones, when it would take like a whole three seconds for that dial to turn back, just so you could dial the next number? Oh, the humanity!

Hyacinth 9-4579, Sterling 8, South 8; what am I talking about? Who else remembers their home phone numbers before it was all numbers?

South 8

South 8-63? :)

And I lived in Brooklyn 15 NY. Yes, I remember pre-ZIP code days. Don't know whether to laugh or cry at that one :)

Mine is a NE8-???? as in Nevins! Number has been in my family for 70+ years; family and friends won't let me change! Sadly, a true story. A Lan phn #

I remember before we had ZIP codes. "Brooklyn 15 NY," LOL. And my phone number was SOuth 8-63??. Ah, those were the days. :)

Yes! St8 was my exchange.

STerling 8. :) I remember that one, too!

UL-ster, EV-ergreen. WY-nagate, ST-yvesant.

HY9.

Same here...HY9-78**.

Amazing; you never forget your childhood number!

My mother has had the same phone number for 92 years! (We grew up with HY 9)

HY was for Hyacinth

There was also STerling

We were ULster...3

South 8-----!

NE8-1062, when we lived on 7th Avenue, and MA5-**02 when we lived on 4th avenue. NE stood for Nevins; not sure what MA stood for, probably Main. Also, I remember our "zone" being 15. Man that was a long time ago!

The MA was an exchange in 4th Ave. Brooklyn was for Market. Quite interesting.

Playground

Visited Ninth St. Playground a few years ago! Brought back a lot of memories; even as a teen I would go there often to play on the swings, just to chill.

Loved them. I spent so many hours on them!

The trick was to swing fast and high enough to clear the fence when you jumped from the swing.

Left more than my share of skin on that fence!

Is the playground still there? Some good memories there.

I remember hanging out with my friends while babysitting my brother John, as he played in that sandbox for hours...

My mom used to take us up to the sprinkler park there during those really hot Brooklyn days. So much fun for free.

I grew up here. Metal seat swings, the square tower monkey bars, seesaws, sand box and sprinkler.

When I got older, hanging out at the band-shell on Thursday nights, waiting to watch the local bands play, I would play on the swings and monkey bars.

The all-metal monkey bars. Broken bones just waiting to happen.

Does no one remember the playground nurse "Alice?"

Inevitably, there would *always* be at least one kid getting conked in the head by a metal swing! Kept the nurse in a job! LOL!

Now, *that's* the playground we grew up in. Back when kids knew how to have a good time!

All the playgrounds—at PS-282, 3rd St. and 9th St.--all had those metal swings. Even the "baby" swings with those slide-down bars. I've seen many a head gashed, but they were the best for flying high and taking the girls for a ride up. They sat while you stood. You just couldn't do it on those "rubber" seat swings.

They were the best. I got 10 stitches from it smacking me in the head when I slipped while doing a dip.

It's just *not* the same anymore...I go there often with my grandchildren, and it looks like someone who doesn't have children designed it...black rubber is too hot in sun...not enough swings...sprinklers are nothing like "back-in-da-day," etc....oh, well...I too have had my "fair share" of fun here, straight into "teen-nights!" lmao @ remembering! Thx for that...

Straight into the teens? Ha, I've been had! ROFL

OH YES...we used to say we were having sleep-overs and *all* of us would hang out in the playground..."da good-ole-days!"

The good ole dayz. Makes me feel old. Darn!

Remember...we as old as we...oh, wait...can't finish, my arthritis is hurting! lolololololol

LMAO!

Where r the monkey bars, lol?

The monkey bars were to the right of the big-kid swings, caddy-corner from the brick building. The seesaws were behind the swings.

I remember it like a photograph in my mind, burned in my memory.

No rubber mats under the swings...how did we ever survive!

What about the hot slide?

Not-so-alert Kids were always getting "conked" in the head with occupied—or un-occupied—swings in that playground! Some lost teeth!! LOL!

I remember standing on the big swings and going so high that the swing went out from under me...my heart dropped and the rush was incredible. Probably my first "high," in that park. LOL.

Oh, wow...the sand box of my youth brings back such memories. I also remember when the kiddie swings and see-saws (teeter-totters, today) were made of wood. Yep, sometimes you'd get a splinter, but we made nothing of it. We just had fun.

I remember how we would clog the drains at the sprinkler and it would fill up with water.

The sand box...I miss Brooklyn.

Me too...until I go back for a visit and see how overcrowded it is now.

Remember the hill going down to the playground from the entrance on 9th St.? Remember how steep it seemed when we were little?!

I know...I remember roller-skating down that slope and falling, and skinning my knee because we didn't have knee pads...lol.

Knee pads?! We played on concrete playgrounds...slid down metal slides...tried knocking each other off the seesaw and jumping the fence off the swings! I loved that playground from when I was really little...I miss being in the Slope.

How *about* those swings? Remember "taking someone up," or "breaking even with the bar?"

I was always there w/my dad...such fond memories.

I still go to that park w/my nieces and nephew, going thru the sprinklers like a little kid. Hell, I'm a kid at heart! I miss the metal swings, too. Got better lift from it. No more monkey bars or see-saws, like when we were kids.

We were so lucky to have Prospect Park growing up...from when we were really little, in the sprinklers, to taking people up on the swings...loved that! The concerts in the circle...ice skating...and when we got older, I think most of us appreciated how beautiful it is. It was our little Central Park. Damn u all....u got me getting the blues...missing HOME.

Also, remember taking some one *up*?!...They would sit on the swing...and you would stand up on the swings...and go as high as you can.

My favorite was the monkey bars; I fell off them lots of times...I remember taking my son to the sand box and small swing set...before I left Brooklyn 21 years ago...

Scariest Moments in Brooklyn

In any life, there are many memories. Unfortunately, some are going to be bad, like getting jumped or robbed.

Your scariest moment while growing up in the Slope? For me, it was my first time walking across "The Ledge" in John Jay schoolyard. I am sure I will remember other times.

4th of July was always the worst for me, between blowing up my fingers and making genies out of all the old fireworks...they once blew up in my face; I had serious burns and had to walk up to the hospital myself...but I still look good.

Wow! I'm not even gonna go there. HA!

Right across the school yard, as I tried to get a Spaldeen off the cafeteria roof: as I pulled myself up to the roof, the fence anchored on top gave way—not all the way, but about four feet. It scared the crap out of me, I shook all the way up—and after I threw the ball down they all walked away, leaving me on the roof to get down myself.

7th or 8th grade, walking home, I was literally two houses away when I heard a noise, turned around and got hit square in the eye with an egg. Emergency room doctor told my mom that if I hadn't closed my eye at just the right time I would have lost it.

It was harder when people would throw Spaldeens at you. Depends on where they landed, LOL.

JHS 51's 1967-68 it was bad, really bad...

I remember 51's had a "bad reputation." It was one of the first JHS's in NY to have a police patrol assigned to it (after a stabbing incident). I was part of the "Math Team" (we competed with other schools, solving math problems), and when we visited the other schools, I was amazed how "scared" they were of us. We would walk through the hallways and the crowds of kids would just open up like the parting of the Red Sea. OMG, we were a "Math Team" (like nerd-a-rama), not the Hell's Angels. I LOL now just thinking about it.

That's hilarious—I saw my parents today, and my dad is always thrilled to hear those memories.

Mr. Sullivan had the wax hand.

Good memory.

Crashing into a suddenly opened car door while bike riding down Garfield. I was more worried about damaging my friend's bike than I was about myself.

Getting lost in a storm in Prospect Park on a mini bike and finding ourselves in the cemetery when the lighting struck. Terrifying!

Being jumped in Prospect Park and having my younger sister to worry about!

Coming home late from work, some guy followed me off the train. He had been staring at me on the train. I had gotten off at the 7th Ave. end. I raced up the steps; no one was around, then when I reached 7th St., I saw some guys and ran over to them. That was the wonderful thing about Park Slope. There were always people around and it made you feel safe.

Talking about the ledge in John Jay schoolyard—I never walked it. I went around the corner and over the fence on 4th or 5th Street, through the alleyway, and collected the balls and threw them over the wall. I am glad I did not do the ledge since you guys thought it was fun to throw balls at people when they were up there.

Being chased across the roofs on 5th St. between 7th and 8th Aves, across from John Jay, by an irate home owner.

The first time we went down the emergency exit grate for the F train in the park. We walked the tunnels to 9th St. station and heard a train coming. There were, however, storage rooms between the Coney Island bound and the Manhattan bound tracks—so, all was well.

As part of the initiation to hang out with us, you had to walk across the ledge. Eventually the school smartened up and put cement on it, at an angle so you couldn't walk across it any more—such spoil-sports!

Riding the top of the F train.

I agree with you; getting hit with an egg hurts like hell. I got hit in the neck with an egg.

I got shot 3 times with a BB gun by some moron who was sniping from a roof on 5th Street. That hurt like hell, too.

This scared me: Suicide Run on Monument Hill had a tree root sticking up out of the ground, about 3/4 of the way down. While sledding, I hit that summit with my tail bone (the sled kept going). I thought I died, plain and simple!

Lots of scary times...especially back then. We grew up in an urban city constantly changing. We saw the good, the bad and the ugly, but I still wouldn't want to grow up anywhere else. The good memories far outweigh the bad ones! P.S. I DO remember being scared to death crossing that ledge, and you had to cross it at some point, it was a rite of passage.

There were times growing up in Park Slope that you would never want to see a kid go through today, Plain and simple, it was a dangerous time to grow up in. Now we have a sense of pride and survival. Time has a way of eroding those scary memories and the happy ones stay fresh and powerful.

I too experienced fun times sledding down Monument. One time I was sledding with friend on my back, we took a bad turn and were heading for a lamp post, I jumped off, she didn't. She hit her head

Will always be anything to do with "Doyle"

WHO DIDN'T GET A BOOT IN THE ASS FROM DOYLE OR HIM WALKING BY AND KICKING OVER YOUR BEER LOL

I graduated from John Jay

The days of "The Son of Sam"

Climbing the fence behind the baseball diamonds in Prospect Park, by lake, and then trying to get down!

The Days of Son of Sam were the scariest thing ever in my lifetime!

The Seltzer Guy

Never really used seltzer back then, but I had it several times over at the houses of a few friends who did get it delivered.

Hammer Soda. We used to have it delivered. Grape, orange cream & seltzer. Etc.

Are you sure it wasn't real antifreeze that you were drinking? LOL! That ethylene glycol in it is poison, but it does taste sweet. Don't ask how I know. LMAO.

I couldn't remember the name of that soda truck. And it was more like a flatbed, with "tiers." The soda bottles were in wooden crates, all just piled high on the truck. Used to come down our block but we weren't allowed to have soda as kids. Mom always said "NO." LOL.

Yes they had seltzer and soda; you would buy the huge container of coke syrup and mix—my friend down the block had this—no soda for us, either! Was it Fox?

It was Good Health Seltzer. My mom had a guy from Manhattan Beach. They kept the seltzer bottles in the hall, and you tried hard not to pick one up and squirt your brothers and sister when they annoyed you.

Back here in the Slope we can still get Fox's U-Bet chocolate syrup and it is still good. I think the soda brand was Hammer (they had celery soda). When you had an upset stomach, your mom would go to the local soda fountain (Henry's on Fifth and Ninth) and buy a cardboard container of coke syrup to settle it.

Made the best egg creams with that seltzer.

Haven't seen this truck in a couple of years...always wondered why people had them delivering...cheaper in supermarkets.

Remember the horse-drawn seltzer guy...?

Remember the horse-drawn fruit guy? I think they called him Jumbo. Old Italian man, yelling at us kids.

But the seltzer did make the best egg creams; had to have that blast. That's why we didn't buy from a store.

Yeah, I remember that truck. I remember always thinking that I would never drink anything that came from that truck!

One summer day, we were all sleeping, and we all thought a gun went off...it was the seltzer bottles going off...lmao.

Street Talk

OK, guys. Here's a "street talk" test. You're gathering together, to form teams to play stick ball (or any other game). Of course, it's been established who gets to choose first by the "hands around the bat" method. Question: What's the worst thing that can happen to you, aside from not being chosen early (the 1st draft)?

Being the last one left after they pick the kid that has a broken leg and crutches.

If you really stink, you would say "no chucking; no taking." Which meant if a better kid came late, you couldn't get rid of the stinky kid.

You're right. The one-word answer I was looking for was "chucked." I mean, really, you were considered the least capable, and so if someone better came along, late even, you were chucked. That's bad. Now, you taught me something, because I never heard of calling out "no chucking." What street did you mostly play on?

Your answer had me rollin'. It was great! Thanks for the laugh.

8th Street between 5th and 6th Aves. P.S. 39 school yard, JHS 51 softball field--played hockey, football, basketball, and softball there.

It always seems that everyone has their own local rules. If I remember rightly, that was usually something that had to be agreed upon. I think the rules of the street you were playing on took precedence.

"No chucking; no taking" was the rule among all the blocks we played stick ball against as kids. 5th St. v. 8th St. was a huge rivalry.

Money games, 5 bucks a man, high stakes.

Guys on 10th and 6th were awesome stick ball players.

Yep! That was MEEE, the most awesome one you ever did see! My legend still lives on!

I never had money to bet. End of story. Secondly, that was the point to my question. Chucking was so bad, so humiliating, that rules were created to get rid of it.

The streets and school yards were the learning grounds for life--no parents holding your hand making you soft; kids that were pampered with over protected parents were looked upon as sissies.

Oh, by the way: we walked to the park and there wasn't a parent to be found at any of the practices to butt in and bitch.

I agree: the more you were outside, the more you learned. Your parents taught you right from wrong, but everything else was outside. Saturdays saw you outside in the morning and home for dinner.

If you were not home by 6 o' clock, no dinner!

The people that came up with "play dates" need a beat-down with a stick ball bat.

A play date in way back time was: "Is Johnny coming out? We need another guy."

I remember playing for the PAL (NY's Finest Coaches) with "minimal" practice. These volunteer coaches really had minimal time to spend with us. Basically these coaches just visually checked us out (height, weight, physique, and how you threw a ball and swung a bat), and that was the "basis" they used to decide place positions. Played a few practice innings, & made "adjustments" as needed. Usually we played against other precinct teams, and the games were always competitive.

When we played "exhibition" games with those "organized," Little League "preppy" teams on those diamond fields near Coney Island, we just plain opened up a couple of cans of whoop ass. They never had a chance. We didn't play great, but we played hard. Ah, yes. I remember baseball!! (Sigh.)

There was guy who coached PAL baseball—his nickname was "Waxie" because he had a wax ear.

His name was Birdy, if I remember correctly.

You're right, Birdy—but he did have a wax ear, right?

Yes, everyone always bothered him about it, but he was a good sport.

70

Things Our Parents Would Say

Well, thanks to the ones who gave birth to us, the ones who put up with us through thick and thin, loved us unconditionally, and navigated us and our families through a unique time in history. Looking back on it now, I still sometimes have to say to my mom: sorry! But whenever we got on our parents nerves, they were still human, and they came up with a lot of things to say in ever so profound and poetic ways, some examples:

"If you don't stop crying, I'll give you something to cry about!" (Me: "Huh?")

My mom: "If you break both your legs, don't come running to me!" (Me:"Huh?")

Never you mind!

Needless to say, I drove my parents NUTS.

Can't "go there."

Jesus, Mary and Joseph; God forgive me! Or, you are going to break your neck!

You'll put your eye out with that!

Me to my dad: "I wanna help [build or fix something]." Dad to me: "You can help me by watching; that's how ya learn!" ME: (FRUSTRATION!!) LMFAO!!

My dad: "Don't be thinkin' you're slick cause everything you think of doing...I've done 10 times over."

How about going through the litany of siblings' names before they get to yours?

" What am I heating, Con Ed?" My mom.

"Money doesn't grow on trees," was a big one.

"I brought you into this world; I can take you out of it!" My mother never said that, but I don't think anyone would say that today.

LOL—I heard 3 boys' names before my own!

"Thanks, Chief!" Thanking any service person who did repairs in your home.

My mom always said, "Eat your carrots, or else you'll go blind!"

About cursing: "A lady doesn't use that kind of language!"

"If your friend jumped off the Brooklyn Bridge, would you?"

In my house "We'll see" eventually meant NO in the long run!! Never got positive results outta "we'll see!!" Unless it pertained to grades!! LOL!!

"Oh, smokin' that shit again, huh? Don't cha know it makes ya LIGHT in da head!!" Just look @ Robert Mitchum & James Dean!! We used to LOL!! Big time!!

Mom: "Go ask your father."

Dad: "Go ask your mother."

Me: Meant they both said "yes," LMAO.

Absolutely! "We'll see"--99.9% of the time, meant it's not happening. "Mom, can I be on *Little Miss America* or *Wonderama*?" Reply: "We'll see."

How about your dad "BREAKING WIND" and blaming the dog!! LOL!! This was always a scream in my house!!

One of my favorite "Dad" memories was of him "fixing" the toaster. Invariably we'd have to buy a new one. He could build *anything* out of wood. He could fix just about *anything* on a car. He could do plumbing & electrical work, and so many other things. But the toaster was his nemesis, LOL.

Here's another two I just thought of: Straighten up and fly right. Take a long walk off a short pier...

Who heard this one? "Wear clean underwear in case you get in an accident."

"Birds of a feather..." I heard that every time my mother didn't approve of a friend choice.

Or torn underwear.

The "ass" of the bread, which was the end piece of a loaf of Italian bread, which nobody seemed to want. That never made it home. I'd ALWAYS break off the end on the way home from the store and then put the loaf back in the bag the other way around. Apparently I figured no one would notice, LOL.

So funny! I loved that part of the bread, too. Great for dipping in sauce!

Always heard "No going out 'till the dishes are done." That meant all eight of us. So whom ever's turn it was to do dishes would torment us all by taking his time.

Do what I told you or else "your ass is grass, and my foot's going to be the lawnmower!"

Come home when the street lights go on.

I CAN'T WRITE WHAT MY DAD WOULD SAY, LOL.

Here's money; go down and buy me a pack of cigarettes.

JUST WAIT 'TIL YOUR FATHER GETS HOME, LOL!

And don't forget the note...

My dad used to ask, "Did you take any pot?" LOL!

Yes, I remember: "eat your carrots so you can see, why, did you ever see a rabbit with glasses?"

Did anyone ever get their mouth washed out with soap?

Yes, "Jesus, Mary and Joseph!" and when things were really crazy, "All the angels and saints!" LOL!

My mom coming into the room after smacking us for a stupid thing we did...she would say, "You want something to cry about; I'll give you something to cry about!" Then we would go into low whimpering, sniffling, eyes downcast and 15 minutes later, back out on the streets playing and getting into more trouble. Child abuse, HA!

Ya neva heard of beta-carotene (for eyesight!)? LOL!! No, saw plenty of rabbits, though!!

LOL! We could not leave the table till every vegetable was eaten. It felt like hours.

Oh yes, I remember that one very well!

That was a *popular* one amongst our folks & handed down to some, too!! LOL!!

(Raised hand for mouth washed out with soap) Blech!

Who heard, "Wait 'till we get home!" I would rather have gotten a smack right then and there and gotten it over with!

"Because I said so!!"

Little fishes should be seen and not heard.

Wait 'til your father gets home!! There was a cartoon with that name too...lol.

You think it's easy...wait 'til you have kids...and I heard their voices again when mine were growing up...I was telling my kids that same thing...lol.

Go up to the bodega and get me a pack of camels! My old man...I miss him...

Blech is right! I remember my poor cousin got her mouth washed out with soap, and there was a big bubble coming out of her mouth! I had to leave; I was laughing so hard it was like straight out of *Lil Rascals*!

I lived on the 3rd floor; my mom once yelled at me for hanging out the window..."If you fall out that window I'll break your neck."?

"Take it easy, you're gonna bust the tuner on that TV!" Usually heard on Saturday mornings.

Don't stay out all night with those other street urchins!

I remember trying to block the smacks, and Mom would tell me: "Put your hands down; put your hands down!" Yeah right, Mom...NOT!!

"Get over here; you want a-beaten?" Yeah, I'll be right there!

Don't make me get up, LOL! Still works on the grandkids today!

Oh, yeah: while driving in the car, my brother & I in the back seat or in the very back (well) seat in the station wagon...Dad: "Don't make me come back there!" Us: "We'd like to see you try!"

I swear; I think I'm still grounded for something all these years later. Probably only got out of it because I moved. :)

Mom would just give us the look; she didn't have to say nothin'; we knew what it meant...but if she did it was in Italian—didn't understand it, but knew what it meant.

Some things just don't need a translation, LOL.

When I was little, Mom would say..."I've got eyes behind my head!" lol.

Pa: "Don't make me get the Belt." Nowadays, they have child welfare after our asses.

Go play out in the street with your friends... and I do not mean in traffic!!

Keep your nose clean.

Don't let the bed-bugs bite.

"What...do you have stock in Con Ed; turn the lights off when you're done!" Alas, I am now the one yelling this.

This is going to hurt me more than it's going to hurt you. (Sure It is.)

Yankees and Mets

There were many rivalries against each other, but there were none bigger and better than favorite teams; everyone would go crazy rooting for your favorite teams, choosing sides; as we got to bar age the rivalries got bigger and more expensive. For me, it was the underdogs, the Amazing Mets—and the Jets. So who were yours? Were you a Met Fan?

Yes. But an even bigger Lee Mazzilli fan. :)

Tom Seaver. My all-time favorite Met.

Next to Wayne Garrett.

Oh HUSH. I had his friggin' rookie card. And Nolan Ryan's. Do NOT go there. Sigh.

Unfortunately, yes I was. Now, I'm a Bobby V fan.

Most people our age are Mets fans.

Yes, I'm unfortunately just a little older than you guys. We used to see them damn Mets at the Polo Grounds in Harlem before Shea was built, and when you left the game you walked out on the field—not touching the grass, but on the warning track--and walked out through right field. Now, try that today and you will go right to JAIL.

NEVER!! YANKEES ALL THE WAY!!

Forever!

Will always be a Met fan.

Was a big Mets fan, will never forget the 1969 season! Seaver, Koosman, Gentry, Ryan, Kranepool, Hunt, Harrelson, Boyer, Clendenon, Swaboda, Jones, Grote and McGraw.

And you forgot Tommy Agee. :)

I went to so many of their games for free. I used to save the Borden's milk cartons and cut out the coupons on the side; you needed to save like 15 of them to get into Shea stadium for free.

Was at Shea the night the Mets clinched the NL East against the St. Louis Cardinals.

I "like" that...except for that last line. :)

I'm *still* a met fan... :,(

I had Tom Seaver, Rusty Staub and Felix Millan plastered on my bedroom walls. Fooey, David Cassidy.

Of course I had Wayne, the other redhead.

I am an old Brooklyn girl; my daughter was born in 1986 when the Mets won the WS. And I like both the Phillies and the Mets. :) My husband says I am not allowed.

76

Were you a Yankee fan?

My dad was a huge Yankees fan. So, I was, too.

I'm a Mets *and* a Yankees fan—why does everyone have a problem with that, lol?

My dad used to take me to the Yankees games. Back then it was Reggie Jackson, and as a teenager I fell head-over-heels for Bucky Dent. Now it's too many to list...lol!!

Still am. And my brothers, as well.

YES! ONE AND ONLY, YANKEES ARE THE BEST!!

As a kid I only had two heroes, Mickey Mantle & the 7 original Mercury Astronauts. Dad was always a Yankee fan & passed it down.

My story of baseball is almost exactly like the story Billy Crystal shared in the movie *City Slickers*. The first time I saw baseball in color, The Mick hit two out of the park that day. I was at the stadium for his retirement celebration. I missed grabbing his hand by inches during his last "drive" around the park.

My dad was a Dodger fan, so we were raised as Mets fans. Around 1970, I followed my older brother to being a Yankees fan EXCLUSIVELY!!

I wish he'd never learned to fly a plane...

I will never forget August 2nd, 1979 as it was me, too. So sad.

Munson was my idol growing up. I still wear #15 on my Yankees jersey.

Thurman Munson's bust in Memorial Park.

Gotta nice picture of him in my bedroom!! RIP THURM!!

It was like a nightmare for me, how many times I had to hear the Yankee fans bragging...yea yea yea...Yanks were a like a high price...need I say more?

First Jobs

77

Any early entrepreneurs out there?

How did you make spending money as a kid?

I sold Christmas cards and we had a lemonade stand once. :)

SUBWAY FISHING: what about how when we needed money, we used to get the fishing line, tie a fishing weight to it, and use Vaseline to fish for change in the subway grating on 9th Street—in front of the YMCA, or wherever there was a grating? It was a skill.

What about selling newspapers...?

Shining shoes with that shoe-shine box on 9th and 5th.

To earn extra money: packing bags at royal farms on 9th St., and walking the ladies to their cars or homes.

I bought my cards through a card company ad in the back of *Boy's Life* magazine. The sales allowed me to select toys and other items from a catalog.

Remember selling the candy for schools to get some products?

Went shoveling...

Worked as a busboy.

Painting the backs of denim jackets.

Where are all of the babysitters out there?!

Who out there delivered the daily paper?

Had to go get my SHINEBOX. :-)

We used to bring newspapers to a place on 15th Street between 2nd & 3rd. We got paid 40 cents or so for a hundred pounds, and it made for good spending money.

We would always have a few WET papers in the middle of the pile, but the guys were wise to us and would catch us and take off a few cents for it.

Bringing the piles of papers down from 12th St. between 5th and 6th Aves on our wagons was something to behold. It was one brother's job to pull and the other two were to keep the papers from falling out.

Only two of us left now, but we both remember the "paper runs" well.

Shoeshine box, then a paperboy, lol.

Babysitting, and running errands in the neighborhood for the elderly.

Worked in a Pizzeria!! A pretty bad one!! LOL.

Baby sitting and then L&J bakery on 9th Avenue.

Warehouse worker in Consumer's. Anyone remember the Consumer's on 15th Street and 5th Avenue?

Delivery boy/stock clerk for Field's Pharmacy on 7th Ave. and 1st St.

Anyone remember bagging groceries for tips?

Delivery boy at Bohacks on 7th Avenue and Carroll Street, then at Ace Supermarket on 7th Avenue and Berkley Place.

First job? I sold/traded comic books in front of my home on 5th Ave.

Babysitter.

I worked at Bohacks. Good tips from sweet old ladies. I helped by carrying their bags to their homes.

Shined shoes and sold newspapers at the bars on 7th Ave. Then worked at Danny's Candy Store doing stock and folding newspapers on Sunday mornings.

Danny's Candy Store....at age 9, I got paid $1 an hour (plus 2 Yoo-hoos).

Babysitter from the age of 8—what were those parents thinking, lol?

Stuffing the *Park Slope Shopper* into mail boxes (or the sewer).

Babysitter and a dog-walker for a pair of pit bulls (before it became chic), then Häagen-Dazs (the original shop, which is where Treasure Chest is now).

Stock and delivery boy at local grocery store.

Clothes Lines

Who remembers when we used to hang our clothes out to dry on the roof...the laundry room was in the basement, but Mom liked our clothes to smell of sunshine...

The original clothes dryer. And it was "green," too!

Hide those bloomers. Lol!

I am going to make you laugh now...I still have a clothes line, so I washed clothes before I left this morning not knowing that wind storm was coming. Well, needless to say, I came home to find my bras and underwear in my neighbors' driveway; you should have seen the look on their faces, lol...really funny. I guess they are not from Brooklyn...omg so funny...

By the way I was going to take a picture of the clothe line to show u with the clothes on it but they all blew off.

Showing your bloomers or losing them. Ha ha!

Hang on to your BLOOMERS!

You are too funny; I lost many pieces of clothing that way...my husband had so many socks that didn't match...if the washer didn't eat them up; the neighbors got them...lol.

Hanging out your jeans in the rain so they would get softer...the smell of the sheets when they came in from outside on the line...

Looks like my old neighborhood. Oh wait, that's my laundry, 3rd row. Lol.

Love it! lol! This just triggered a great memory for me. I remember my mom having me come to the window to look at our neighbors' laundry line...we screamed with laughter...all of the clothes were horrible-looking, all stained and discolored...I guess you had to be there... :(

OMG...lol...

Hanging the clothes out on the line to dry, like most back yards back then.

Yes, I remember hanging out the second floor window, hanging clothes for my mom I was always afraid I would fall out. Especially when I had to hang the heavy, wet towels! :-S

You could tell a lot by those clotheslines!!

My bedroom window was the one that had the clothesline outside of it. I hated when my mother would come in to hang clothes or to take it in while I was in bed—especially when it was cold out.

No dryer gets sheets smelling like the sun...there were days when it was so hot, that by the time I had hung them all on the line...they were dry and I could take them down almost right away..

In the winter, everything froze on the clothesline; when it was windy stuff would blow off the line & my mother would have us run all over the neighborhood to find it, & when it started raining you had to rush to reel it all in.

Funny story...my parents' family house lined up exactly with my grandmother's...we lived on 3rd; she lived on 2nd...so we had two yards comprising one large one...she would yell: "Tell your mother to take the clothes in off the line!"

That's great. I remember, all it took was 1 lady to yell, "It's raining," and the hands would rush, grabbing the clothes off the line...my cousin and I yelled it one sunny afternoon, and without fail the hands started grabbing those clothes, lol!

Oh, yeah...definitely a Brooklyn backyard.

I miss that a lot. There is nothing like the smell of fresh clothes off a line...hmm hmm, good!

I miss the smell of clothes dried on he clothes line...what about the winter? Everything was so stiff that your jeans could stand on their own. :)

I always hung my clothes out to dry and they smelled so fresh.

Nothing smells as good as fresh laundry and bed sheets that were hung out to dry.

Winter- frozen clothes!

I loved the sound of the squeaking clothes lines as the clothes were pushed out on the lines. Bags of clothespins near the kitchen window--good memories.

Think about it: if it weren't for clotheslines, how would we ever have invented putting baseball cards on the wheels of our bicycles?

My mother would sit with her back out the window and her clothes pins in her mouth and talk to neighbors across the courtyard. She did that when she washed windows, too.

Whatever happened to the days before clothes dryers? My mother used to hang clothes on the roof to dry—aw, those wonderful freshly cleaned clothes, washed with Clorox bleach.

Whatever happened to Duz laundry detergent? I guess the Amway guy changed that.

8 Track

Just another piece of technology that littered the ages as yet another invention, but it is one of the predecessors to the digital file that we are using today, like a hard drive is to a flash drive.

Who needs an iPod when you have your 8 track player and your suitcase full of tapes?

I still have some 8 tracks but no player, lol.

Those 8 tracks could be a drag; if you wanted to hear a song again you had to go back to the track and go through all the songs. But the 8 tracks themselves were indestructible.

Especially when they would change in the middle of a song.

We had an 8 track player; I remember listening to the 5th Dimension's "Age of Aquarius" on 8 track, loved it!

My first and best car stereo was 8 track. Man, did it sound good!!

My 1970 Olds Toronado had one installed in the dash from the factory. It still worked in 1979 when I bought it secondhand.

Listened to the Beatles, still have a few on my shelf.

Remember when we though that nothing would replace the 8 track.

The Mail

Remember when we used to wait for the mailman to come? With a letter from our girlfriends or boyfriends that went away for the summer, or moved away...

Or those who joined the service, looking to keep in touch. To have a piece of home with them getting through boot camp...

Maybe getting letters from your brothers, sisters, cousins, aunts, and uncles who lived far away. That was another thing that is lost in the passage of time…

Those days are no more. With the rate of technology, even the post office has suffered and everything is sent by email. Instantaneous, no more waiting, taking away the human emotion or feeling of missing...losing part of the human element has changed our lives over the years.

The Boom Box

Mom still remembers the old days, with all of us teenagers hanging out on the stoop, blasting the radio!

Hey, I still have that radio!

You mean that suitcase that played music?

Yea that big-azz Sony that was heavier than a stereo.

Hey, I might even have a pic of it sitting on my lap; it takes up half my body.

The boom box was always blasting...good times! Until the neighbors would scream out the window..."Shut the friggin music off!"

Anyone here remember hangin' out on Manhattan Beach with the boombox, and us girls (that was then), wore shorts and high heels, strutting our butts...with our beach chairs, and running for the bus to get to the beach.

Silver Panasonic boombox, dancing to planet patrol.

Taking your boombox everywhere, in the late 70s and early 80s...back then, I had this big boombox. I went everywhere with it, also taking my suitcase with 50 cassettes in it. All I remember from back then is wishing I could carry all my music with me. Now, I carry all my music with me on my iPhone—over 700 Cds—and plug it into my radio in my truck. I had the idea back then, lol.

Handball, beer and the Grateful Dead on the boombox!! What a blast. :)

There were times when our corner had as many as 25 people just hanging out, boomboxes blasting. But no one complained, really, because they knew that we kept the neighborhood safe.

My boombox also had a built-in TV & a cassette player, (or maybe an "8 track," lol! j/k). TV was always static-y tho, impossible to get a signal back then, lol, & maybe that's why my back is sooo screwed up & I'm hard of hearing nowadays-- 'cause to be cool, we had to carry it on our shoulders & crank the volume up to blow out our ears!!

Haha, crazy!!

In 1976, the coolest thing for a guy to have was a radio with a cassette player/recorder. I had a Panasonic - woofer / tweeter - it was silver, with the antenna on the left side. I listened to Boston's first album on that radio - I'll never forget that! It was an analog radio - the dial never moved from 95.5 WPLJ!

Summer of '77 (Black out & Son of Sam)

No matter where you were in Brooklyn, we all remember both of these moments.

I just gotta say one thing...where were you when the lights went out in NYC? Well, don't you know that I was making love!!

Where were you when the lights went out in 1977?

Looting? LOL.

On the corner of 8th & 8th with The Gang. For some reason, we had the Mets game on the radio. One of the announcers said, "The lights are going out here at Shea one at a time..." and just then, the street lights went out.

6th Avenue...not too far from home

I was right in front of my house. My dad called out, "Come on upstairs." I put a cool, almost dry sheet on myself that night and went to sleep. The lights were still out the next morning.

What a night. Forgot who I was with, but there is a lamppost on 10th St. between 5th and 6th and when you kicked it at a certain spot you could make the light go out. Well, at the time, I kicked it. And I freaked, 'cause that's the night the lights went out in NY CITY!

You were responsible!! LOL!

16 and stupid, I didn't know what to think! All I saw was the whole block go out and we ran...and the rest is, well, history...didn't it last 3 days?

Home watching the intro for *Baretta*, then the TV went out.

Don't remember what the episode was about, was just upset the damn TV broke.

On July 13, 1977 at 8:37 p.m., the lights went out.

I was at a social club. I believe it was on 12th St. & 6th Ave. My memory isn't what it used to be.

I had just moved to 13th Street, in a small apt building near 4th (I was 18 and on my own), when the lights suddenly went out. I thought it was from having the fans, the radio and TV on at the same time. When I looked out to the courtyard, I saw that the whole building was dark. Sh*t, I thought to myself, I blew out the whole building!

I remember running to Carvel for the free ice cream.

We had the best night on 6th Street. Everyone was out, and we cooked on the barbeque, made drinks and stayed up all night outside. What fun...all the cars turned on their headlights so we had some light. We were with all our families and friends from the block. Great time...

Stoop sitting on 12th St. with my dad, looking towards the GOYA sign, Gowanus Expressway, and Jersey. We saw the lights start to go out from the Expressway to the Goya sign, and it worked its way up through all the street lights and houses, until we went black.

9th ave and 16th st, or Prospect Park!! lol.

The party really took off once the lights went off!

I remember being very hot, and not able to sleep.

That's why we were "sleeping in the park with the one I love"...lolololol...

You got that right; thank God we made it through in one piece! And I don't remember any one of our friends or anyone in the hood getting hurt--and yes. it was very very HOT!!

I thought it was 3 days long. I remember all the looting.

The park was never so jam-packed as it was during those 3 days. Was it an entire swath of the mid-Atlantic?

I guess it was just a day. It just felt like 3! Lol.

The blackout was localized to NYC, and it was July 13 and 14.

Was anyone worried about Son of Sam, at that time?

Maybe not right away, because of the "what the heck is goin' on?" mindset, but I'm sure it started to cross people's minds that he was still out there.

We took all the meat out of my mom's freezer and had a BBQ.

I was in Central Park at a Richie Havens concert. Had to walk home to Brooklyn!! It was actually a fun night.

He was apprehended 28 days after the blackout of '77.

I was 7 years old. I remember being able to stay up late, and I wished it happened during school, LOL.

Almost busted my ass walking down a flight of stairs across the street at my friend's house. I thought I went freakin' blind, lol. The next day, went straight up to Häagen-Dazs for some free ice cream. I think that was one of my good summers.

It was the summer of SON of SAM!

David Richard Berkowitz, also known as Son of Sam and the .44 Caliber Killer, is an American serial killer whose crimes terrorized New York City's young couples until his arrest in August 1977.

Born and raised in Brooklyn, left when I was nineteen. I miss Brooklyn. Wow, Son of Sam was a very scary time—yes, you are right, like you said it was especially scary for a teenage girl with long hair that was parted down the middle, yet we all still parked with our boyfriends at Marine Park...thank God we all got through that scary time.

I was only 13 when Son of Sam was terrorizing Brooklyn. Although I was not old enough to go on dates, just the thought was scary enough.

Shortly after his arrest in August 1977, Berkowitz confessed and claimed that he was commanded to kill by a demon that possessed his neighbor's dog.

Prospect Park-Suicide Hill

Did anyone sleigh ride in Prospect Park at Suicide Hill?

Blackberry brandy always kept me warm. Mr. Boston was the brand. We would sleigh ride down Suicide Hill drunk and numb as hell; if you didn't have a sled you could just take someone's plastic garbage lid on the walk up to the park. It was so easy then.

I remember going to keg parties after school, and then trying to get down the hill afterwards. That was an adventure.

Yes, lived on 8th St., easy to get there.

Plenty of memories and broken Flexible Fliers from Suicide Hill, double jump and triple jump...

Yes, it was great fun.

Yes, we used go all the time. We used to stack 5 or 6 of us on one sled. I don't think we made it to the bottom intact.

Went down that hill many times; one time I veered off to the left, hit the walkway where there was no snow, went airborne and hit a chain link fence. Painful memory.

Yep we'd go down the hill on our wooden sled. Lived on 6th Ave. , and we'd walk up to the park on 9th St.

A favorite sledding spot, as well as the sugar bowl. We had a very old Flexible Flyer that was much higher off the ground than todays are Lots of fun.

Sure did. I lived across the street from Prospect Park.

I tried it once, and then stuck to smaller hills.

:) Lived across the street from the park; it was thrilling. Loved sleigh riding on my American Flyer, and then coming home and getting into newly, just warmed-from-the-radiator Pjs. Such a pleasure!

No, but we used to ice skate. Had to take the Hamilton Ave. bus from Red Hook to get there.

The Train Pit

The train pit was by PPSW, below Cherry Hill. We got busted by the cops for melting quarters and spraying fire extinguishers.

How many of y'all remember the Tunnels? Walking through them has got to be THE stupidest thing I ever did. Entered right by the Hill on 10th Avenue, walked the Tunnel, and exited by Prospect Ave. (and Terrace Place I think). I remember it all. Yeah. Dumb dumb dumb us. LOL.

Oh my God, the train pits. That crazy metal door in the ground. Well, I went down there once, and we walked the tracks and found another way out. When we came back above ground, we were somewhere around Prospect and Terrace Place, and totally dirty.

Was the train pit where you had to jump on the door a certain way and it would pop up?

Don't forget about the train pit! When it was extremely cold, we were hanging out down there and drinking; I think there were a few in Park Slope.

Statue of Liberty

There was another prominent, iconic figure in the Slope that stood as tall as the skyscrapers in New York City. It was and is the Statue of Liberty. You always had a view from the rooftops of many buildings in Park Slope, but my favorite was the one that was visible if you stood at the corner of Fifth Avenue and Fifteenth Street. She has stood with her torch for over two hundred years, welcoming visitors. Just growing up with the Statue of Liberty was always a reminder of where we lived, and the freedom for which she stood. We lived in the greatest land in the world, the land to which many people over the years flocked to make the United States of America. And she, and the freedom for which she stood, were always a symbol never more evident than at the Fourth of July, when she would be lit up by a display of fireworks.

The Trade Center (Twin Towers)

I remember watching the Trade Center being built from the Park Slope rooftops, and watching it rise up from the skies in my youth. When you went up to the rooftops, it was the New York skyline. Seeing it go down was devastating to say the least. But as a tribute to the Trade Center, though not in Brooklyn, it was still an iconic figure in our lives. In its history, it was so iconic that a few daredevils tried their luck and survived their feat. In 1974, a tightrope walker named Phillip Petite walked from one building to another. In 1975, Owen J. Quinn used it like a cliff to parachute off. And in 1977, 2 WTC was climbed by daredevil George Willig, a.k.a. Spiderman.

2 - Best of Our Memory

- Best Magazines
- Best Ice Cream Truck
- Best Pastries
- Best Sicilian Pizza
- Best Pizza

Like every kid, each of us had our favorite hangout, favorite friend, favorite street, even favorite teams, but these I consider to be the best of the best; these few things kept our lives going. We can still argue about it today, because it's not a fact, it's our opinions of what we thought was the BEST...so lets start off with...

Best Magazines

OK, what were your favorite mags of the day? My first is *Mad*, great writers and satire...and of course, *Circus Music Mag*...And the music mag with the lyrics? Otherwise, I would not know all the lyrics to almost every song, especially "Blinded by the Light," which is my fave by Manfred Mann...

Man, I bought most of my mags from that little wooden shack on the corner of 9th St. and 5th Ave.

Cragars SS...oops, my bad. *Nat-Geo, Popular Mechanics, Mad, Omni*, just to name a few. We're keeping this family friendly, right? ...8>)

8> <8 Just noticed. That looks like *Spy versus Spy*.

The three you mentioned plus, *Omni* and *Psychology Today*. Don't ask, LMAO.

I used to dig the *Farmer's Almanac* as well. City kid, go figure! Started buying that sometime in the 70s.

Railroad Model Craftsman and *Model Railroader Magazine*. My dad was into H.O. trains and I got into it when I was young, as well as Aurora cars.

Mad and *Betty and Veronica*. I loved my *Archie's*!

Seventeen, Glamour.

Boys' Life, then also the grammar school version of *National Geographic*. Always loved *Mad*, though!

Grit—the magazine advertised in the back of comics that you were supposed to sell to get points. Just kidding—I know of no one who ever saw a single issue.

Mad, Cracked and *Heavy Metal. Outlaw Biker. Iron Horse.*

Highlights Magazine. I still do the puzzles while waiting at the Dr.'s office.

The hidden object ones? Those were great. :)

My favorite mag was *Tiger Beat* (always looked forward to either David or Shaun Cassidy in the centerfold...xoxo).

With a 6th Ave. sign over my door, I'm back in the SLOPE!

Anyway, I think the lyric mag was *Hit Parade*...or *Creem*. And I still have those David Cassidy and Donny Osmond posters from *Tiger Beat* hanging on opposite sides of the room, so I can see them both when I walk in. HA!

Anyone know if that newsstand next to Tony's record store is still there?! That's where I use to buy all the mags, that little wooden shack, like a shanty town shack. Or did the yups jack up his rent for a studio apt and kick him off the corner? That guy had so many mags packed in the little shack.

He's gone. Last time I was down there the corner felt so empty.

Yes, Leif was on my walls too, and I loved Les from the Bay City Rollers. Both became total heroin fiends. Hmmm. *Tiger Beat* and *Sixteen* for the posters--*Mad* to read.

David Cassidy, Bobby Sherman and Jack Wilde, who was in *Oliver* - all over the bedroom walls - *Tiger Beat* and *Sweet 16*.

Best Ice Cream Truck

OK...Which had the best Ice cream truck...Mr. Softee, Jolly Roger or Mike?

MR. SOFTEE!

Mr. Softee.

OMG!! Mr. Softee.

Mr. Softee.

Bob the Ice Cream Man...

Benny's Breyers ice-cream cones...

Mike...hands down.

Mr. Softee....hands down!! Double cone, vanilla & chocolate w/chocolate sprinkles...yummmmm...

Mr. Softee, hands down.

That's why you still see those trucks around.

Mr. Softee was good.

Mr. Softee.

Mr. Softeeeeeeeeeeeee!

I remember kids used to scream M...I...K...E... if he took off too fast I think he did it on purpose, and liked to see the kids run. He was a nice man.

LOL, I remember Mike and he always showed up before dinnertime.

What about the Good Humor man?

Yum...I liked Mr. Softee

We used to chase the Bungalow Bar Truck off the block and tell him it was Mike's turf, LOL!

Lol...I can see that...

Mr. Softee, hands down. But if ya missed the truck, you could always walk up to 5th Ave. and go to Carnival. Anyone remember Bernie? :)

The Carousel Truck!!

"Bungalow Bar tastes like tar, the more you eat it the sicker you are!"

Sorry guys, the Good Humor Truck was the best on wheels, but to me there was nothing like getting a "fudgy wudgy bar" from the man on the sand at Coney Island—of all things, out of paper shopping bags with dry ice. Anybody remember that?

OMG, yes! I can hear him yelling out "fudgy wudgy bars heeerrrre."

Bob the ice cream man! On Friday nights he would hold a contest where he would line all of us up and if you picked the right number you won a free ice cream. He always worked it that no kid was disappointed.

Bob also give us free ice cream on our birthdays.

I use to hitch our Good Humor man's truck on 10th St.

Best Pastries

Who had the best pastry in The Slope? Lillie's pastries on 7th Ave. and 5th Street...or if u felt like walking...25th St. and 5th Avenue...xoxo.

No one. You had to go to Court Street. Still do.

Leave the gun. Don't forget the cannoli. LOL.

No one! You had to leave The Slope and go to Bensonhurst. (Alba's.)

You have to leave The Slope; they use imported ricotta from Sicily.

They made great pastries at 21st St. and 5th Ave....NOT!

We always got good pastries from Court Street.

We got ours at a little bakery on 86th Street called "your baker"...still go there.

I agree. One of the best pastry Shoppe's In Brooklyn: D'Amico on 5th and 24th or 25th?

D'Amico it is!

Villa Abate is like art. You walk in there and it is incredible! But actually *in* The Slope? D'Amico. But for Italian cookies, good old Regina's Bakery on 9th Ave. and PPW.

The place we bought bread and communion cakes, etc. was Harbinger's; it was a great bakery as well as Cushman's, but not really for pastry. Wow, wish I had some right now!!

Gotta agree...D'Amico...and it was 10 blocks away.

Bit far, but we went anyway.

Best Sicilian Pizza

The best Sicilian pizza in Park Slope HANDS DOWN is Lenny's Pizza!

OMG, you are so right!!

Slammin' Squares...LOL.

I want one right now.

Hate to say it, but Lenny's replaced Pino's during my IS 88 years...no doubt.

Pino's can't hang with Lenny's...LMAO.

Lenny's Calzones were great too!

Played hookey here many times from 88.

OMG, yes!

I used to stop here on the way home from 88. This is where I acquired the taste for rice balls with sauce. Never had their Sicilian.

Didn't they deep-fry the Calzones? I had many a slice at Lenny's. My friends and I would play two-hand touch football on Sunday morning and then we'd go to Lenny's. Good friends, good fun, and good food.

Agreed. Best Italian ice too. But Pino's had the best slice—and baby pizzas...

Loved Lenny's Zeppole with extra, extra powdered sugar. Always had a sweet tooth.

They did have great Zeppole--however it's spelled--I don't know, lol!

It only took a few minutes for the grease to soak thru the bag. Sounds soooo delish. LOL.

That grease was amazing, and yes tons of sugar. Amazingly, they do not make these in Florida? Hmmm, may have to start.

You might need some BKLYN water...

Aniello's Pizza on 11th Street and 5th Avenue - THE BEST!

U r also right.

Yeah, great, delicious stuff, but it's probably why I no longer have a gall bladder. LOL.

Best Pizza

How many of us remember where the best pizza place was and how much a slice was back then?

I remember a slice and soda cost 25 cents...there were many good ones back then on 5th Avenue. Loved the ices, too.

That's when you would buy a slice and a soda, then a lemon ice. 2 scoops.

I remember a slice and a small coke for 50 cents.

I remember the pizza place on 5th Ave. between 10th and 11th Streets. The name started with A.

Aniello's.

The family still owns it but they changed the name after all these years.

That's right; does anyone remember eating there?

I remember Pino's on 7th Avenue between 1st and 2nd Streets. 50 cent pizza & soda.

That was another good one.

Hung out there many nights when it was too cold to stand on the corner.

I remember him as well; he used to own a pizza shop on 5th Ave.

I think those were the days when you would walk in with a dollar, get 2 slices and a soda, and get change. Who remembers that now?

Remember the jukebox? Three records for a quarter. All the pizza shops had one.

Yup, I do.

Yes I do, and all the kids would hang out.

Favorite pizza hands down was Mike's on 5th Ave. btw 11th & 12th St. Lowest price I remember was .50 a slice. For hanging out on cold nights, Aniello's on 5th Ave. btw 10th & 11th St. Led Zep on the juke, too.

I remember when Aniello's had the jukebox in the back & a huge hand-painted wall of a scene from Italy...

Best pizza was Lenny's on Prospect and 5th Avenue; I remember my grandmother would take my sister and me to Joe's Pizza between 13th and 14th Street on 5th Avenue after we would get out of school at Holy Family.

There was a place on 5th Ave. and I think 11th St....can't remember the name.

We would hang out there, too, for awhile...but then we were thrown out.

Joe's Pizza on 5th between 13th and 14th St. Slice and a coke for 25 cents!

Camille's Pizza on 5th Ave. & 11th St....25 cents a slice!

Aniello's Pizzeria at 5th Ave. btwn 10th and 11th St. Hung out there for hours eating pizza, drinking soda and listening to lots of music on the jukebox. I think pizza was 50 cents. They didn't mind my friends and me hanging out as long as we weren't loud. They called everyone "paisan." Was disappointed when they sold it.

Slice and a coke – 25 cents!

Yeah, the lowest price I remember was 50 cents per slice. Our family always ordered pizza on Friday nights from Aniello's (5th Ave btwn 10th & 11th) & then at other times we hung out there with our friends. Great pizza! Good memories!

Always went to Pino's on 7th Ave. I miss NY pizza. I live in Cape May now, and all the pizza is Philly inspired. Totally sucks.

Joe's on Prospect Ave. near Holy Name.

There was a place on 7th Avenue, maybe off 8th Street. Can't recall the name. In 1967, you could get a slice and a cup of coke for twenty-five cents.

I loved Lenny's on Prospect Ave. When I moved to Brooklyn in 1980, a slice was 85 cents.

Also, Dino's on 9th Street, same price.

There was a little hole in the wall pizza place on 7th Ave. near 8th St. on the Methodist side. I would buy a slice and a small coke for 25 cents.

I don't know; remember Joes' on 5th Ave. and 13th St.?

Does anyone remember the songs in the jukebox in the pizza shops that played back then?

Joe's on 5th btwn 14th & 13th Streets: $0.35.

50 cents for a slice & soda at Joe's lunch special...boy, that place would pack 'em in!

Frank's on 7th Ave. between 7th & 8th street. #1!

Smiley's on 9th and 7th. Used to get a knish with sauce and cheese after a night of drinking!! Great!!

Luigi's special, 21st and 5th.

Prospect Ave. is the cut off. Lol.

I have to say Pino's on 7th Ave. across from PS321 had the best Sicilian.

Always had a square from Pino's on Fridays after the Iron Horse.

And Slimeys (as it was affectionately known) was okay...best for that late night, while you were intoxicated, pizza run.

I can't stop laughing about "Prospect Avenue is the cut off," very funny but so true...we never went past that Avenue, so funny...

You're so right, I always heard about Lenny's, but living on 8th St. 6th to 5th you would never go that far for a slice. Especially when you had your own good place.

We could always go back and forth on who was the best, but let's face it; they were all good in Brooklyn back then.

Aniello's, btwn Rolee and Sepe's on 5th: school lunch special, coke and a slice for 75 cents.

I remember when you got a slice and Coke for 25 cents in Aniello's...

3 -Things We Ate and Candy

– Bungalow Bar

– Cereal Box

– Cracker Jacks

- Chocolate Snaps
- Gold Nugget and Gums
- Good Humor
- Deli Meat Cakes
- Old Candy and Food

Bungalow Bar

Ow, Bungalow Bar!! Think they used to advertise on Soupy Sales's show!!

We didn't buy from Bungalow Bar or Good Humor. On my block, it was Bob The Ice Cream Man...

He owned his own truck, with "Bob" written on the front fender...

"Bungalow Bar...tastes like tar...the more you eat it...the sicker you are."

Bob was not with Good Humor; it was his own business. I worked for him as a kid, and used to love going early in the morning to McDonald Ave. to the wholesale ice cream places to get his stock.

Yep...the best was on Friday nights, when he would come around and have all the kids line up and pick a number. If you picked the right number, you got a free ice cream.

Wow, you bring back memories!!

The Bungalow Bar man would have "draw the truck" contests. Best picture won an ice cream of your choice.

Okay, that's just scary.

OK, that guy is creepy. Pretty sure if he had been driving the truck when I was a kid, I'd have run *screaming*.

Then again, maybe it's only now as an adult that I'd do that, LOL.

Don't move. Raise both hands slowly and put them behind your...cone?

I know this is wrong...but...I don't think he would have lasted too long in the old neighborhood! OK I've prepared myself for a** whippin'!!

Some of us might not want to admit it, but we all know somebody...somebody would've abused him!!! I'm sorry ppl. but I'm giggling just thinking about it!!

No need, no temptation to do such a thing. He would eventually just melt. LOL.

Picture this: This guy running for his Mr. Softee life along 7th Avenue with the boys right behind him!! LETS MAKE HIM A SHAKE!!

Whipped up on Sundae...LOL.

He came to work vanilla and went home chocolate with sprinkles!

I admit it I am one of those people that would have abused him.

He got his banana boat Rocked, ROFL.

I'm guilty too; poor Mr. Softee woulda been in trouble...

It's all good. As an adult, I've managed to make amends for some of my misspent youth!

Yeah, I will be working on making amends for just a little longer. The word "troublemaker" is synonymous with growing up in Brooklyn.

Key word: "some" of my misspent youth. It's gonna take awhile!

Oh, I'm right there with you, LOL.

I think we all have some "it seemed like a good idea at the time" amends to make! Let's face it...in our youth, they all sounded like good ideas!

Mzz Smooth was the best ice cream.

Well, maybe I have made amends since I am now "respectable." If the people I work with now only knew!! LOL.

Cereal Box

Remember the cereal boxes that had 45s on them?

Wow! Forgot about that! And the Monkees too!

We used to actually cut them out and play them.

Don't forget SUGARBEAR!! Honeycomb Spokes Bear!!

Honeycomb's big! Yeah yeah yeah!

Oh I forgot about those. Amazing they actually "played" fairly well. Don't get nothin' for free now!

OMG, yes, I remember. What a nice memory I had forgotten about.

Yes! I remember a Jackson 5 record. I couldn't understand why I wasn't allowed to play it on the hi-fi (remember when they used to call it that?); the record played pretty well.

High fidelity, how sweet the sound!

I just remembered this too. The prizes inside of cereal boxes. We had--and my mother still has--a bunch of them that we collected over the years.

Cracker Jacks

All the prizes in cracker jacks! One year we tried to collect a series of little monsters.

103

The prizes suck in cracker jacks now. I had some a couple of weeks ago and was disappointed. First they made the print so small that only the youngest of eyes would ever be able to read it.

There were always lotsa plastic *cars*!! Specifically cougars!! Circa '67-'68!!

Remember the Oscar Mayer whistle?

I popped the question by putting a ring in the prize-- she didn't budge and didn't notice it was real, or that it weighed more and wasn't plastic when she opened it. I tried to be romantic; how that worked out is another story for another book.

Chocolate Snaps

These are without a doubt the most remembered thing we all ate, so many memories. There were 3 different kinds, but all tasted great with milk

Love these.

Please stop. Otherwise, I'll be tempted to print out that picture and eat it--wait! You know...it ain't half bad. Gonna get some milk now. LMAO!

I miss them soooo much. I use to bring them to school on Wednesdays 1/2 day of school with a bologna sandwich.

I used to put them in a glass of milk, crush them, and eat them with a spoon.

Now that I've seen a picture of the chocolate snaps and the ginger snaps--sooooo good.

Yum--it's like yesterday when I look at this box.

Man, those things were sooo good. I loved, loved those cookies!

Gold Nugget and Gums

Remember the little cloth bags of chewing gum? It just popped into my head and I can't remember the candy's name.

Ooh, yes. And Chiclets.

What about the gum that was like sand. I think it was called "Quicksand."

This came later, but what about Bazooka in a toothpaste tube? And Hubba Bubba and Bubblicious.

Remember Razzles? They were like candy tarts but when you chewed them they turned to gum.

I think they were called gold mine or gold nuggets.

Remember the Razzles Contest where you wrote in answering the question: Is a Candy or is it a Gum?

Gold Rush Nuggets!

Always kept a bag in my pocket.

I loved that gum. I used to get it at Pop's all the time.

Oh, *now* I remember this stuff!!

I loved them!!

WOW, I loved this stuff!! GREAT FIND!!

That's what I was talking about!

Yum!

It was so good that I couldn't help myself, going thru the whole bag at one time. Couldn't stop chewing, and was awhile before I can start speaking again! "Gold Fever"! LMAO.

Good Humor

Everyone had their favorite treat, but mine was always the Good Humor man and the toasted almonds; but my all-time favorite was the chocolate-covered chocolate candy bar inside the ice cream

Some Park Slope memories!

Wammy Bars for 10 cents; toasted almond for 25 cents

Mmmmmmmmm!!

Wow!! I'll have strawberry shortcake, lol.

Push ups, 10 cents.

Cannon balls with a gum ball at the bottom!!

Bungalow Bar, tastes like tar...great truck. Good ice cream.

Lol, I remember saying that!!

Oh, the many ways of poisoning us! But we became immune; I guess...if you lived through those large pretzels that had a lye-based salt on them, you can live through anything, lol.

Anyone remember the Good Humor man on a bike with the ice box mounted on the front?

When my friends came over to buy ice cream, they would give me a dollar for the ice cream and I would give them back a dollar in change so it was free, as long as the drivers saw money change hands.

Typical girly choice: strawberry shortcake, although I love the fudge pops too!

Toasted almond for me, please!!

It was stick ball time out when he rolled by...a Good Day chocolate fudge bar was 25 cents...okay, a Day wammy bar for .10.

Chocolate Eclair, yum!

Yeah, how 'bout the truck that sold pot? LOL, Mr. Softee I think.

Wow!! I thought I was the only one who remembered that!! You GO GIRL!! ;-)

Fudgesicle...I have not had one in years.

Vanilla pop with chocolate crumbs on the outside and hard chocolate candy on the inside. Loved 'em!

Coconut on a stick...they discontinued that; it was SO GOOD...also love the strawberry shortcake and the choc eclair...yummy!! Good Humor...

We should definitely have a truck available for the next reunion...

Good Humor had the bells; Mr. Softee had that (now quite irritating) tune, LOL.

The Crunch bar with the chocolate in the center-- can't get them anymore, either?

OK who around First Street remembers a particular incident with a Good Humor truck--the one where the door for the ice cream was in the back? Let's just say some people had a lot of ice cream that week!

Mike the ice cream man had the only truck we allowed on our block.

Cho Cho bars, mmmm!

Deli Meat Cakes

Does anyone remember meat cakes from the deli? They were a meatloaf-like cooked patty, made from the ends of the cold-cuts. Cheap and tasty!

Did they sell them at Medoro's?

They sold meat cakes in the deli on 7th Ave. between 5th and 6th St., and Herzog's.

At Herzog's they were shaped like little footballs. My brother worked there and he would bring them home and we would eat them cold.

Weren't they better cold? Or cool-ish. Mom & Dad are forever on a mission to get meat cakes again.

Remember Joe's place on 5th Street and 6th Ave.? Everyone used to hang out there and have soda floats!

WOW!! Herzog's...I worked there as a teen...I don't recall the meat cakes.

Cold was the only way to eat them!

The best one came from that deli on 8th Ave. & 12th St., lol.

Meat cake sandwiches with mayo.

Old Candy and Food

Can you name foods or drinks from your childhood that no longer exist?

Coconut Yahoo.

Purple Passion.

Koogles flavored peanut butter.

Coco-Marsh chocolate syrup, with a "pump."

Do they still make Bosco? Used to love that stuff, LOL.

Chock Full O'Nuts stores, with the hot dogs, orange drink, etc. Remember the little paper dish they put the mustard in? Every trip downtown usually ended there...

Ebinger's Blackout Cake.

The "soda fountains" in the Woolworth's stores.

Bazooka Bubble Gum (with the little comic book on the wrapper)?

Wetson's Hamburgers.

Scooter Pies, OMG. Down here they call 'em Moon Pies.

Yeah I want my Scooter Pies back, not Moon Pies. Lol.

I hear you. I don't like moon pies, but they LOVE them here.

I buy them when desperate, but I still love Mallomars more.

And it happens to be THE Moon Pie Mfg Headquarters.

LMAO!! No Way!! What are the odds...

Bond Bread... Remember the baking aroma you got when you were within blocks of the old factory on Empire Blvd?

Razzles, cuz I can still buy them...lol.

Got it!

I'm still thinking candy. Sugar babies and sugar daddy?

You can still get those; I see them in stores out here all the time.

They still sell them though...

Those colored popcorn were 3 tiers.

Chocolate Snaps!! They came in that box that was the same size as the animal crackers box, right? I LOVED those!!

Frozen melon balls, and Fluffer Nutter?

Razzles. "Is it a candy or is it a gum?"

Does anybody remember those licorice candies that were individually wrapped, about the size of a men's shirt button?

Oh, and I don't think Reeds candy rolls are around any more. Preferred them to Lifesavers...no hole!

Oh, I remember Reeds. They were really good. Hey, how about Jiffy Pop Popcorn?

I would just love to have Mallows again...those vanilla wafers with a hunk of marshmallow in the middle. Or Melody cookies...the large thin chocolate cookie with scalloped edges and sugar sprinkles. And ...the spicy "kettle cookies" that came in those large assortments.

Hey, this is not a food or drink, but does anybody remember a plastic ball (about the size of a tennis ball) that had two "tubes" at opposite ends? And this ball came apart at the middle. The way this worked was, you put a scoop of ice cream inside the "ball", one tube you put into your favorite soda pop bottle, and you drank from the other "tube". The idea was that the soda went thru and mixed with the ice cream as you drank. You now had an ice cream flavored soda. Does this ring any bells?

Chocolate Ice Cubes.

Maypo cereal, Kellogg Sugar Smacks, Hawaiian punch?

Quisp Cereal. Shasta Cola.

What about Tab, the soda?

Chocolate Cow.

One single Ring Ding (large size).

I think Butoni was the maker, but do you remember the pizzas that you put in your toaster? Wish I could still find them.

I remember those too. Loved 'em.

I think they make something called pizza hot pockets now.

I saw a box of Quisp cereal yesterday and the market.

King vitamin.

Sometime in the early 70s, Mom went on a health kick and declared, "no more sugared cereals." My brother and I would pool our change and sneak boxes of Quisp, Quake and the like into the house. Mom found a box behind the couch one day. Busted. :-)

In my house, my brother and I would fight over who was going to have the last Devil Dog, Ring Ding, or Hostess cupcake.

I see you grew up in my house, LOL. :)

OMG! My very favorite!

Treat potato chips. Reed's butterscotch or cinnamon hard candy (like lifesavers).

Sunny Dew (the original version).

Brown Cow chocolate drink (similar to Yoo-Hoo).

King Vitamin! Forgot all about that---LOVED it.

My dad used to carry violet candies, and when he came to visit he would give me one—haven't seen those in years.

How about the marshmallow sandwich cookies? Nabisco vanilla wafers with marshmallow centers, only sold in small boxes of about ten cookies? THE BEST.

Large dill pickles from the jar on the counter. Sold in any bodega for a nickel or a dime. Then wrapped in waxed paper so you could hold it without getting the juice all over you.

Anyone remember Burgerama near the cemetery, where they would serve you in your car?

Screaming Yellow Zonkers.

Nabisco raisin biscuits. Flat with scalloped edges.

Chocolate Snaps in the original small box.

Sen Sens: little black ¼ inch squares.

Windmill cookies with the slivered almonds.

Were those called butterfly cookies? I weirdly liked them.

This is so wrong...I am *completely craving* Chocolate Snaps. Not fair. Just not fair. LOL.

They have organic ones at the co-op, but they're like rocks.

I wrote to Kraft foods through their website about discontinuing Chocolate Snaps. They said that the marketing felt there was no calling for them any longer, but he would mention it to them (Bullshit). I told them even if they don't want to mass produce them, Could they make me a couple of dozen to hold me over. LOL. Send them a note; maybe we could put pressure on them.

There is a FB Nabisco butter cookies/ Chocolate Snaps page - who wudda thought!

The marketing person said there are no plans to bring them back – boooo. But maybe we could flood their page - Chocolate Snaps for everybody!

Pop Rocks...they crackled when placed on the tongue.

There was a green-colored Hawaiian punch drink that looked like anti freeze, and does anyone remember blue Nedicks?

Did you know that if you drank it while having Pop Rocks in your mouth that it would literally explode?

Schrafft's...I used to get it at the local pharmacy...vanilla, coffee or banana were the bomb...

Lady Fingers...those awesome little cakes my grandma used to have all the time!

Hammer Soda. We used to have it delivered. Grape orange cream & Seltzer. Etc.

Entenmann's blackout cake was diabetes in a box!!

U bet was the name of the syrups.

Ebingers? Do they still exist today? They were good back then.

Shake-A-Puddin'.

I loved that stuff!! LOL!!

Marathon Bars - the long weaved chocolate and caramel....and good ole' Danny's Candy Store penny candy items.

Then there was the fruity stripes zebra gum which lasted all of a bout 3 seconds before the flavor ran out, but it was a good 3 seconds.

Sunny Dew orange drink and Sixlets chocolate candy.

Remember the guys on the beach with the shopping bags that sold knishes and Sunny Dew?

Sara Lee chocolate pound cake!!

Charlotte Rousse...hmmmm.

Not sure if they make it any more but it was a favorite - refrigerated Sara Lee layer cake - vanilla cake with creamy delicious chocolate frosting.

I used to go to Germain's on 5th Ave. and either 15th or 16th St. They made the best Chow Mein on a bun I have ever eaten.

How about TAB soda?

Sky Bars? A chocolate bar divided into four sections - each one with a different filling.

Zero Bars.

I know you said childhood, but what about Schaffer, Rheingold (Chug -a-lug), Stroh's, Schlitz etc.? LOL.

Ahhh! Adult carbonated beverages!!

Oh, and then they made Milk Chocolate Chunky and I was in love :) Or Raisin Chunky.

Fried Crocodiles and Lik-M-Aid Fun Dip - what beats flavored powdered sugar eaten with a sugar Lik-A-Stix?

Well, I know they took it off the market because it was being mistaken for anti-freeze. If that was what I was drinking than that explains a lot, LOL!

What about Mallo cups? Like peanut butter cups but with marshmallow.

Delfa Rolls Red Licorice...remember they were like an inch wide and rolled up, 5 or so in a package...

Nabisco chocolate covered graham crackers were my favorite.

Cherry Lime Rickeys from your local fountain shop!

What about the layered, flat fig sheets-_like two crackers with a layer of figs, which comprises a Fig Newton.

I saw Bonomo's Turkish Taffy @ a World Market store in Florida recently. Would have bought it, but it was my least favorite flavor...banana.

Yes, I remember.

Bought Bonomo Turkish Taffy at Dylan's Candy Bar not too long ago & it wasn't as good as I remembered. :(

114

You had to be a kid with good teeth to eat that.

What about the blackjack gum with the kid pirate on the wrapper?

I remember my brother used to send me down to Jim's on 10th and 6th for Loggins and Manix; he used to say, "I just bought them there; don't come back without them." Well, after sending me a lot of times--I used to search and ask the owner where they were and when they were coming in--my brother told me he had just bought a box...only to find out at a later time that there were no such things, probably a play on Loggins and Messina and Manixx. Funny, big bro, I see you got the looks and the sense of humor too!

4-Games We Played

- Atari

- Flipping Cards

- Games

- Handball

- Old Games We Played

- Rides

- Roller Skate

- Scooters & Go Carts

- Skelzies

- Skitching

- Football–Baseball

- Stick Ball

- Wiffle Ball

- Wirlycorns and Noses

Atari

I found a bag of Atari cartridges and started playing Asteroids.

I still have like 100 cartridges for Atari...

I just saw 6 cartridges in my grandma's basement last week.

PONG! That was the greatest game, LOL.

Those two little lines; that's where it all started.

Yo, that's insane...they still work?

Don't know. Imma hook it up one day for kicks.

Try making your kids play this; they will laugh...

Just bought one at a yard sale. The kids look at it strangely when they see the tennis with 2 lines (paddles) and 1 white blip (ball), LOL.

I had one of these. But it all started with "Pong" and I was hooked. LOL.

You know, a year ago they renewed all those games. I can't believe how far we've come and today the world is going to end, lol.

I remember playing with my brother when he got his Coleco Vision, lol...

My boy had one and I had the Atari.

Oh shit, Johnson, my first computer was the Commodore, then the 64 came out later--used for hams early packet radio, lol.

I only have one word for this...wow...

WTF...u still have this...lol!!

I owned one too!! Hahaha!!

I have 2 Atari's with 25 games...lol

Still have my Atari, brother!! Plus games.

Spent lots of time & quarters too at the candy store on 4th Ave. btwn 8th & 9th Streets. My favorite was Defenders.

If you go to the Museum of the Moving Image in Astoria, you can still play one that works, plus some other arcade games like Asteroids.

My kids had a blast playing these old games.

I have a bunch of these games. My husband collects old arcade games and they are still so great to play!

Flipping Cards

Guys, remember when we used to play Flip with our baseball cards? You have your deck and flip them, and if yours lands face-up with the pic showing and the other guy's is facing down, you get to keep it. You play until one of you loses your deck.

You don't hear about kids collecting baseball cards anymore. When I was growing up, we all collected the cards. I would go up to the candy store and buy them for 5 or 10 cents a pack. And if I had extra money I would buy the whole box. We traded away the doubles or flipped them. I bet if you asked a kid of today what flipping baseball cards was he couldn't tell you...

Still have my baseball & football card collection! Pretty big collections, too!!

I wish I had all of the priceless cards that I've used on the spokes of my bikes...lol.

So true! Baseball cards and comic books were "my trade" while livin' on 5th Ave. Always traded, with my wooden "milk-crate stand" on the street. Never exchanged money. Guess I was never a businessman. Later traded cards from movies & TV shows. Anybody remember *Planet of the Apes* cards? The backs of the cards were like "puzzle pieces." When you got the whole set, you ended up with a poster from the card back.

Remember when we used to put the cards on the bikes and ride around, as well as the clothespins on the spokes?

Man, I used to walk home from school with boxes of them; I flipped them during lunch time. I loved that game. It was almost like war, too. If the flip was the same color you would go again, and the pile would get even bigger. When I moved from 6th Ave. I left them with my toys In the cellar--probably about 20 thousand cards from 1969 to 1975, all the great players

Who still has their old baseball card collection?

See what they are going for on eBay or Craigslist.

I have boxes of cards; they may be worth something someday.

My cards are on my bicycle spokes.

With the right cards, your bike could be worth thousands!

If those cards are in mint condition...lol.

Games

What could keep you busy for hours on end? How many different games could you play? I remember climbing walls, roofs, fences, and sewers to retrieve a few hundred of these just to play a simple spaldeen.

118

I could play the card game War for hours on the beach.

The best "toys" we had as kids were the appliance boxes, and the absolute best of those were the refrigerator boxes. We made everything out of them -- clubhouses, slides, tunnels...whatever. It was great!

Appliance boxes...

Remember all of the things we made from appliance boxes found at the curb?

We played "tank," wherein we'd crawl inside it and make the box travel around the block!

Of course there always the guy who would jump on us while the tank was in motion. That was part of the fun!

This was common. A refrigerator box was a day's worth of play, maybe two if it lasted. Somebody emptied a brand new big TV out of this box.

We cut windows out of tall refrigerator boxes and made a door. It was fun until some big kid came along and knocked us over!

I used to love when we turned those boxes into a tank!!

Who needed any toys when you had a big box? I think every kid loved them.

Not something kids would consider today...sad.

No - they have too many expensive toys and wouldn't think of playing with a box and having some real fun. Sad...

With a little imagination and some colored markers or chalk, a simple box can become anything.

I made a lemonade stand out of one of these boxes.

It was fun to build, and we sold out! Except for what we drank ourselves.

Fridge boxes: great clubhouses. Held up in the rain pretty well, too. Loved it.

I loved when they started putting "landing gear" (and takeoff) on those wooden planes.

Jacks: I can't picture any of today's kids playing that.

Believe it or not, my mom was the best at jacks. She was best I ever saw. I was amazed to watch her play. I think she "retired" undefeated. LOL.

Jacks was one of my favorites!!

Like Lou Costello, even I "played" (tried, all thumbs) jacks and ball, all over the place. Found the jacks fairly easy. Usually at the bottom of my feet. Ouch!

Jacks was awesome! Remember the first time you got "twelvsies?" As for the box, that was such a great find; It would start a clubhouse, then a fort, then it would lose its shape and become a tank--then we would roll down the street inside it, then down the stairs...that hurt a little, though.

I loved my slot cars. They were great.

Brisk on the stoop.

We loved jumping rope...three had to play: two to hold the ends to turn, or tie one end to the fence, or just jump by yourself and sing those silly songs.

Long double dutch jump rope!

Chinese jump rope.

Loved building models. Only stopped a few years ago. Just don't have the "eyes" and steady hands anymore.

Monopoly.

Stratego!

Skully...melting a perfectly good box of crayons to fill the bottle caps.

Loved jumping rope! All all all in together girls, not last night but the night before, Lincoln, Lincoln I've been thinkin'...

REMEMBER KINGS?!

Yep, Kings Hitting Babies; we also played a game called Errors. This was throwing a ball against the wall, trying to make them miss. The loser of either game had to put his ass on the wall.

It was called "asses-up," and you tried to hit the person. If you were lucky, they missed or hit you on the ass. It hurt the most when they hit your legs.

It's a shame no one plays this game around here anymore.

We had so many good times playing outside every day, especially in the summer! All the kids on our block used to go in the johnny pump, line up our towels alongside the church sidewalk & we would chase one another with milk cartons full of water having fun...a great summertime memory!

Who remembers playing "king of the mountain" when the sanitation trucks made snow mountains? Or picking up the acorns by the library and throwing them at each other, or making slingshots out of hangers, or carpet guns from a board with a cloth?

How about building condos out of the A&P boxes?

I remember so well, and I think you're right about kids growing up today...even If I sound like an old fart for saying so. I think of you and the whole gang a lot! I hope you are well!!

Yes, I remember making houses out of the A&P boxes. I remember collecting the acorns, too. The A&P condos were great.

Everyone would stay out the whole day. Everyone would cry when it was time to go home.

Who remembers the Hookman? My mother said if we didn't come home before dark the hookman would get us. I used to run up the block when it got dark. Lol.

I remember those days, also. We had so much fun then--my how times have changed for 8th Streeters. How many remember the huge pile of snow in the A&P parking lot that we dug out and made a hangout inside of it?

We made igloos to hang out inside and I had multi-story card board condos outside that A & P.

I really miss it. I will be back one of these years.

Anyone remember "coco levio?" Don't even know what that meant but it was a fun game. Had to grab and hold while you said it 3 times, then 1, 2, 3 , no break away. Never knew that game was preparing me for my job. Ha ha.

We would make a little Eskimo igloo fort. Snow balling one another! Snowy days were so much fun!

That's a good one!!

Kids today don't know how to make their own fun...

What about Hot Peas and Butter--come and get your supper?

Spin the Bottle is a party game in which several players sit and kneel in a circle. An empty bottle is placed on the floor in the center of the circle. A player spins the bottle, and you must kiss the person to whom the bottle points when it stops spinning. It is popular among teenagers and is very embarrassing to most. There are a very large number of variants.

7 minutes in heaven.

All that I did...but I didn't see kick the can!!

Red rover.

Kick the Can, you're in a *Twilight Zone* episode. LOL, we ain't *that* old.

Come on, ur telling me u never played kick the can...lol.

I don't know if any one else did this, but we used to tie black thread onto a tin garbage pail top and put it on the top of a stoop and the thread down by the sidewalk. We'd tie it on a car door and would wait for someone to pass by...thus getting caught up with the thread and pulling the top of the garbage pail down 13 or 14 steps, so funny...got chased a few times; my mother was not happy, lol...I guess we called it "cans;" dumb name but a hell of lot of fun...

Puff, puff, pass.

Chinese jump rope, with the rubber bands we made ourselves.

We did the same thing using fishing line from the lamppost to a gate, and watched the delivery guys walk into it and drop whatever they were delivering.

Well, I had my own version of that. On 5th Ave. when they were building the Burger King, we used to tie dead rats to the string and as the people passed, it would swing and hit them on the face...yea, we did the bottles, etc. but that became boring.

Do you remember getting a pink belly or giving one?

Yes, and I give them to my 9 yr. old.

Yes, how about a Indian burn? How about this one: you hold your breath and your buddy wraps his arms around you from behind, lifts you off your feet, and squeezes until you're knocked out, lol. We were sick kids.

What's worse than a tornado? A titty twister...

I never heard of that one. LMAO.

Oh yes, from friends and from my two older brothers.

Haven't heard that term in years.

Don't forget a purple turple.

Wasn't it a purple nurple?

How to Give a Purple Nurple!

Bullies throughout the ages have given many a painful purple nurple.

And let's not forget bangcock.

How could anyone forget...especially pink bellies and purple nurples...ouch, lol.

Lol, I remember them all!

Handball

Name the park u would go to, to play handball, baseball etc.

Handball: 51's and 39's schoolyards.

I use to go to Douglass Park and 3rd Street Park to play handball and softball...

Prospect.

Holy Name.

124's schoolyard, 51's schoolyard, and the garages on 14th St. just below 6th Ave.

Couldn't beat Brighton Beach courts. Couldn't beat the 60 yr. old (and *up*) players on those courts either.

Holy Name & PS 10.

John Jay schoolyard.

3rd St. for handball. The Bandshell circle (back in the old days) for baseball. Stick ball...Grandma's block, 7th St. between 5th and 6th.

Handball: 3rd Ave. and 10th under the train. Baseball: Prospect Park.

Handball—Grady High School. Any other sports—Prospect Park.

Prospect Park for baseball and football.

Handball & stick ball were in the parking lot across from the nurses' residence at Methodist Hospital (8th Ave & 6th St.). Softball was at Prospect Park.

Handball: back of 51's. I miss that wall.

My grandfather used to play bocce ball there on Sundays.

Anywhere there was a brick or concrete wall. We would play anywhere. But Brighton Beach had some serious players...

The wall in the school yard of PS 10 (doesn't exist anymore).

What about stick ball in the schoolyard at 13th St. & 4th Ave.?

There used to be a park between 23rd and 24th St., between 4th and 5th Ave. Now it's condos.

Handball, football, stick ball, baseball, softball or just running like a fool all happened at the schoolyard of P.S. 321.

Oh yeah, and throwing beer bottles to see how far you can throw them, and not thinking—like an ass—that you might get cut by running around the yard, lol. Youth well-missed.

Playing handball in the schoolyard...

Paddle ball, also. 5th St. Park and 51's.

Handball was on the 1st Street side of P.S. 321.

I did most of my handball playing when I was at JHS-51. We played along the Back of the building. We "never" played in the "Third Street Park". That was where the "bigger" guys played, and they were very "territorial"

Handball in the back of the YMCA all day.

Also PS 39. Smaller wall, but we managed.

10th Street Park and 4th Ave. under the train.

The YMCA: basketball, handball, wiffle ball, and pitching stick ball.

I remember the wall on 5th Ave. and 3rd St. The steps going down to the handball courts being there, and the two single courts down the block that were not knocked down or re-done; they were the original tournament courts for the high schools.

Yes, I remember the little Old Italian men throwing their little balls, too.

Old Games We Played

Who remembers the street game "Red Light, Green Light 1..2..3...?"

Remember having to choose with the amount of fingers out, or "my mother said to choose this one and you are not it?"

It was called freeze tag, I believe.

Nah!

We never included you in this game!! LMAO!! ;-)

How about when we used to sit on the stoop and play truth or dare--consequence, promise and repeat of course!

May I?

Red light, green light and freeze tag were two
different games on Tenth Street!

How about Buck Buck?

Of course, but it was too "simple" a game. Now take
Coco-leevio (spelling? anyone remember that one?);
this was a game that took some tactic (stealth) and
speed. Now that was a GAME!

I went to P.S. 321 in the 70s. We used to play early
in the morning in the small playground in front of the
school before we had to go in. Boy, wish I could run
that fast again, lol, coco-leevio 123!!

I loved Coco leevio!

We played Buck-Buck on 7th St. with the Lincoln
boys on those hot summer nights. You could get a
broken back playin' that game.

How about getting thrown in the "johnny pump" (no
silly sprinkler caps)?

They would spray water with soda cans.

Absolutely...that was the only way...

I would be all dressed for the night and the guys
would throw us in - we had so much fun!

WAIT...how about Skelsies (not sure of spelling)?

Yes, I remember Skelsies, and hop scotch (jumping
rope).

And the more we complained, the more the guys
would hold us "under"...ha ha.

What about Simon Says?

Who remembers turning soda cans into shoes, and
trying to run the block?

Sometimes they would pierce your sneaks if ya had cheapos, lol.

I liked putting M-80's into the garbage cans of douche neighbors...

Or stepped on thumbtacks on the back of your shoes so they would click when you walked like tap shoes? I know, looking back now...dumb idea! LOL.

OMG...that was so much fun...drove adults crazy...OK, now I want to do it and show my kids...now if I can just find some cans.

Remember playing "Johnny on a pony?" We called it Buck Buck. Lots of fun!

I Buck bucked once into the fence we were playing against- five stitches later, ouch -I remember thinking no one is gonna beat this jump.

Usually the fat guy was "the pillow."

My friend's father played one day with us; he hurt his back badly.

Forgot all about the pillow.

Buck Buck, how many fingers are up? I prefer hot beans (or peas) and butter...

Hop scotch: toss the chips in the numbered boxes and had to do it on one foot, etc....

"I declare war on.........you!" Throw spaldeen on.

Country (written in chalk on the street) and run! Fun stuff!

Rides

I loved growing up in Bklyn; how about the rides on the truck and the fun we had?

I always loved when the King Kong ride came around, always sat on the top seat. Until the day I saw it tip over...

The Whip...a.k.a. the "whiplash?"

Loved this one, too!

The whip was a favorite ride...all of us kids on my block would be so excited & run to line up to go on that ride!

Would jump over cars for a spaldeen, in the middle of traffic on 6th Ave.--fly over a ramp and jump 10 garbage cans, on a banana seat bike (with my CAPE on of course), but was too chicken to go on King Kong...LOL.

I liked King Kong the best.

Back in the 60s, when the ride still had the gorilla head over the cab, we used to hang outside of the seats instead of in them. They'd never let kids get away with something like that today.

OMG! I was afraid to sit on top!

I was petrified of all rides!

That tip-over was called a full moon.

Lest we forget about "The Whip."

My favorite...I just loved going around and around...

That was great when the rides came down the street on our block! We were all so excited! Unfortunately, it has not been continued through the years!

I would hang off buildings, but I was scared of this whip, go figure; glad I got that off my chest.

Higher, higher, higher...

Hands up!!

It tipped over? Anyone seriously hurt?

I never heard that.

The tip-over was called the full moon...BTW, remember the guys who worked those rides? They were *nuts*!

Wow, never did one on 5th Street - the operators of those trucks were psychos, all right.

Remember one of the guys was a body builder he used to pretend he was making it rock with his own strength. Silly me, I believed it then.

I loved growing up in Bklyn how about the rides on the truck fun we had

Remember the block party back in the day? But remember the King Kong ride on the back of that truck? U get on top and that was the best. Miss my childhood.

I remember the whip, that ride that used to swing back and forth and everyone wanted to sit on top.

How about the "King Kong" ride? You got to ride for--what was it? $.25?

How about the mini Ferris Wheel?

Roller Skate

Depending on whether you enjoyed it, rollerskating was a great way to wear yourself out and work off anger; we went to the roller disco and played roller hockey in 51's, in the park, on the streets and in the Fort Hamilton League. We even had roller derby teams knocking the heck out of each other, with iron wheels no less.

Rollerskatin' in the 60s and 70s. Remember the red clamps and having your very own skate key that you wore around your neck?

Wow, there was great roller skating in Park slope.

130

Still got my skate key.

Still remember that God awful feeling of your sneaker popping out of that front clamp...

You would wind up with your skate, flapping if you had a pop out; what a pain - but PS was great for roller skating all the way downhill from the park to 4th Ave.

I was the ONLY kid in Brooklyn (really!) that couldn't skate...it sucked - but I did love watching the boys play street skate hockey.

Skinned knees, scraped elbows & hands. Boy, was that *fun*!

Those skates were my favorite "toy" of all time. Second to the spaldeen.

What about playing roller derby and knocking yourself out?

Future Scooter! Although they look like the "My First Skates" type. Wouldn't really hold up.

Oh yeah...I remember I'd always lose the key. I used to steal my father's wrenches and use those. I was constantly in trouble for touching his beloved tools. LOL.

Oh, I've got a brand new pair roller skates and you've got a brand new key...God I loved my roller skates!

Oh, yeah! These are the "older" type that worked best with shoes that had soles. Can you imagine that we skated with shoes on? It wasn't until they came with the larger wrap-around front clips that you could use your sneakers. I rode those 'til the wheels wore out & fell apart, since we only used them on those tough concrete sidewalks with expansion joints. It wasn't 'til later that we were "big enough" to skate on the asphalt streets.

You reminded me of those "strap on" blades they had before they made actual ice skating shoes. They make great wall decorations now. LOL.

Actually I have more "memories" of Roller-Girl of *Boogie Nights* than I do of my own roller skating. LOL.

Scooters / Go-Carts

No one bought us scooters. We built them. LOL.

That was the best part of go-carts and scooters: building them.

What do you do when you "lose" the bolt & nut that holds the two main parts of your skates? Good ol' Yankee thrift!!

Yeah, we made go carts with, like, wooden milk crates and a skateboard--or roller-skate bottoms?

How did we fit in a milk crate?

Big crates, little people.

My older brother use to make 'em. Wow, great memories.

I built a few of those in my time...miss the old wooden milk cartons.

My brother scavenged the garbage and built his own bike, too!

If I built one for my kids, they wouldn't know what to do with it!!

I hear u, brother. My kids would ask, "Where are the wires to make it move?" Lol.

So many kids only had one roller skate in those days, lol.

The good old milk crate and 2x4 and broken roller skates...and a few nails...instructions not included.

LOL, those were the good ole days.

A 2x4, a milk box, nails and old skates made for many fun days in my life.

No steering wheel--we used rope or our feet to steer. Yeah, kinda killed the sneakers too.

My sis made a skateboard out of parts of a broken ironing board and wheels from broken roller skates. Then she got in trouble for skateboarding down the ramp in the subway station! Don't ya just love it?

Skelzies

This is my all time favorite game next to stick ball; this requires the motor skills and just the right flick of a finger to make it around the board and home first. I played this more than any other game and longer than any other game.

Loved this game; we used to steal the bottoms off the school chairs; they worked best--or we would scrape the tops of glass bottles against coned grills on the ground and the top of bottle would pop off like a ring. Then, of course, fill them with melted crayon. I tell people about it all the time here in Florida.

If you want to confuse the kids in your neighborhood, draw this skelsy board in the street. They will never figure out what it is.

Killer!

Remember melting crayons and or was in the bottle tops?

We used to rip the glides off the school chairs; they made "killer" skelzies caps.

Almost all the chairs at I.S. 88 were uneven from the missing steel caps at the leg bottom...the teachers had no idea why. Lol.

Just last week I made a Skelly board on my children's table and melted crayons into bottle caps. They love it!

I remember doin' it all. Got best results by "carving" (with a pocket knife) the board into the asphalt. It lasted a long time.

The "slickest" caps were made of glass. Yes, strange and not easy to make. Using the "old" coke glass bottles, you "gently" rubbed the top of the bottle, at about 45 degrees, along a "sewer cap" (it had to be a specific type), while at the same time rotating the bottle. The intent is to separate the smooth top (where the cap is fastened) from the rest of the bottle. You end up with a glass "ring." Works best on smooth asphalt. Anybody familiar with this method?

Yes, those where the best, and you described it perfectly--a very delicate operation. One slip and it was back to the drawing board.

You put a lot of thought into your skelsey game. LOL, I never heard of that method.

You know! Playing in the streets of Brooklyn. It's an art...friendly competition (but you had to win). Kids now only play inside, with A/C, and always with some kind of electronic device. Sort of what we are doing now. LMAO.

This is a missing ingredient in my life! If I went back and drew this in the street now I'd be arrested. I also can't remember the last time I played stick ball (I guess I didn't officially retire--that's what happens when you're careless with your career!).

Just sit right back and you'll hear a tale, a tale of a fateful trip...

Typed in the wrong spot. Hah, but I did like skelsey, too. We also used the chair glides. Although I do not know who procured them, exactly.

I also remember carving our Skelseys court in the asphalt. We carved ours in front of the Johnny Pump because we knew cars couldn't park there.

On 8th St., above 8th Ave., there was almost a permanent one in front of Charlie's Candy Store; he sold the soda that we got the caps from...Kids don't play in the street anymore on 8th.

It just shows how ingenious and creative Brooklyn kids were back then; nowadays kids only play with other kids when their parents arrange a play date.

Does anyone remember taking the glass Pepsi bottle & slowly scraping it on the sewer until the rim came off? Then you spent hours rubbing it on the concrete to make it smooth.

I loved playing this game & yes we were always outside making up games. We didn't have a stick so we played punch ball (sorta like baseball but you hit the ball with your fist).

CLASSIC STREET GAME.

With today's games, there's nothing left to the imagination. When was the last time you saw kids playing two-hand touch football or stick ball in the streets? I remember when we couldn't wait for it to snow to play rough tackle in the street, or cleaning out a vacant lot just to get some sort of game going.

Did you use melted crayons or candles, and who cheated and put a dime in the bottom of the bottle cap, lol?!

No dimes; that was a lot of money then, a penny maybe. Hershey candy bars were a nickel then (I'm 51). We used to rip the glides off the bottom of school chairs.

I'm 48 and you're probably right about the pennies. But I forgot all about ripping the bottoms off the school chairs, classic -- still cheating, but classic.

It was just too good not to share....anyone who grew up in Park Slope back when it was a "real" neighborhood played skelsies!!

Played all day long!! This was the best. Great memories.

Yep, it was either skelsies or stick ball during the day and either Buck Buck, off the stoop (point), or Hot Peas & Butter at night until our moms screamed at us about 10 x to come inside.

Melted crayons... :)

I never even thought to put a dime under the wax! Damn! I used crayons, though. But I remember getting the glass ring from the top of a Yoo-Hoo bottle.

Yep, remember that too. Sorry about you not knowing the "cheap inside skelsy tricks," lol.

GET THE MATCHES, CANDLES AND OR CRAYONS & BOTTLE CAPS! LOL!!

My kids love the game...it makes a mess but I love watching them make the bottle caps.

I use to love to melt the crayons in the bottle caps & mixed different colors to get awesome looking caps...

Gee, how many hours did we spend making those caps and playing in the street...lol...

I loved melting the crayons - made custom colors for my friends and brothers - favorite colors - rainbows - designs - sports team colors - so much fun.

The old Yoo-hoo bottles had the best caps.

Now I know how to spell it. Thanks, although on my block, It was Skellies.

We always said it with a Z.

BTW, I should still be able to kick some butt. The only problem is that I may not be able to get back up.

As a matter of fact, some called it Skully...

How 'bout sending the other player's cap down half a block when you were close to him, so it would take him a few shots just to get closer to his square?

Yeah, I remember we played dirty. We yelled cross country and kicked the shit as far as it could go. Ahhh, sweet memories, lol.

I got to make my game pieces out of glass, so unless they came out really thick, they were not strong enough to do that. I always saw it as a game of "fineness," if you can call a "street game" that.

We could kick it down the street on my block.

The bottom of a school desk filled with molten crayon...YES!

It was all fun.

Sometimes you wanna go...where everybody knows your name...and they're always glad you came...

Thank you all, for sharing our awesome childhood memories.

I loved this game...I taught my kids this by making a skellzies board on my living room floor for a few years...don't have to tell you the wife flipped!

Funny, great stories. We can all share this book; it's like *Cheers*..."Everybody Knows Your Name"...LOL.

Skitching

No matter what they did to the bumper we found a way around it, even though it was the most dangerous thing.

I tried this once & my uncle caught me. I think they called this "Skitching." It was dangerous, and I know some of you crazies attempted this? LOL.

This is "hitching" & we used to do it all the time. That is how we used to get to Sunset pool and back. The MTA finally caught on and put slanted metal along the bumper, but that didn't stop us; we then started holding on to the inside of the back window and resting our feet on the outside of the bumper.

Skitching was holding onto the back of the bus or garbage truck after it snowed, using our shoes as skis.

We use to "Skitch" in the slush & snow!! ;-)

I wasn't far off. I remember women on the bus telling the bus drivers that boys were riding. He would stop, get out and the kids would run away. When he got back in, they got back on. LOL.

There was a kid I knew from the neighborhood that was hitching a bus and fell off on 9th Street and 5th Ave. and was killed...

I think most boys had to do this to keep their "rep." It was easy on those older buses with the big bumpers.

We held onto the back with roller skates on and would ride for blocks.

Blackie the cop was always yelling at someone for being on the back of the bus.

Hitching rides on the back of the 63 bus on 5th.

Or on a skateboard or bike. -- the good ol' days. Dangerous, but good. LOL.

Football-Baseball

1 Mississippi, 2 Mississippi 3 Mississippi...when you were playing two-hand touch.

We'd play tackle football out on these streets with just some $5 plastic NFL helmets from Modell's...

In 2 hand touch football, the sewer covers were the end zones. You called plays like "go to the black car and do a button hook or on the Ave."

Little League baseball: we were the Robins in the early 70s. MLB would not let us use their team names; I'm not sure why.

The Robins sounds familiar, what league was that?

Not sure; I played there when 8 and 9 yrs old. I do remember the tryouts were at St. Thomas.

I went to Holy Family. St. Thomas ran it, I think.

I played for St Thomas. 7, 8, 9 was the Popcorn League; all the games were played in Prospect Park.

Ten and eleven was called Bantam. We played in the Dust Bowl on 65th and 8th Ave., and on the fields along Shore Rd. The league was called BBB Build Better Boys.

Popcorn is ringing a bell right now.

The softball games in the PS 39 schoolyard always bring fond memories. A ball, a bat, and a glove and we were on our way. It didn't take much for us to have fun!

They put a jungle gym right in the middle of the field. God, how small were we then? Hitting one in the dungeon was a shot, or pulling one down the third base line over the tower or off the wall. Shit, I was so skinny I didn't need to climb the fence; I could squeeze thru the bars, lol.

We always found gloves in Prospect Park early in the morning on the baseball fields on the way to the little lake to fish.

Most of the gloves we used had Magic Marker on them from crossing off names, lol.

I miss those days! And football in the library yard. It all seemed so big to us then. Lol.

The best games as we grew up were at 51's park. There were always games going on; we had to wait for the field to clear, but great games.

Stick Ball

The ultimate street game against other blocks and for great rivalries against other blocks. It was great playing on the Avenue and in between cars and that almighty elusive 4 sewer shot.

For stick ball we used to get someone to unscrew somebody's mom's mop handle. Or if we saw a mop in someone's garbage, we would take it and customize it.

How many sewers? If not for anything else...those cars!

And the cars used to actually stop for us.

What do you mean? The most fun was trying not to get hit by the car and catch the ball at the same time! As they were honking and trying to hit you...that was the skill of playing the Avenue.

Well, the ones that didn't stop needed more than one spare tire when we saw where they parked!

We had the schoolyard for stick ball. You could play the short way, or the long way with running bases. Either way, it was always a fun time.

How 'bout climbing the fire escapes to get the Spalding ball after you or a pal knocked the ball over the roof!! HOMER!!

Not anymore; kids today stay inside and play on their game systems. It's pathetic.

I agree.

Football and stick ball: good times!

In my day on 3rd Ave. Prospect - 18th depending what we were playin'.

Yeah I remember playing baseball on 21st Street...and street football with our block teams...also kick the can, red light/green light and a bunch of other activities that these kids these days just don't know about!!

Chips on the ball!

I remember these guys used to play a great game of stick ball on this block, 11th Street between 5-4 Aves.

We grew up on 9th St. btwn 2nd & 3rd Avenue. Memories.

Growing up on 5th St. you were in the park from 8 a.m. 'til you had to go home for dinner, then you came back for some more fun.

Lost many spaldines on 51's roof from playing stick ball. The only person I ever saw hit a hardball over that roof from home plate.

And nobody ever got hurt.

Ups: you never hear a kid say, "let me get my ups." My father would call me in for dinner and we would all stall by saying, "I gotta get my ups." Playing stick ball all day long.

All the great games we played against other blocks...those were the best.

We used to say, "chips on the ball and bat."

Chips is great. Thanks for letting me remember that.

Remember choosing sides with the bat?

Ok...memory tests for us senior citizens: How many strikes did you get in stick ball? And if you roofed a ball was it an automatic out? Besides having to pay chips...lol...enjoy your Sunday.

And when you got to try to kick it out of the person's hand after he palmed it.

We let one kid play 'cause he was good at climbing roofs to get the ball.

2 strikes in stick ball unless it was a "slow roller" and you called it right away. Different rules for different blocks, but for the most part roofing the ball was automatic out.

Always good to have one of them around...designated climbers.

Stick ball reunion gets mixed reviews from Brooklyn neighborhood: Play ball or get lost!

Is an annual game of stick ball a hit - or a foul? Some residents of Carroll St. in Park Slope ran for home when a squad of old-timers returned to their block to play the classic Brooklyn street game.

Been playing for the last 25 years...

I'd like to meet the commenter in person and...well, you know. Butt heads. Sorry.

There are *always* going to be detractors that have to complain about something or other; apparently they have nothing better to do. I believe they're "Scrooges" that wish they can do the same, but can't or choose not to. Them Bums. LOL.

The new residents have no clue that it was like "that"--every nice day for months in Brooklyn there were kids. Be lucky it's only one day Carroll St. Bear with us "REAL" Brooklynites.

All the guys that played when we were kids would come back every Labor Day and play; nobody bitched. There would be people on the stoops watching, cheering, and laughing at us who lost their skills; it was a blast. Now even if we did go back the trees have grown so big you couldn't play, and I'm sure the yuppies would be calling the cops.

RIGHT ON!!

Yeah, stick that ball where the sun don't shine. Goin', goin'...gone!! LOL.

One more thing...they moved the things that we had done to an art form, to be discussed, to be viewed under the microscope as to why we did that, the bringing together the community--guess what? We did what we did because it was fun, get it? Fun, we enjoy it. We had no way of knowing that what we did was going to change the world; it changed our world; it forged friendships that last forever and a day. We never wanted to be in a SoHo art gallery or a op-ed piece in the NYT; we wanted to play stick ball, sit on the stoop and be stupid, funny and be the best at Brisk. OK, the rant is over.

Wiffle Ball

Though this was not as tough as baseball, it still took a lot of skill and was lots of fun. The only drawback was that swinging at air pulled your arm!

"Ups" meant your turn at bat—or, the older kids' way of hijacking your stick-ball or Wiffle ball game. It would start out with an older kid waiting for the littlest kid/path of least resistance to get up, go over to him and say, "Let me get an up." The bat would never come back, and the game was over.

"Ups" was also a way to piss your parents off when you were called in for dinner. "Come on, let me get my ups."

"No penny tax; no gum ball raps," was said at the end of a choose-up, as an assurance that the rules of whatever game you were playing could not be changed mid-stream.

Getting kicked out of a wiffle ball game was called getting "chucked."

Whirly Corns and Noses

Such a childish thing to do, but we were children, and it was fun.

Oh, how much fun we used to have collecting acorns...those were the days. :)

Making whistles out of them!

Outside the library on 6th Avenue there were lots of acorns on the sidewalk in the fall...

"Polly noses": sticking them on your nose. I looked them up and the name is a "Brooklynism," LOL. Was that the library on 6th Ave. bet. 8th & 9th Sts.? We had these three *huge* trees on the 8th St. side. That's where we got all our acorns. And those trees were kind of an "age gauge." Depending on how old we were, we could either go as far as the first tree, the second tree or (finally!) the third tree. LOL.

"Polly nose" is the name? I never knew that. Does anyone remember being able to whistle really loud with a blade of grass? Or with these also: "Pinocchio noses?"

Just throwing a bunch of them up in the air and watching them come down was fun, even at this age.

Acorns and a sling shot.

5-Hanging Out On the Stoop

–   Hanging Out On the Stoop

Hanging Out On the Stoop

Remember how many late nights were spent with whole families on the stoop, talking about just anything 'cause no one had air conditioning? How did our parents do it? They would be up all night only to go to work the next morning. How about waiting for a space on the stoop to sit, only to have an adult come up and you had to give it up. We had respect back then, and didn't dare sit while an older person stood.

Yes, "the stoop." Used to spend hours on the Stoop-- it was just something everyone did back then.

I've lived in N.J. for 6 yrs now... lived in Brooklyn for 39 yrs. They say, what's a stoop? Omg... Only BKLYN...

Now the yuppies will call the cops on anyone who does that.

"Stoop, what the hell is a STOOP?"...lol.

I remember on hot nights, all the old ladies would sit on the stoop with Shower to Shower down their bras and a wet rag on their backs--who needs air conditioning?!

A few months back, a man got a ticket for drinking a beer on his stoop.

The stoop...the original social network!

We used to sit on the stoop and play games and cards all night. We had so much fun.

Remember how the first floor people would hang out their window while we would sit on the stoop? At times, a four-step stoop would hold about 8 people with two people on either window. LOL!

Yes, I remember, and my uncle would yell at us to be quiet.

It was a good way to spy on conversations! No one had secrets for too long in our neighborhood!

Absolutely; I miss those days.

You bring back great memories of "the stoop." Back then, everyone sat outside on the stoop and friends were family. Good times.

Loved those days!!

I remember people sleeping on the fire escapes in summer - I don't think they do that anymore. But yes, we did have respect for our elders, and that is sorely missed these days.

The big question was, whose stoop would you hang out on that night?

My stoop was on 8th Street, just off 5th Ave. between 5th & 6th Aves.

Great memories. It's funny how there were always those stoops that were more "popular" than others. I was lucky to have "my stoop" as one of those.

I remember the early *ahem* gentrification/ YUPification of the Slope, when *fences* were put on certain stoops to keep ya from hanging out!! Some still remain!!

Unfortunately, it was also the times - some fences were put up to keep the drug addicts from using your vestibule as a shooting gallery and your front area from being trashed. And we weren't the yuppies that moved into the area. And the neighbors were original Slopers, too. This was from living on 5th St. just below 7th Ave.

THE STOOP: how does one explain to those who do not know? We'll give it a try. A lovers' lane, casino, altar, confessional, kitchen table, night club, haven, healing stone, pulpit, starting point, ending point, café and playground.

Wow!

Someone should write a poem, "Ode To A Stoop." Like the "Ode To a Spaldeen."

I remember, even as a little girl, sitting on the stoop and walking to Carroll Street to get lemon ice at night.

A stoop is home away from home.

The stoop...generations mingling and intertwining; communication and sharing between family and friends; neighborhood interaction. It was funny, you could go on any block and see people and sit and talk for hours.

My stoop was huge. Therefore, it was the hangout for us kids.

I remember being really little and waiting for my father to come home. I wasn't allowed off the stoop at the time, and it took my father 20 minutes to get from the corner to our house because he would be stopped to talk to so many people on different stoops along the way.

What is your favorite memory about hanging out on the stoop?

Wow, Knuckles!! Almost forgot; double ouch!! Bleedin'!

Wow, too funny!

Hanging out with real friends, people who accepted you unconditionally and with so much less drama.

Waiting to watch the pizza guy deliver pizzas to the people we hated, after we called the order in!

Knuckles, would you take the 52 or the sandwich? What moron would put their hands between a full deck of cards and let someone stomp on it? (The Sandwich). If you scraped their knuckles while dishing out the 52, you got the 52.

52 Pickup was better!

The constant games of Brisk and Hearts - Shootin the moon and endin' up with the Mullins...

So many memories. First kiss - stoop on 9th St. by McDonald's; breakups and make-ups; flying down on a fridge box...and oh, yeah, those funny cigarettes.

It was my whole life as a kid. Sitting on the stoop listening to music with about 10 of us. First boyfriend, and best friends.

Only someone from the old hood will understand when I explain how I got a scar on my hand from playing knuckles.

When the pizza guy caught on...we sent Chinese food!!

I just remembered that after the pizza and Chinese food delivery guys caught on, we would send a car service around 1-2 a.m.

Playing cards all day and night on the stoop.

When my mom and aunt sat on the stoop and talked for hours, my cousin John and I would snap our tee shirts at each other. When you're 11, that's a lot fun!!

When we were young and stupid, we would snap the girls' bra straps.

Stoop ball.

Chipping in for beer or MD 2020 or Mad Dog.

Then Ripple came along.

How could I leave out Thunderbird?

Playing 45s and dancing!

But you forgot Boone's Farm and Tango! - hurl city!

Some things are still a blur, lol!

We have some great memories of hanging out on the stoop I loved when it got so hot in the summer that everyone was out on the stoop until all hours of the night! Lots of fun times!!

So much fun. Hot summer nights, and the entire block was out, or so it seemed. Parents, grandparents and kids. Laughing, talking, having ice cream. It was a comfort zone.

Singing Italian songs!

The stoop on the corner of 5th Avenue & 13th Street...you would always find someone to hang with. I don't think that stoop was ever empty. When we stopped hanging there & moved into the Lucky Buck, the next set of kids took over. Oh, the memories. Oh, let's not forget Officer Doyle's visit every couple of weeks. Ha Ha! He could have made a fortune if kept everything he found, instead of destroying the dubes.

Remember jumping off the side of the stoop onto the concrete aerie (13 steps)? I am surprised we didn't break our ankles

Is that the same Doyle that patrolled John Jay?

Officer Tommy Doyle passed years ago, of cancer....the officer that patrolled John Jay in the 70s was John Mann.

Boom box playing, and dancing in the street.

You all know that *everything* happens & happened "on the stoop." For me, it didn't start until we moved to 2nd St.

Life was loads of fun "on the street" anyway. Ice-cream truck, King Kong ride, "Officer Joe" always on Union & 5th, helping kids cross the street. The local Italian "social club," it made the kids feel safe, and always made things "very interesting."

Eating 10 cent packs of sunflower seeds and quarter juices while listening 2 some real hip hop on the stoop.

We had the two biggest stoops in Park Slope: the library and P.S. 39 on 8th Street and 6th Ave.

Just hanging out...everything!!

Laughing...someone was always doing or saying something funny. Sometimes we'd have a boom box and do the "Hustle," that was fun too.

150

Hanging out with my girl friends on the stoop as we played 45's on my Victrola and sang girlie songs.

Loved the girlie songs on the 45s..."He's So Fine"..."My Boyfriend's Back"..."Johnny Angel"...to name a few...and "Big Girls Don't Cry."

Everything -- not one bad memory of hangin' on a stoop!!

The stoop...the original social network!

6-Holidays in the Slope

- Easter

- 4th of July

- Halloween

- Christmas on 5th Ave

- Childhood Holiday Memories

It's the most wonderful time of the year! Yes it was, no matter which holiday, it was always special in Park Slope...now everyone is trying to shut down the celebrations, rename the trees; they probably never had many good memories and are stopping millions of kids from experiencing them also, but we will always remember.

Easter

Happy Easter memories! Loft's on 5th and 10th street. Chocolate eggs that opened up and had jelly beans inside, gold foil, happy Easter greetings. The best toffee, too. New shoes from National and a pink coat from Miracle Corner. Had to have a hat and pocketbook, too.

Oh, how I remember that. You just had to have a new hat and shoes. And if Dad and Mom could afford it, a new spring coat. I remember when they had hat shops, too.

Oh, YES--I remember!

And white gloves!

OMG, you brought me right back to Park Slope! Happy Easter!

Loft's!! Thanks for the memories!

OMG too bad the avenue doesn't have those stores anymore...I used to love shopping on the avenue.

Going to church and getting all dressed up in our little Easter bonnets.

4th of July

While growing up in Park Slope, I loved the 4th of July and the fireworks you could go get—and m~80s, cherry bombs, blockbuster. But my absolute favorite fireworks were helicopters and plain ol' bottle rockets. What were your favorite fireworks when you were a kid?!

Sparklers.

Everything you said!! plus something called crako balls similar to cherry bombs but more powerful!!

Blockbusters were the best!! Helicopters, too.

Got some bad burns from sparklers one year, LOL.

M80's, Ash Cans, cherry bombs, roman candles...

Burnt face, blown-up fingers, genies, yeah 4th of July!

Roman candles.

Yeah ....Genies...I forgot about them!

152

Cool...smelled weird. COOOLLLL!!

I always liked Jumping Jacks, Silver Jets and bottle rockets.

Lighting an M-80 and putting a metal garbage can cover over it. That M-80 would blow that cover way up in the air.

The entire street was thick with red paper shreds of firecrackers on July 5th. :)

My own cherry bombs in garbage pails.

Bottle rockets, roman candles, Lady Fingers and helicopters. Miss being able to light fireworks.

My family always had a great day. They'd come to my house to swim in the pool and BBQ, and when it was getting dark we'd shoot off the fireworks.

My uncle would come w/bags full of fun stuff. AHHHHH THE GOOD OL' DAYS!!

Remember all the great firework shows that went on all over Park Slope? Some blocks were shut off from traffic.

We had ours in the John Jay school yard.

My favorite was on 5th and 5th.

23rd Street between 4th and 5th Avenues.

Third Street.

We had ours right in front of our stoop. Our "super" at the time was a pyromaniac.

Could always head down to Chinatown and get the works.

14th bet. 3rd & 4th would have the annual block party, loaded with food, rides for the kids etc. At the end of the day, we would have our fireworks from several neighbors....when it was over, we would then sweep it up into a huge pile, set it on fire to blow up any firecrackers that didn't go off, and then turn on the johnny pump to wash away the mess...lol.

What good times on 10th St. btwn 5th and 6th Aves., setting off fireworks.

The John Jay dungeon! Best place to light up Christmas trees.

We all know who had the best fireworks on 10th Street...lol. Mr. P's birthday every year was the best display, and every year it was the only day when I got hurt in some way or another...

It's nice to see the pride for your favorite fireworks celebrations. It's one of the reasons I loved growing up in Brooklyn. You never had to go far to do, see, or get ANYTHING!

Ur right, ANYTHING, LOL!

Yeah, watching the fireworks from the rooftops, looking at the Statue of Liberty and the bridge.

Had to sneak down to the piers to get some fireworks.

Halloween

As if we needed another day to cause mischief...but we'll take it! And we did...and caused lots of good fun...and also got tons of candy.

Halloween brings me back to my youth. Coming home from school, my sister and I would get dressed up and go out trick-or-treating.

Going door to door with our shopping bags, we hit every house on 11th St., 10th St., 12th St., 5th Ave. and 6th Ave. We got so much candy, we would have to go home, empty the bag, and go back out.

Our mom had a good time picking out the candy that she liked...

We used to hit the apartment buildings on 8th Ave. and 5th St. to 3rd St. We'd be in there for hours.

We would just put on plastic masks with the elastic and get a brown shopping bag, and off we went for hours (no parents).

We would go up and down 8th St. and 9th St. and along 8th Ave. and PPW, and occasionally 7th St. I remember once going to the nun house when it also opened up on 7th St., and I think they gave out apples...we didn't go to the 6th St. entrance...and never the rectory!

Some years were pretty good - I remember quarters were great, and a dollar was like a miracle! I think one year I hit 5 bucks - but that was some heavy duty all day and 'til late trick-or-treatin'. Hitting all the apartment buildings on 8th Ave. and PPW was rough! Especially at 8, 9 and 10 years old!

It was a 100 percent kid venture. We would wander around the whole neighborhood, houses, apartment buildings, stores. And yes, run home to get another bag. The final stop was Pino's; they gave out free slices. Those were the best days. Hanging around with our free pizza, examining each others costumes—which sometimes consisted of nothing more than some makeup and our mothers' wigs.

Remember the costumes in a box? The popular one for girls was the fairy princess. Plastic mask, one long piece of polyester cape and a wand! The masks were a bit sweaty and you could hardly breathe with them on.

And that rubber band broke within the first 30 minutes of you wearing it, LOL. My mom then started making our costumes; she used to sew a lot.

I remember all of the above. Yes, we used to get money on 8th and 9th Ave. and then went to the movies at the Sanders.

Blast from the past! ;)

Made of wax...those were cool!!

Oh wow, this took me back!! Remember, they had the wax lips, too? U played with them and then chewed them for hours, lol.

I was in a store the other day & they had "wax lips" in the Halloween section. Couldn't believe it. Of course, they were obviously collagen-enhanced; must update for today, you know. ;)

Lol, that is too funny. I was also thinking how nowadays kids would probably choke on the wax. Or it has a warning on the label "chewing this may cause cancer," lol.

You know, for wax, they tasted pretty darn good. I'd stuff that whole harmonica in my mouth until my cheeks popped out. De-rishious! Chomp, chomp.

You're killing me! I think I still have some of that wax in my teeth!

I don't think I would eat them now--but I used to love them—the coke bottle ones.

Remember the chalk socks and the eggs on Halloween? We would go to the candy store and buy chalk, put it in a sock, then get a hammer or rock and break up the chalk. Then we started with the eggs, and we were bad with the eggs...lol...throwing them at people and bombing the houses of anyone that pissed us off that year.

Hitting moving cars, trucks and buses. Not just at the bus; we would wait in the bus stop on 5th Ave. When the bus stopped, a friend would hold the back door open, then we went up the steps and threw the eggs at the people sitting on the bus. It was funny back then, but looking back, it was wrong...

We got the eggs by the case, 72 dozen from Harry's Fruit Stand on 5th Ave. bet 9th & 10th Streets.

Don't forget the shaving cream!!

Some stores wouldn't even sell eggs on Halloween.

We put baby powder in the socks, and I was never allowed to throw eggs so I didn't...lol...but we did shaving cream!

I remember when Mom would pat me down as I went out the door to break any eggs! I was trying to sneak out of the house...do u remember that?

Yes!! She would keep the eggs hidden and she counted, too!!

They always had rotten eggs to sell at the Union St. chicken house.

How about dunking for apples at the Halloween parties down in the basements of your aunts' or uncles' houses?

Or the bad times, when some one decided to start putting razor blades in the apples and handed them out to the kids.

Christmas on 5th Ave

Who remembers how 5th Ave. was for the Christmas holidays—how the Ave. and stores were decorated? How the cold weather and snow would fall, and all the people were shopping? The kids looking in the store windows. Your parents buying Christmas toys and cooking for the holidays. Those were the good old days.

I remember the Christmas lights on 5th Ave. from 8th St. to 16th St. Three sets on every block, strung across 5th Ave. My sister and I would walk down 11th Street just as it was getting dark on Thanksgiving Eve, and watch the lights come on for the first time. That marked the start of the Christmas season...

And the Christmas shopping would begin on 5th Avenue, and we all would go to Germain's to see Santa...

I loved it at Christmas time, trees on every corner with that beautiful scent. It was magical...silver tinsel on your tree, colored lights, everyone dressed up, and your relatives were so close by. No driving in traffic.

And during the Christmas season, I remember stores selling Christmas trees on the sidewalks. My dad, sister and I used to walk down to 5th Ave. and 12th St. where we'd pick one out and carry it back up to the house. It smelled wonderful.

My mom used to buy a real tree from there and also in front of Timboo's, as well. Brings back the good old days.

That's right, they used to sell the live Christmas trees right there, and when you walked by you could smell the pine.

We bought our Christmas tree on Fifth Avenue and 3rd St., and it had to be on Christmas Eve or the day before because that's when it was the cheapest.

Walking along 6th Ave. with my entire family, going to midnight mass. Then back home, where the adults would have black coffee and homemade cookies, and we kids would be allowed to open one present each.

Neighbors who would be visiting out of the neighborhood on Christmas Day would come by to wish us Merry Christmas. Great times and great memories.

My parents would get out the 78 records, pull down the Victoria from the standup radio and play all the Christmas music.

How exciting it was at Christmas, because I sang in the choir at midnight mass in St. Francis Xavier. It was just wonderful...

I loved the Christmas lights along 5th Avenue!! From 9th Street to Prospect Ave....Great memories!!

Life seemed so simple then. Midnight mass at all of the neighborhood churches was packed.

Besides all the great memories of Christmas in Park Slope, it wouldn't be the same without the Johnny Mathis Christmas album.

I remember the Christmas lights on 5th Ave, and how a man had to walk up to each one with a pole to turn them on, one at a time. And midnight mass at Holy Family, standing room only, three priests at the altar, and the choir singing in the back above the congregation.

We belonged to a club, and every Christmas they would have a party in Prospect Hall. My father would walk my sister and me all the way to 15th Street to go to the party, and then we'd walk back. It was soooo exciting for us; what great memories of Christmas in Park Slope.

Remember 5th Avenue this time of the year? All the trees out in front of the stores. The smell of Christmas. The lights along the avenue. I can still see it. I can still smell it. I remember walking with my mom and all the needles from the trees were on the floor and you would walk on them.

Going to Germain's to see Santa, and how beautiful they would decorate the upstairs where Santa was.

My dad always bought the tree from 5th Avenue on Christmas Eve, and I remember him taking the saw out and cutting the top, and the smell of pine. Yes...when we got up, the tree was all decorated like Santa did it and the toys were there. We had a real chimney that we never used, of course.

One year I got a dollhouse and found a piece of furniture on the steps in the hall like Santa dropped it, and sand from the chimney was all over the floor. How I believed...

We went to A&S the same night we went to see the windows. Apparently I didn't quite get that whole "Santa presents" thing yet, LOL.

Germain's—having to walk upstairs to see Santa. A&S was always beautiful and felt classy. Then when I had our first son, we went to Macy's the day after Thanksgiving - what was I thinking? It was not called "Black Friday" back then - it was just an extra day off!

There's something very special about Christmas in NY. Funny I never "visited" Santa during my entire childhood, though.

I cannot remember if it was A&S or Macy's, but I remember going to see Santa and when it was your turn, they led you to a room but I could see there was more than one room with Santa's inside.

Lay away at Al's Toy land, Santa at A&S, and my Uncle setting up my Lionel train set.

160

Lets not forget "POPS" (Levine Bros., Jack & Julius) which served as a major hub for many parents throughout the neighborhood!

The street lights came on last week on 86th Street, but I don't know about this year on 5th Avenue yet; I remember last year there was only one string of lights, maybe for just a few blocks. Nothing like back in the day. Remember how crowded 5th Avenue used to be around this time? You couldn't even walk; people were shoulder-to-shoulder.

Since the weather's getting colder, gettin' to that time of year - who else had a 'Christmas Club' account at the Dime Savings Bank on 9th St. and 5th Ave.?

I think mine was at Greater NY Savings Bank, which was right next door. Apparently, NY State is still holding money that was mine from an account I had with them, LOL.

I had mine at the Greater New York Savings Bank also.

I used to have mine at the greater New York...I would feel rich when I was a kid at Christmastime...lol.

I think everyone did, lol.

Greater NY!!

I had mine at Atlas Savings Bank!

I remember that.. I think I saved 98 dollars and thought I was the shit...lol.

You were at the time; we *all* were. That was so much money back then. We could buy so many Christmas presents with that! Oh, yes.

Childhood Holiday Memories

What is your favorite childhood memory from the holidays?

Going to see Santa at A&S downtown.

Heading up the old wooden escalator from the Hoyt St. IRT station. Getting into the elevator that kinda tickled because it moved so fast. Waiting in line to see Old St. Nick...

Burning the tress in John Jay's underground school yard - after bringin' all the trees, and startin' them up, the police came with the Fire Dept. and we ran!

A&S is a blast from the past...been going to the Macy's that's there now for many years...thanx 4 sharing your memories.

Santa @ A&S.

Going to bed on Christmas eve with great expectations!

That too; Xmas morning was always worth the wait...special shout-out to Big Al's Toyland & the lay-away plan.

I remember going to Germain's and seeing Santa, and having a toasted corn muffin and a Brooklyn egg cream. Those were the days!

Going to See Santa @ A&S (now Macy's) in downtown Brooklyn and sleigh riding in the sugar bowl & Monument Hill in the park!!

Seeing Santa at Germain's on 15th Street!

I loved that on Christmas Eve we'd have a feast with the family, then we'd run down the block to our grandmother's house to see that side of the family.

On Christmas Day, we'd open our presents, then run back down the block to see what the lil' cousins got and play w/their toys. Afterward, making the rounds to friends and family we didn't see. I miss those days.

Playing outside with the snow coming down, with no traffic anywhere, rubber boots all buckled up and not even feeling the cold. My dad used to take my sisters and brothers and me to Fifth Avenue to count the lights that were hung. They went from 9th Street to 15th Street. Good times.

Keep the stories coming!

Early on, it had to be Germain's Santa and the 5th Ave. lights. Then Christmas morning itself. In my teens, it was midnight mass and visiting friends and family. When I got a bit older, it was hanging out in some bar with my large group of friends and going to someone's house for breakfast.

Interesting how profound that A&S memory is...

Who can forget walking into that store with the gold elevator doors, the store totally decorated and the Christmas music playing? What better memory for someone?

As soon as my parents went to bed, we knew that the gifts were underneath the tree, and we would run downstairs and wake them up; it was still dark out. Oh, the excitement!

Do you remember the sensation you would feel when those elevators moved? The speed of light, or some such...

Going to Radio City Music Hall to watch the Christmas show, then heading over to Rockefeller Plaza. Also, going down to Fulton Street to view the A&S window displays.

The Macy's Thanksgiving Day Parade! I was always so happy to see Santa at the end of the parade. To this day I still watch the parade, but on TV.

163

My favorite memory is sitting at the table on Christmas Day with a huge Italian family, comprised of grandparents, parents, aunts, uncles, cousins, etc., as we begin to eat a ten course meal. Most of them are in heaven now and I would give anything to go back in time. Heart warming memories that live in my heart forever...

The elevator operators were always trying to freak us out with making those things go fast.

Had to love those A&S elevator ops!!

Xmas Eve at Gma's with the whole family, eating fish and everything else.

I can relate to those who mentioned the feasts with the big Italian/Italian-American families...still doing that to this day....lots of fish & other yummy foods...I love my family & the fond memories we have created!

Going shopping in Macy's dept. store, then stopping off in McCrory's dept. store...taking the escalator to the basement and sitting on the stools and eating Sharlot rouche desserts with my mom...

The times spent alone with just you and your mom at holiday time are forever etched in your mind. Merry Christmas to you all!

Oh, and stopping in Chock Full O'Nuts for a hot dog and an orange drink.

Seeing Santa at Germain's and all the Christmas lights on 5th Ave., and the sound of Xmas songs coming out of every store as you shopped, and pretzels roasting on the BBQ by a street vendor.

I *loved* shopping on the avenue and being able to get whatever I needed at a good price. When I was little, at Christmas, my parents would give me like $5 to add to the money I saved from my weekly allowance of 10 cents, to buy gifts for my 5 older siblings, my parents and grandparents. I would shop in Greyshell or Dee and Dee, buying stuff for like 4/$1. Still have a few of those items to this day. It was nice seeing all the places decorated and all of the hustle and bustle. Thanks for the memories.

Oh, wow, everyone—thanks for the trip down memory lane...and the good old days...esp. the Christmas trees lined up along 5th Ave. We also used to go get a tree and walk back home...miss those days.

I still make sure I go Christmas shopping on 5th. Yes, I use the Internet or catalogs, but it makes Christmas special to buy in the neighborhood.

7-New Park Slope

Park Slope: my home, my birthplace, my life, my memories; what else can I say?

- Park Slopian
- Ugly Buildings
- Who Saved Park Slope
- More About Park Slope

The Park Slopian

This is the name of the book and the reason for the definition, to separate and differentiate the Park Slopers.

Here's another difference between real New Yorker/ Brooklynites/ Park SLOPIANS: My wife and I always take our "granny cart" to do the weekly shopping a block away at C-Town (aka: Royal Farms and the Prospect Theater before that). Watching these people run to get their orders in before the delivery time closes is just nuts.

I remember: If we didn't take the car, my parents would push around the granny cart all up and down the neighborhood to do the shopping. Rode in it until one day my dad let it go and I got a hell of a bump when it fell forward...

I still got one. Last year when they did not plow the streets, I used it to go food shopping. Worked like a charm.

I swear ta gawd, I am a bit older than you and I never, in my 33 years in Bklyn heard the term Park Slopians. That has to be a new word. I know, I know, I am no longer a New Yorker, being 20 years gone, but we were never called that!

No, never heard it either but like the new name. Park Sloper almost has a negative rep now because of the invaders. A friend of ours said we should call the invaders Slopies just to distinguish them from the regular folk.

Eh, just call them what they are, newbies, Johnny-come-latlies, carpetbaggers, a mess...lol.

I don't think Robbie thought this would cause quite a stir but, it was rather funny! You must admit...Robbie has a great personality & no insults are intended by Robbie, I can assure you. He's a great guy!!

Far from serious.

Definitely far from serious...call it Brooklyn Banter...stoop talk, if you will...

Hey, so its official, MY FELLOW PARKSLOPIANS...maybe that's what I will call my book...what do you say about the invaders who call themselves Park Slopers today? Or, pardon the expression—yuppies, who think they created park slope and made it better, and call themselves Park Slopers because they live there *now* (HA). When in fact, they actually ruined it: they took away the culture as well as raised the rent to $8000 a store rental (is that true?). Just so they can sip a small latte and eat a 4oz. pizza. That money can feed a small neighborhood in the USA (don't get me started). For all the memories that are on these pages, our kids will never experience like we did, so there has to be a re-definition between the people who share the memories on these pages and the people who occupy that part of Brooklyn now. They are just visitors to a place in time that we grew up in and where we shared all these wonderful memories, that all their money in the world can't buy: well, actually maybe one day they can *get real close* when I finish my book, LOL; we'll see if they'll spend some of that money on a real Park Sloper!

We used to call the people on the "drug maintenance program" Methadonians. They always hung around 5th Ave and 9th St.; they still do. It always amazed me how they would double over and never hit the ground.

O.M.G., not too long ago I was showing my daughter how they'd be waiting for the light to cross Fifth and how low they could go and not fall. She thought I was messin' with her.

Lord forgive me, but it was amazing.

I recall; sometimes they were around 5th Avenue yrs. ago... They looked like zombies from a scary movie!

167

Hey, didn't they have one right across the street from John Jay, halfway up the block? I sort of remember some clinic and the guys in suspended animation motion waiting for the place to open.

Yep, 6th St. (I think) right below 8th Ave and like 23rd and 3rd Ave on the corner. That's where they're giving out the Orange Magic.

What's sad is that when I drive by the 3rd Ave. site, I see many familiar faces. Some of these folks are in their 60s and 70s now. Many good people lost themselves and their lives with heroin from the neighborhood.

The junkie lean: they never fall over. I always found that the good people who dabbled in heroin would OD, and the junkies who would steal from their own mother would live on to be senior citizen dope fiends. No offense to anyone who is recovered; I'm glad you made it through, I just could never understand how some people's bodies could take so much.

I have lost friends to the drug and have known some to recover, thank God...but ya don't know the sadness of it when you're a kid.

Totally sad.

So true.

Heroin was a major factor in the downward spiral of the 'hood in the '70s. While many of us have fond memories, we all know blocks or people we avoided. The Slope is a lot safer now.

Weebles wobble but they never fall down. As a cop, this was a common sight; occasionally when interviewing this type of person they would go into a nod mid-sentence and fall right back into the conversation when they reemerged--sad but fascinating. It truly was the scourge of the slope; we lost lots of neighborhood people to this; some were really good friends.

The clinic was on 5th St., just below 8th Ave. and on the opposite side of the street from John Jay.

Ugly Buildings

Now look at what they have decided to build...

It's horrendous. It doesn't even come close to blending in with the original or existing architecture. Dislike. :(

It's been happening all over Park Slope for the last couple of yrs.

That sucks. Seriously.

U-G-L-Y !!

5th Avenue and St. John.

You know you're not from the neighborhood when you don't put up curtains or shades and let everyone see everything you have, and when you are not home, etc. These new buildings look like they came from a building in a weekend kit.

It's funny you mentioned that. I noticed on my last trip to the Slope, and questioned why so many apartments (and ground-level ones, at that) didn't have any window treatments. Those same apartments were "lavishly" furnished too. I mean pianos, classy artwork, fine woodwork details, expensive furniture, etc. Then it struck me: these folks were "showing off" their ritzy lifestyle. I even saw guys playing their guitars, saxophones, etc. while standing in plain view of the windows, like they were putting on a concert.

In many cases, there was nobody else in the apartment, and the volume was crankin'. They're either exhibitionists or idiots (though they did have elaborate security systems), or just plain both. These people are just not normal.

They are so arrogant! It is as though the world ends at the tip of their noses!

It is amazing how they let stuff like that go up next to vintage buildings! There are building codes so it doesn't ruin the rest of the neighborhood; even fake brick would have looked better than that, and blended in. Someone paid off the building inspector! and I guess the rest of the new Slopers were to busy sipping their lattes and didn't have time to protest.

I agree, like at Grand Army Plaza they put up a cheap looking condo against such beautiful classic masonry. What is worse, they give some of these people 5 year tax abatement's to live there, so that the taxpayers are the old school "Park Slopians" who don't have a say in how their neighborhood has changed.

Yes, this is what they did in NY, when they drove the rents up too high there, they came to the Slope-- and when they finish here, they will move somewhere else and drive those people out of their homes, but the memories ,they cant take that away from me...no no no, they cant take that away from me...

170

They've already gone across the river to Hoboken; that was back in the late 80s/early 90s when they ruined it. I assume they've now migrated to Weehawken & every *other* formerly nice little NJ town with a view of Manhattan. Kind of tired of seeing it, even from afar.

They're going up all over.

Yes it's disgusting - flaunting what you have - I take pleasure in knowing that that glass hunk of crap at Grand Army Plaza is still half empty – ROTFL!

Yes, I looked at the building because the views are spectacular, i.e. Grand Army Plaza Monument, the Brooklyn Museum, Brooklyn Public Library, Prospect Park and the Botanical Gardens. That's why there are all-glass walls. However, how do you cross all of that traffic?

Who Saved Park Slope

This is my 2 cents regarding an article and a popular misconception amongst the yuppies.

Am I the only one who is outraged by an article wherein someone stated, "the yuppies saved park Slope?"

What do you mean "saved" Park Slope, like from what exactly? Termites?!

"Looking Back: How Yuppies Discovered Park Slope," A magazine providing cutting edge news on the real estate market in New York City and beyond. Ha.

Like Columbus discovered America. Despite the fact that indigenous people already lived there.

Yes, back to the war with England: once yuppies cross a certain threshold of stupidity, when do they stop? Someday they're going to have to start cracking down on spinning around in circles really fast.

They pat themselves on the back as though their presence truly improved the neighborhood until they can no longer afford to live there anymore, because really wealthy people decided it's chic to live there.

When my daughter was in high school, she mentioned to a few of the yuppies' guppies that her mom had grown up in Park Slope. A number of them sniffed that I had "lived there when it was a slum," and some even said that *their* parents had *saved* the neighborhood. Saved it from *what*? A super-cool, working class place to grow up where everyone seemed to know each other? Right. We really, really needed snooty restaurants and fifty dollar cheesecakes. Lol.

Exactly! I was told once "Well, I live in Brooklyn, but thank God I'm not from Brooklyn." I laugh 'cause they paid 100 times more for their houses and in rent than we did, and last I checked apartments and houses didn't grow extra rooms on their own. Couldn't just live in a neighborhood cause you liked the place, had to make it trendy. Morons!

Having grown up on 2nd St. and 6th Ave., it fascinates me what the neighborhood has become when I go up to visit friends. How many organic food stores does a neighborhood need? I guess painting all those bike paths down the street require the purchase of a $5 slice of pizza.

172

What the YUPS have done to the Slope (now more like slop!!) is horrendous!! When we were growing up in the 60s through the 80s, the place was a cool place to hang, with great characters, hangouts, fun people & fun places to be!! In a little more than a 1/4 of a century it's been turned into a PC, sterile, commune-type setting. Oh, bring back the fun times of the 70s & 80s!! Elk & ostrich burgers? WTF?!

I'm still here and when I tell people where I live I add, "Not by choice, by chance." By the way, the people who saved Park Slope are our elders who couldn't afford to move!

And this has always--since the 50s anyway--been a mixed ethnic community. That was the best part of living in the Slope.

I remember as a kid, there wasn't one block that I walked down where people didn't know my mom. Okay, back then we called them nosy bastards, but they looked out for everyone's kids...

I lived there for 29 years, and I've seen it change just like the rest of us did, but now when I go back to NY for a visit--I'm sorry, that is not Park Slope!! All I see are snobs with overpriced strollers, and they look down their nose at you!! They are not Slopers; there's no memories there anymore, they built over buildings and the prices are crazy!!

My mom's rent was 35 bucks a month and that was for 4 1/2 rooms! The same building is more then 2 grand a month!! Screw that!

They saved Park Slope? That is the most ridiculous thing I ever heard! How? Who?

I grew up in the heart of the Slope. The reality is the Slope had everything. Writers, poets,, artists of all kinds, museums, music--we had the best that New York had to offer; we didn't need to go to the city of Manhattan. Brooklyn already had it. The bottom line is: the Yuppies moved to Park Slope because they wanted to be *us*. They wanted to work, play, love and live the way we did. In a magical place, in that magical time. But they can't, because it's not something you can buy or steal or just walk in off the street. It's something they can never have or appreciate. *It's home.*

Very well put, its our *home.*

We see them come and go, and we are still here. I am raising my kids with good old Bklyn values. IT'S HOME!

It needs to be saved from those yuppies! Park Slope is not what it used to be!

They need to go back to Manhattan.

They will someday, when their "precious" Park Slope is too expensive even for them. Then they will have to crawl back to the who-cares-where suburbs cause they can't handle real city life if doesn't have a food co-op and segregated schools. That's another thing they are doing to the neighborhood.

I know, I heard of a woman in a bar telling some guys to keep it down cause her baby was in the stroller sleeping. They believe the world revolves around them and everyone else is supposed to accommodate them. Stupid twerps.

They need to go back to their tower in the sky!!

Yeah, maybe they can make condos out of clouds.

WTF, yuppies *discovered* Park Slope.

I really miss the old Park Slope...kids out on every street playing something, you knew everyone on the block & if you *ever* did anything wrong, moms would know about it way before you got home....lol.

Maybe save Park Slope from other yuppies...lol.

The only thing the neighborhood needed to be saved from was gentrification itself. The neighborhood has lost its characters, its character, and its authenticity. I feel like I live in a tourist trap. The people that "saved" this neighborhood and defined its true spirit were our parents. So many of our parents had values that were admirable. They cared for and protected their own families and for others.

That seems to be the missing ingredient in the neighborhood today; it is a value that serves as a fundamental piece of building a true community. In the 60s, 70s and 80s, we had it stoop by stoop, and block by block. It can't be bought; it can't be fabricated. I wish our parents were still around to help save us from these selfish new residents. I deserve it; my family built this neighborhood.

This is not Park Slope anymore – racist, rude, arrogant, snobby, sloppy...

I hate when people say how seedy this neighborhood was - that's just cause they were afraid of Brooklyn!

Always loved my neighborhood, just hate what it's become, I can't even sit on the stoop of my family's brownstone because I get looks from everybody.

I always say - what's missing from Brooklyn...Brooklynites!

It's where they live; to us it's home.

Park Slope has lost its "Brooklyn feel." It's now filled with a fake, soulless atmosphere! That old Brooklyn spirit is gone!

I don't know what that article means because Park Slope was great in the 70s and 80s. Fifth Ave. was great for shopping and had great stores. It's always home to me!

Park Slope was the best place to grow up. I visited 5th Street 2 years ago. It broke my heart to see what the block had turned into.

The only thing yuppies did was drive up the housing prices!!

Property is worth a lot of money compared to what my mom and dad paid for it 55 years ago.

I'm proud to come from the real Park Slope, where people got your back and when right was right.

You're right. The real estate is sky high. I will be going back there to visit pretty soon. There was no better place to live or grow up than Park Slope. I cant wait to be back there and relive some of my fondest memories. :)

I am also proud to come from the real Park Slope. We all know who we are. The others aren't worth our time.

A Look Back At Park Slope

Though Park Slope may have had different names and boundaries in   its history, hidden treasures still remain among the new tenants. A few examples: where there are sprawling streets of stores on Fifth Avenue, there used to be an elevated subway back in the 30s. It was taken down as recently as the 1950s. A few movie theaters also adorned the streets of Park Slope. The only one left standing is called the Pavilion; in its heyday it was called the Sanders. It is located at what is now the edge of Park Slope on Prospect Park West and 15th Street at the park circle. There were plenty of theaters; even Snooky's was a theater in 1911-1916 that was called Touraine Theater. Other theaters in the Slope: the Garfield, on 5th Ave. between 1st St. and Garfield Place, which closed down in the early 50s. The 16th St. Theater was on16th St. off 5th Ave. The Globe was on 15th and 5th next to Larsen's Baker. And of course, the more recent and more popular one we remember is the RKO Prospect on 9th St., between 5th and 6th Ave. Also, the Avon, which was on 9th St. between 4th and 5th.

If you bought this book, you will also able to see Park Slope in its yesteryear by visiting theparkslopian.com, where I have compiled iconic images of people, places and things from the time period, plus a historic profile of Park Slope--with many more pictures that I couldn't fit in this book.

8 -Places We Ate

- Bickford's

- Bonanza

- Chinese Restaurants

- Chinese Takeout

- Delis
- Fran's Pizza
- Gleason's Deli
- Heritage Diner
- Herzog's Deli
- Ice Cream Stores
- Lewnes
- Pizza Places
- Restaurants
- Santo's Deli
- White Eagle Deli
- Polio's Deli

Bickford's

Bickford's Restaurant - 315 9th Street, Brooklyn (btwn 5th & 6th Aves).

What year?

1965-1970? Good coffee!!

Great, thanks again for the memories.

Thanks...I just got permission to use this in my book...I did a little more research, and for those of you who are unsure of where this is...it's where Bonanza used to be--the cigar store, the barber, then Bickford's.

Great detective work. If you have a link to some of your photos, please send it along. Have a very Happy New Year.

Find all photos and many more memories at theparkslopian.com

Many a pre-dawn morning was spent there, eating, fighting, sleeping, puking, falling off the stools, having food fights; it was like goin' to rehab without the nice scenery!

Wasn't there another restaurant on 9th, a little closer to 5th Ave. called the Cube Steak? I took my girlfriend to eat there after a movie at the Prospect Theater. I would have taken her to Bickford's, but my friends might have been there!

I don't remember a restaurant named Cube Steak.

The Cube Steak was there also, a few doors up from Bickford's.

The Cube Steak--did that later become the Heritage Diner?

Ah...now Bonanza I remember...my folks talk about Bickford's. I remember the Cube Steak and the Heritage House.

My parents think there was an old-style diner where the CVS is now, further up from this one. Never saw a picture of that, though.

Yes, I think there was an old-style diner up the block, between the pet shop and the YMCA. There was a large parking lot there, also...

WOW, I sort of remember that spot...I used to play there in like 1970. Then they tore that down and put in the A & P; I used to play in the big hole...don't know the name...but I do remember that there was something there before the A & P.

I remember the Cube Steak, used to go there with Grandma! :)

My dad thinks that they towed away the diner car from that spot. Moved it on a flatbed or something like that.

Ice cream soda & french fries & spinning around in the counter chairs were the highlights @ Bickford's Diner...I was very young at the time but...still remember!

Bonanza

Who remembers Bonanza Restaurant on 9th bet. 5th & 6th?

I remember during my nite time newspaper route, where I use to sell the early edition at a few of the bars and diners on 5th Ave., I used to stop by Bonanza's and get all kinds of foods that had so many different things.

I use to work there; it was one of my first jobs.

Hot dogs, burgers, corn on the cob...etc....

BEST FROG LEGS IN BROOKLYN!

I kinda remember it. Damn, you have a good memory, lol.

I never had the guts to try the frog legs.

OMG, that brings back lots of memories.

Open late at night even on weekdays.

I think the people who owned the Heritage Diner also owned Bonanza.

It was like having Coney Island right there in Park Slope. Oh, what I would give for a potato knish right now. (Did I spell that correctly?)

Knish...they were great.

Rotisserie chicken and my favorite - Colombo frozen strawberry yogurt!

Or the shredded barbeque meat on a roll and corn!

They had the best BBQ beef on a bun!! Sloppy but delicious!!

Wow, forgot to mention all the arcade video games inside. That was my favorite spot & also the YMCA was right up the block.

Bonanza! Used to play pinball and other video games there back in the day...I don't recall the food being any good tho. Not that we went there to eat.

Chinese Restaurants

Hey guys, what's the name of the Chinese restaurant on 5th Ave. near 9th St.? Remember u had to walk up those steps?

Can't remember the name but ate there all the time.

The name was Hom's.

I always went to Sun Joy.

Yummy...Sun Joy...

No steps into Sun Joy, were there? The "upstairs" Chinese place was across the street over Optimo...never had a name...just a sign that said, "chow mien"...am I right?

The best one on 5th Ave. was and still is Sunny Bo Bo's, between 10th & 11th Streets.

Come on, every Chinese place in Park Slope was amazing!!

I don't remember seeing a sign...lol.

Sun Joy!

SUN JOY!! Thank you, I remember they gave out cookies with an almond in the middle instead of fortune cookies. They were also the only Chinese restaurant for miles!!

My mom used to take us to Sun Joy every Friday night because my dad worked nights on Fridays. Great memories...

It was called the Bathroom in the Sky, as the whole place was tiled in white bathroom tiles which doubled for NYC Subway station tiles.

The Chinese restaurant above Optimo was named Hom's; I remember it well. I got food poisoning there when I was about 7 years old.

Chinese Takeout

Who remembers the Wing-Wah Chinese take-out restaurant between Garfield & 1st on 7th (near Greasy Jacks), Ate some of my 1st Chinese dishes there!! Great food, especially the fried rice & the dumplings!!

That place was so scary filthy...but that fried rice (or fried mice, as we used to call it) was quite tasty!

I remember it well, but honestly, when I was really "in the mood" for Chinese, I always went to Chinatown. I actually liked going to Greasy Jacks just to see the soda cups and dishes "slide" on the counter tops!! LOL.

They produced sooooo much in such a small space; it was amazing. Pots & pans were clanging or hanging everywhere!!

Yeah, now you pay TOP DOLLAR to go to places like Benihana to watch the cooks do basically the same thing, in front of you, like a production show! LOL.

Until about 5 yrs ago, Chinatown in NYC was still cheap. Now it's really expensive compared to what it was when we were younger & even old farts too!!

Loved their pork fried rice. Ate it all the time. I remember a really nice guy! He used to deliver the Chinese food by bicycle.

Wow, I remember that same guy; a couple of times we ordered and had it delivered right to us for free, if you know what I mean!

OMG--that was all I would eat for so long!! For at least a year--then I sampled everything else; it was all *great*!!

Wing-Wah - now that's going way back!

That pork fried rice was all I ever ate for the longest time, too! Straight out of the pint size carton. It was the first Chinese food I ever ate in life.

Funny, last month I was thinking about that place, but couldn't remember the name for the life of me.

Delis

Do you remember some of the delis and bakeries on 7th Ave. had cats hanging around the store? You got to know the cats as well as the owners.

I remember the cat that sat on the floor and the shelves of the deli on 7th Ave. between Garfield and Carroll (not Durells'). There was also a cat in the Regina Bakery on 7th between President and Union. This cat just sat on a shelf right behind an open bread counter. I remember thinking, is this really sanitary, and has anyone complained about it? And of course, there was the Doberman pincher at the Neerguard Pharmacy on 7th and 1st Street.

Iconic of the times. :)

I think that's the deli with the cat. I remember it from the 70s.

Don't all delis have cats? LOL.

I will always remember that deli.

You guys have great memories! Not sure about the cats though...Kenny and Bobby ultimately bought the deli before it went out of business...wonder if Kenny is still around? I'd love to get the deli's potato salad recipe...or a picture!

Ahhhh, BLIMPIES!

Mike's Deli always has fresh chocolate and rice pudding.

Only a hero from Pollio's could compete w/ a Blimpies sandwich.

Pollio's! I was trying to remember that place. Their heroes were the BOMB! :-)

Remember the cast of characters that owned/worked there at one point or another? Anthony, Little Vinny, Ronnie and Artie.

The two delis on 10th Street were on opposite corners; that was my first stop to school in the winter. I used to wear my Harpo Marx jacket (trench coat) and walk out with enough candy to last the day.

Who remembers Louie's deli on the corner of 7th St. and 6th Ave.?

What about Ralph's, or Garry's Deli on the corner of 6th ave and 11th?

They had good heroes.

Used to go to Ralph's to buy munchies and subs on the house account.

Sandwiches and a twelve-pack Rein gold.

1/4 pound of cheese and spiced ham or olive loaf.

13th & 5th made great heroes, too.

You could buy butter by the 1/2 lb or the lb, cut and wrapped in wax paper at 13th and 5th.

Or Herzog's on the corner of 3rd and 7th Ave. I worked there for a while.

I remember The Cantene when they had the corner place, before moving next door...great sandwiches...

9th Street off 4th Ave. Roast beef hero on a 3/4.

Great calamari and great sandwiches!

Breaded shrimp in the hot and spicy red sauce , Italian heroes with oil and vinegar, and great roast beef heroes.

Anyone remember Madora's on 5th Avenue? It reeked of the stinkiest cheese, but boy, they made the best Italian hero.

Fran's Pizza

Fran's pizza on 7th Ave. between 7th & 8th Streets.

It was nasty for sure. I used to go to Smiley's...

Everyone went to Smiley's, but the best Zeppole were at Lenny's on Prospect and 7th.

A dive, yes, but the pizza was good. Tom was Fran's son and there was another guy with a Hitler mustache--named Joe, I believe--that ran the place at night. He was a character! Lol, I worked right across the street at "Chick 'n Chips," another hang-out. :)

I love Chick 'n Chips...playing pinball.

Well, the guys at Smiley's were cute. :-)

I did have a crush on the tall one...what was his name?

He had these beautiful blue eyes, and he was tall and knew he was good looking.

Fran's Pizza was oily as hell.

He was great! He was outta control. He would tell us to "watch the place for a minute; be right back," and go across the street and play cards. He had so many stories he would tell, and loved his cigarettes. But he did look out for all of us and his pizza was great.
Great times, bro!! :)

Best pizza !!

Fran's had the best pizza...loved that place...

I remember that place; it wasn't bad, but L&B's, forget about it. Love their pizza, the squares.

Fran's *sucked*.

Gleason's Deli

Remember Gleason's Deli up the block?

Was that deli right next to a penny candy store? I forget what the name was. The first time my mom sent me to the store to buy a bottle of coke, I was 7. I fell, and the bottle broke outside the store. The deli man came out, picked me up, brushed me off, dried my tears and gave me another bottle of coke.

That would have been Frank who picked you up, and Charlie's Candy Store; I lived up the block.

I used to play Kings against the wall there before they put up the fence. Booty's up for the losers.

I lived on the avenue until I was 8, then moved to 11th St. between 8th and the park.

It was Frank's Deli; then the Gleasons took it over...I remember when my mother used to send me to the store for 50 cents worth of bologna...LOL...it was a lot.

Kings ruled on that wall for years; Charlie's Candy Store with the salted pretzels and Frank Mongello's deli.

186

Yeah, I used to get two nickels for the offering at Sunday mass, but sometimes I would forget to put the second nickel in and then head over to Magoo's for a salted pretzel. They were great people.

Yeah I know, I lived right up the block on 8th Street; I loved Charlie. My mom was the crossing guard on 8th Street and 8th Ave. when I was a kid.

Yes, OMG, I remember the list: get 50 cent spiced ham, 75 cents olive loaf, and ¼ pound of cheese from the bodega on 6th Ave. and 10th St. Once in a while I still get that at a supermarket just to go back in time for a few moments.

Heritage Diner

Does anyone remember the Heritage Diner on 9th Street between 5th and 6th Ave., not too far from the YMCA? They had the best cole slaw.

I'd go there at 2 a.m. and get a chocolate shake and a hot pastrami on rye, the friggin' best chocolate...hot.

I agree, or after the YMCA dances everyone was hungry and went there to eat. They made awesome cheeseburger deluxes.

Heritage House, no?

That's it. The Heritage Diner. Thank you; I was racking my brain. I knew it was close in name.

Loved the Heritage!!

I remember going there every Sunday--burger deluxe, or grilled cheese sandwiches and soup.

A very good friend of mine was their best waitress. Her name was Lydia.

Remember the little Greek momma...always in black? She used to make sure her boys were on their toes working! Little Greek momma was sweet & feisty!! Good local diner!!

Herzog's Deli

Remember Herzog's Knishwich?

YEP!! I liked their fried chicken & various pasta dishes. Ziti was great!!

Yes! Do you remember Herzog's always had a 20-25 lb. turkey in the deli show case? *Delicious*!!

Loved it, and Durell's on 7th.

If I remember correctly, Herzog's was the only deli to stay open 'til 11p.m. Best dill pickles!

I loved Herzog's. My friends and I had a crush on a guy that worked there; I asked him his name, but we called him Wa Wa 'cause he only said "what else?" We were kids, but we kind of stalked him. Poor guy. Durell's was a great deli. Anyone remember Bill's on 7th Ave. between 1st and 2nd?

Herzog's chocolate donuts were 2 for $.25.

Nothing like Herzog's Deli!

Yup!!

Hey, didn't they make Belly Bombers? I used to work there for a while...and broke the sound barrier. Until I worked there, they never let anyone play music. Well, that was a no-go in my book, and of course they saw things my way.

Ice Cream Stores

The Carvel store on 7th Ave. and Carroll Street, boy I miss all that free ice cream!!

I loved that Carvel store.

I helped myself to lots of ice cream when working at Carvel!!

I loved the Carvel store, except for the time I fell down the stupid open cellar door. Spent many a summer evening there with my friends.

I loved that place.

OMG, I lived around the corner on Carroll bet. 7th & 8th...that store is so prominent in my childhood memories! Cones were 35 cents, and since the counters were so high they could never see me waiting, so I'd tap my quarter and dime over my head on the counter-top to get the attention of whoever was working! Ah, soft chocolate on a wafer cone never tasted so good...

I just saw this today. Oh my God!! This was home!!

OMG, the memories I have of this place. I lived on Carroll bet 7th & 8th from 1970-1979. 35 cents bought you a cone. I loved this place.

Great memories of working there!! And me & the rest of the Garfield crew hangin' out inside & outside of the store!! Who can forget Jody the dog chasing us out all the time!! Lol.

Also great memories of your dad.

Best ice cream cake in the world.

This was a big part of my childhood!!

I so miss those parfaits where you took off the top and put it on the bottom to stand up. I actually bought my wedding flowers from the florist that bought the store afterward. The door made me very nostalgic.

One of my favorite places to be...

I worked there.

First two-way mirror in The Slope.

189

Wasn't there a Carvel--or maybe a Dairy Queen--on 7th Ave. (8th & 9th)?

That was Dairy Joy, on 7th between 8th and 9th.

There was a Dairy Queen on 5th Ave. bet 8th and 9th St.

In the summer I used to bring home a shake to my mom all the time...after I sold newspapers at night. Even as a teen, I continued the tradition...walking up 8th St. with two shakes, though mine would be done by the time I hit 7th Ave....ha!

I remembered as soon as you mentioned it. It's funny how the mind works!!

Always at Nick's Dairy Queen on 5th and 8th St. Best flying saucers and ice cream sandwiches.

Carvel - flying saucers - Fudgie the Whale cakes - the owner would give us extra sprinkles, even on my flying saucer! I loved that store.

Mister Misty's brain freeze!

The Chocolate Thick Shake Float!

With an extra scoop of chocolate thrown in for good measure.

I remember it well.

I loved going there! My favorite was marshmallow syrup over vanilla with sprinkles. Beats Häagen-Dazs any day.

Oh...the things the boys who worked there used to do to the food items there...frightening...you know who you are, and you know what you did...naughty ones...I used to play it safe and stick to getting the soft ice cream cones, armored with far too much knowledge...

I know the names and the perps! Ya wouldn't be surprised!! LMAO!!

It was only aimed at the real "problem" customers, though. The "pains in the asses," as they would say!
:-)

I hope you never had the orange drink!

I remember the shop well. Or maybe my mind doesn't work well enough to know. Anyway, I loved going there.

Smooth, best ice cream.

Who remembers the name of the ice cream store on 5th Ave. between 10th and 11th Streets?

The name was Carnival; it closed.

It was first Carvel, then changed to Carnival.

Lewnes

The ice cream store & diner on the corner of 9th and 9th--I think it was called Lewnes...

I think we're still paying off the bill for all the ice cream sodas I had in this place. Wow!! Brings back old memories. :(

It was Lewnes, & then it became a restaurant. The building was demolished at least 8 years ago, and an apartment building went up.

Loved this place, especially after sleigh-riding at Monument Hill...

OMG, so many fond memories of this place. And the Park House Restaurant next to it.

Lewnes had great burgers & shakes!! Better than Benny's!!

All right! Our famous hangout after work on a Friday night!

My brothers and I would sleigh-ride in the park (Monument Hill), then stop here to get hot cocoa, then go down into the subway and walk underground 'till 4th Ave. to keep warm.

That's the place!! Lewnes!! Benny's was cheaper, tho.

Yeah, wow...sleds and Ivory soap and money for Lewnes...that was all we needed.

The Ice Cream Parlor was at 9th St. and Prospect Park West.

Lewnes Restaurant: spent many Sunday mornings in there.

I used to walk to Lewnes or to Benny's many nights with my father to get the news. All the men would stand around smoking and talking and the news; the truck would pull up and the driver would throw the bundled papers off, and they would stand around waiting to get their copies. Sometimes I would get a roll of butter rum life savers...

Benny's was on 8th Ave. and 9th St. I don't remember Lewnes.

Lewnes, LOL...it had been called the Ice Cream Parlor since 1962. Lewnes...LOL.

This is definitely Lewnes, on the corner of 9th St. & PPW. I grew up on the corner of 10th & PPW and the Lewnes owners, a husband & wife, lived in my building.

Last time I drove by, all gone...now new condos.

In the 80s it became Rain Trees.

A word from an elder - in the 1950s, teenage couples would always go to Lewnes for an egg cream before a romantic stroll in Prospect Park.

Benny's was Tony's in the 50s.

The only problem is that Lewnes opened in 1906, so it was there in the 60s, too--and as I said earlier, some people know a store as one name and others will remember it as another. Either way, the store was still the same.

Yeah, back when a scoop of ice cream with a cherry on it was like a big reward.

Then the world will seem right again...

Went for ice cream there after playing Knights of Columbus baseball.

Pizza Places

Smiling Pizza on 7th Ave. and 9th St. *Best* pizza!!

THE BEST>>>>> OMG...

Before Smiling Pizza expanded, there used to be a cleaners on the corner and Smiling was half the size.

Never really liked their pizza. Camille's on 5th Ave. & 11th St. was much, *much* better. Anyone know if it's still there?

Of course my absolute favorites were John's on Bleecker St. and Grotto.
That last one is or was on either 20th or 21st Aves off 86th St., and Spumoni Gardens. Oh, never mind, LMAO.

I think it's just a novelty now.

We did Pino's a lot. Only one that would deliver to Eastern Pkwy...

Pino's - their Sicilian right outta the oven - hands down - for me!

Now I remember that one! Oh, yes...

You can't get good pizza out here because the water sucks. :(

For Sicilian, L&B Spumoni Gardens was and is still king!

House of Pizza and Calzone down on Union St. were our favorites. Pino's and Smiling were good, also.

Gotta agree - Pino's, through and through - still crave it to this day. Loved the orange oil, when it actually dripped down the cracks of your fingers if you forgot to put a napkin at the spot where you bended the crust...mmmm...took my kids there once - time to go back!

I liked Fran's on 8th Street.

Fran's had that orange drink that went great with their slices, and man did Pino's make the best Sicilian and individual pizzas with the onions--mmmmm mmmm goooood.

When I was a kid, I'd have "pizza lunch" every Friday @ Fran's. I remember Mom would give me a dollar and the slices were like fifteen cents each! But Smiling put them out of business. It was sad; I always thought Fran's made much better pizza.

My first date with my hubby was at this place---the pizza was so good.

Tell me about it. I made my whole family troop it over 2 bridges just to get a pizza pie after 21 yrs of not having one. Believe it or not, the place looks great. Pizza is still great, and one of the men who used to give me slices as a kid was still there and even *he* hasn't changed much. Love my Park Slope!

Chicken parm hero, my favorite!!

The best pizza in Park Slope!! :)

I still miss Brooklyn...*especially* Brooklyn pizza. :)

What I do when I walk by the place. I inhaled deeply, just to see if my memory would let me "taste" that smell. (Sigh.)

194

I could actually hear the guy screaming, "Who's next?" With the open door...LOL.

7th Ave. entrance.

I guess these guys would rank #2, next to Lenny's...

I got it; I got it! LOL...

Yes, #2 after Lenny's. Not before Pino's though. I know others may disagree...

I love Pino's slices and love Smiling's squares...

Smiling: I grew up on it; I would call and Tony usually answered...RIP. I said it was Junior, and he knew: large pie, xtra sauce, pepperoni, burnt. :)

I never forget to eat at Smiling once a year.

Back in the day, I was always a "Pino's guy." Lived on 2nd, between 6th & 7th. So close, why go anywhere else?

Marino's Italian ices! *The* best!

Ice, hands down! I liked the lemon.

Aniello's pizza on 11th Street on 5th Avenue – *the best*!

Who had the better pizza...Aniello's on 5th between 10th & 11th, or Camille's on 5th between 11th and 12th?

Camille's, totally! *But* Anellio's had the jukebox!

I think the guy at Aniello's sweat onto the pizza more. thus giving it that true greaseball flavor!

But Camille's taught me my only Italian words: "Che fa?"

I think she had a face...pretty sure she had a face...I think her father shipped her out...

Camille's--the cheese was great!

Camille's, also known as Mike's.

Camille's was the *best*...Aniello's has the atmosphere (jukebox)...anyone remember the tiny hole in the wall, Joe's, on 5th between 13th & 14th?

Yes, I remember Joe's, and then there was--and I believe still is on Prospect--Lenny's. From 7th and 5th Ave. to Prospect Ave. we had 6 pizzerias.

Lenny's is still there...they have the best Calzones

Camile's, hands down.

Omg, that's awesome!! There's a place in South Beach in Miami with the entire NYC train map on the floor of the pizzeria. I asked the guy behind the counter; sure enough they were also from Brooklyn.
=)

The jukebox had Jethro Tull..."Living in the Past." And Led *ZEPPELIN'S* "D'yer Mak'er!"

Camille's had the best pizza in the world. No duplicates. Ever. Mike made the best pie. Mom & Dad don't eat pizza because it doesn't taste like his.

Camille's was the best--every Fri nite with my gf for pizza and a soda!!

Come on now; there was a time when all the pizza in Park Slope was good and made by Italians.

Lenny's *is* on Prospect Ave. & 5th, and it was good, but no Camile's.

It was Camille's. Best squares in Park Slope!

Who remembers Frank's on 7th Avenue and the corner of Prospect? Among many things, they had the famous 3 pieces of chicken for a dollar! I would stop there on the way to I.S. 88 with my brother and split a meatball sandwich.

What about Dino's Pizza on 6th St. and 5th?

Nico's Pizza on Fifth Ave. between Carroll and President Street.

What was the name of the pizza place next to Tony's Records we always use to hang out at?

Restaurants

One of my fondest memories of Park Slope was Snooky's.

I was a hostess there...loved that place!

The best salad bar and shrimp Newburg...yum...

I loved the Shrimp Newburg; it was so delicious.

I hear you; I'm in the process of changing back myself...lol.

Christmas Eve after mass at Snooky's was always an adventure. You never knew who would show up each year.

French onion soup in the small crock pots...yummy. My favorite waiter was Al, a big guy, bald, with glasses...everyone loved him.

I was there every Friday night!

We really, really, got to groove, lol...ring my bell?

Love Snooky's: onion soup, french fries, and Pac Man.

Shrimp scampi!! Ordered that every time I went there.

It was the place to hang out and I got pretty drunk, lol.

I remember hanging out at Snooky's.

Was a great place for food and fuel (booze that is)!!

We sure had a good time.

I was there every Friday, beer bottle in hand! Lol.

And I was sitting right next to you...

Does anyone remember the bouncer at Snooky's?

And I was in the middle, lol...

Isn't Snooki on the Jersey Shore, lol?

Raising the elbow in Snooky's every Friday night, lol.

Ha ha, you're too funny, lol.

"Burger in a basket" was my fave from there to my hub. We both wanted Snooky's back, at that moment. Oh well, can't have it all...there's 9000 places for organic food now in Park Slope, but no burgers in a basket.

I saw a place on 7th & 3rd that has organic food, organic wine & organic beer?!

Isn't beer by definition "organic?" Hops, barley, rice, water and yeast? They sound pretty organic to me.

Had this mirror back in the 70s: "Man made beer. God made grass. Who do YOU trust?"

Why did Snooky's close?

Remember how Gov. Carrey used to come down from Albany to hang out at Snooky's every now and then? You'd see this limo out front. Go inside, and he's in there bending the elbow with everybody else.

Snooky's will always hold a special place in my heart.

The manager was a great guy!! One of the bouncers' names was Steve; that's the only name I can remember.

That was a great place to work: great co-workers, great customers, great food, and great tips!! It was a party every night, a lot of great memories there.

Remember how crowded it got at the bar, lol? Henry was always after me to fix the salad bar; I would dream of mixing it all up and playing Pac Man instead!! Al always told him to lighten up...loved Al!!

Sweet memories.

Santo's Deli

This place has been there a while now. I used to work at Methodist (in the early 90s), and it was there

Used to be Santo Aniello's 7th Street Deli.

Old Man Santo. WOW! That man put up with a lot...he put up with us, didn't he? How many times did we raid his beer freezers? God bless him!!

When I worked there, I used to stash a case of Bud near the dumpster and come back and get it later...good times.

We would just walk into Santo's & walk out...know what I mean?

I worked in many a deli in my day, also did some time there.

White Eagle Deli

Ever go to Eagle Provisions ? Great Food...

It had a *great* smell when you walked in, like any really good deli. Another thing I miss about Brooklyn. :(

Great beer selection, too!!

Polio's cheese aroma hit you right in the face. Ahhhhh, yes.

Yes, White Eagle on 5th Ave. near Prospect; we would go in for kielbasa and have to double the amount as it never made it home to 8th St.

Great polish sausage.

Is this place still there? I don't remember it?!

For sure, decades. The best kielbasa...

Since the 40's...

Now *that's* the sandwich spot! 5 dollar heroes...real Italian bread...fresh cold cuts and oversized sandwiches...not to mention over 100 different kinds of beer.

The White Eagle...great Polish food.

When I lived on 23rd St. I did all my food shopping there. They would bone a fresh ham for ya so you could stuff it yourself, or they'd stuff it for you - I made my own...best kielbasa also, and fresh sauerkraut out of a barrel, like pickles.

There used to also be a White Eagle Bar on I think 23rd and 5th.

Yep - very clean taps - good beer and lots of parties, weddings etc. in their back room...

White Eagle has been in the same spot for 100 years. We always went there for Easter to get our Polish food...

As a little girl we always went there to get our Easter Polish food...because my dad was Polish. All my relatives shopped there. Great store...

Polio's Deli

Now we can't forget Polio's Deli, the best Italian deli in The Slope.

It smelled Italian just walking by outside.

Yea those were the guys who worked there, HA!

The best subs in The Slope.

I had the subs everyday for lunch.

What about all the salamis hanging there and the cheeses? You could barely see the meat case to order.

And all the specialties: the marinated mushrooms, and the artichokes...

And the tapioca puddings, MMMMMMM.

We would go to the original Polio's to order our Christmas Italian Platters. Great heroes. The aroma of the store is what a true Italian specialty store should always smell like; the dried meats and cheese hanging and on the counters; we need stores like that in the neighborhood again.

Rice pudding with cinnamon on top was my favorite, after getting money from my brother's boss on 7th Street & 5th Avenue.

I could never forget Polio's and Medora's. I lived on 6th Street between 4th and 5th Avenues, so these delis were a short walk away. It's rare today that one could find such delicious, fresh Italian delicacies. Mom and Pop stores are becoming a thing of the past.

9-Places We Went

- Avon
- Bars
- Farrell's
- Timboo's
- Clubs We Went To
- Prospect Park Carousel
- Pool Halls
- Sanders
- YMCA
- Horse Stables
- Kate Wollman Rink
- Prospect Park

Avon

Who remembers the movie theater on 9th Street?

Avon was on 9th St. and 5th.

When did it close?

I went everyday to see *Where Angels Go, Trouble Follows* until they changed the movie.

Closed around 1970, I think. Then McDonald's came to Park Slope. Hamburger, fries and a coke under $1.00 (it was actually 99 cents, LOL).

I saw *West Side Story* there and probably a lot of other ones, but that was the last one I saw.

I saw my very first movie there - *Blackula*! Yep, that one! When I was 8 or 9 I think. And of course - the McDonald's came in...I think in about '75, I could be off a year or so.

202

"feel" for you brother. I'm so sorry that you actually paid to see *Blackula*.

I went every Sat. It was only 50 cents...

The good ol' dayz.

The Avon 9 St. bet. 4th & 5th Ave. It's now McDonald's.

Yep, and there was a diner right next to it...

I think the diner was called Sonny's....and on the other side was the locksmith and the bar.

The Avon showed porn. The Prospect was between 5th & 6th.

Don't believe it always showed porn...

Do you remember the matrons with the flashlights walking around looking for whoever was throwing candy?

Something funny. My mom brought us to see Fritz the Cat not knowing it was X rated. She thought it was Felix the Cat. We left in a hurry, lol.

Pretty much...never first-run movies though, even before that. They premiered *Gone With The Wind* in 1968.

Back in the day the Avon was a family theater...

The Manson family.

Yep, I forgot about it till now.

Which one? The Avon or the RKO Prospect?

I went to see an Elvis Presley movie at the Avon on Easter one year. When I went in it was sunny; when I came out it was a blizzard. I'll never forget that.

I saw the first two Beatles movies as a double bill at the Avon – *A Hard Days Night* and *Help!*...

203

All I remember of the Avon is the huge King chair that was placed between the male and female bathrooms in the basement.

I saw *The Bible* there when I was elementary school.

I remember it has a lot of horror flix before porn.

Yeah, I remember the horror flix also.

I saw *Mary Poppins* in there.

I remember but we used to go to the Sanders on Prospect Park & 15th St.

I'm not sure if it was the Avon or the RKO, but I remember going to triple features in the late 60s & early 70s. Usually horror films.

Weren't there two movie houses on 9th? One was below 5th Ave.; the other was above 5th. Does anyone else remember this?

The Avon was below 5th Ave. and the RKO was above 5th; it's now a supermarket.

The Avon was where McDonald's is now: 9th St. btwn 4th and 5th Ave. The RKO was on 9th St. btwn 5th & 6th Ave. We were lucky to have them at the time, lol--always at the Avon Sunday matinee.

Hey, that locksmith is there 100 years.

Oh yes! Both theaters on 9th Street, were where I went most often to see movies.

The Avon on Saturdays used to show Elvis Presley, Jerry Lewis and Vincent Price movies back in the early 60's. My mother was a ticket cashier at both the RKO Prospect and the Sanders. Always got in for free!!

We used to get in for free also. But we did so the hard way, sneaking in.

That vintage-style house next to the post office was Higgins Ink...

Used to go to the Avon a lot when I was kid. Our parents used to let us go alone at the ripe old age of 10. Our parents would give us 50 cents: 40 cents to get in and 10 cents for two nickel boxes of candy. That was before we learned how to sneak in, then we had 50 cents for candy. The stale candy-coated peanuts in the red box were the best to throw at other kids. They started showing X-rated flix before it closed down.

THE PROSPECT! My daddy calls the supermarket that is there "The Prospect"--between 5th-6th Aves.

I remember seeing Jerry Lewis' *Way Way Out* at the Avon, LOL.

That movie made me fall in love with Connie Stevens. By the way Jerry Lewis's son, Gary Lewis and The Playboys, sang the theme song.

Bars

As we grew in age (and some underage) we were able to get into bars...and we found a new drink, beer. And after a hard day's work or play, football, stick ball, or hockey, we would hang in the bar; at playoff time the crowds would be maddening.

There were quite a few bars along 5th Ave. Matty's 5th & 5th, Luisi's 6th & 5th (which later took the spot of Matty's), Dom's 7th & 5th, Jackie's 5th Amendment (His & Her's) 7th & 5th, Smitty's, Roundhouse & Dinky's between 8th & 9th...Ok I tipped a few back in my day!! But the list goes on!

Which was the one that was literally next door to your old apartment? Matty's?

Yep, Matty's which later became Joe Luisi's.

Anyone remember Rocky's on 9th Street between 5th & 6th Ave...?

MUENSTERS BAR--9th & 6th...Oh boy.

The list goes on!!

Nick the bartender...Good guy...Very good guy!!

Muensters was in a class of its own. Good/Bad?! But it was MUENSTERS!!

Remember the After-Hours? 12th & 5th upstairs...Port Royale...Irish Haven...The Club Prospect & 7th.

Star 5th & 5th.

I think Ryan's, Snooky's, Mooney's and every other Park Slope bar gave us a lot of BAD MEDICINE back in the day which actually explains a lot really !!

That's funny but so true. Walk in, scope around, grab a stool, listen to some music, and drink to your health. LOL.

Ya forgot a few!! Coach Inn, Gaslight, Stack 'o Barley/City Lights & Iron Horse of course!! The later named after me of course!! HEH HEH!! ;-)

Leave it to you, for not forgetting a bar! He, he, he!! How 'bout The Roost on 7th Ave. and 8th Street?

That was one of my haunts; grew up on 8th St. bet. 6th & 7th Aves. LOL.

How 'bout Diamonds Bar on 9th and 7th Ave,, and the Motherload disco that was in the same place many years later?

I remember Diamonds and there was another bar right across the street on the corner.

Lucky Buck....5th Ave. between 13th and 14th Street.

Clancy the bartender at Muensters. Always had new jokes every time I went in.

Clancy also did time at the Gaslight...

206

I lived above "The Wagon Wheel" on 10th St. and 4th Ave. when we moved from 5th St.

My first illegal beer was at Dom's, across from the pool room.

My brother used to tend bar @ Dom's. My whole crew drank there way before we were 18.

16 here. Basically, it was here's your beer, go sit down and don't cause trouble.

Totally different neighborhood then. We might not have known the bartenders and owners at 16, but man, they knew every one of us. Knew our parents, uncles and aunts. Lol, we thought we were getting over one, when in reality, they were watching us.

Celebrated my 16th Bday at the Coach. Bartenders: Dave, Al and Rich. They were the best.

How about Munster's and Rocky's, we had a few in there...

It didn't matter where I started my night; 99% of the time I would end up in Muensters. This says something about Muensters...I'm not quite sure what it says, but it says something!!!

Muenster's Bar, the poor man's "Cheers."

I remember shortly after I moved from the Slope, I went to a bar not far from my house and the looks I got from "the regulars"...bah. Humbug. I'm a homebody. LOL.

What was name of the bar at 9th St. and 7th Ave., lol?

Diamond's.

Joyce Jack's Pub....my dad used to stop by there after work. I'm sure it is called something else now.

The bars on 9th Street & 7th Avenue are all long gone.

Jack's on one side and Diamonds on the other, Jack's was the original Denny's that since moved to Church Ave. and is still in operation...

I had a girlfriend who loved Jack's; I asked why and she said, "Because the old men don't bother me."

Underaged, wearing my dad's old army jacket when the bartender proofed us, Joe tells him, "They didn't ask how old we were when they sent us to 'Nam, what are you having, gents?" Diamonds rocked.

Timboo's 11th and 5th is closing at the end of this year.

Lucky Buck. It was an old man bar even when we were young!

You're right...most of the bars were old man bars on 5th Avenue... back then...or we thought they were because we were so young.

Lucky Buck, there was a blast from the past.

I know this is off the Slope a bit, but I spent more than one St Patty's day at Farrell's on PPW in Windsor Terrace.

Timboo's closing!? that's crazy talk! Say it's not so.

Sorry... it's true.

Was never in Timboo's. Wonder what's gonna go there, another nail place?

Never in Timboo's? You were so close! I think another yuppie bar with clever sayings blocking the sidewalks is more likely!

Mcfeelies.

Who remembers the bar on 12th St. & 7th Ave.? What was its name?

I don't remember but I do recall getting my ass handed to me.

208

That is unbelievable; I was just talking to a friend of mine tonight about how I used to play softball for Rockies Bar on 9th St. against that same bar, and I cannot remember the name of that bar either!

Was it the 2 T's?

9th Street & 7th Avenue - The Alamo.

Nobody bothered you for drinking outside of Farrell's in those days.

Carrying 16 big white cups to the park without dropping any...priceless.

Minsky's, later REX, then Miracle Grill, now a burger chain Chee-Burger, Chee-Burger!!

That goes further back than Minskys then.

Yes it does, I truthfully forgot about Minskys, it was the Blue Eagle back in the early sixties...

I loved sitting in the outdoor section sipping banana daiquiris and waiting for their fabulous spinach salad (back when I was skinny, LOL).

Spinach, that is, at Minsky's.

Drank at Farrell's, too!

Coach & Snooky's too. Remember?

When my father went there it was the Blue Eagle Saloon.

I remember the Coach & Snooky's..real well...and the Palm Pines on Union Street...Blue Eagle...

There was a pub on every block..maybe even two...there was Caulfields, Roaches, Diamonds, etc...so many I can't remember all of them...and they all did well...

Does anyone remember Moonies Pub?

It moved from 8th Ave. quite awhile ago; it was on Flatbush Ave. for at least 15 yrs closed about 3-5 yrs ago for good!! There is a group on FB dedicated to Mooney's.

Moonies...vague memories...

I remember Moonies.

Farrell's

Missed it by that much!

You know how we get about our beer; when it comes to staking a claim about our territory, just one block off the newly drawn lines of The Slope sits a bar with a great beer on *tap*.

Know it isn't technically Park Slope, but we all hung out there...

Yes, we did. =) The best was right after the Irish Day parade standing outside with your containers of beer and green bagels.

Oh FARRELL'S! THE BEST TAP BEER IN TOWN!! :)

Hey, they split us up like Ma Bell; this was all south Brooklyn.

I think Farrell's opened 1931.

It gets honorable mention.

Sorry dude, it's the Slope, hello!

No. Wrong. It's Windsor Terrace.

I lived on 13th between 8th and PPW...

Best tap beer anywhere!!

Never been there...heard it was great!

It is technically Windsor Terrace but that's ok.

True...Windsor Terrace it is...but if you ask a realtor...it's Park Slope South...which evidently according to them runs into the 30s (that's street!).

That's da Slope...just on top.

According to the map, the slope's boundary was 15th Street...so it's close enough to include in my book!

Mine too, literally speaking.

Besides, most of the beer we were drinking on the parkside came from there. :-))

I remember all you guys with the tall white paper cups after a game coming back from there...I never hung out there though---seemed like it was more of a Cheers for guys...

Back in the day, weren't women not allowed in there?

They could go in, they just couldn't purchase from the bar.

And the women had a separate side entrance and rang a bell to enter.

Apparently they couldn't use the front door. But what I remember is you had to be buzzed into the bathroom.

Women had to sit at the booths with the gentlemen that they came in with and rang a bell on the wall (still there, not operable, at least the last time I was there) for service. They were not allowed at the bar. I don't know when the buzzing into the ladies room started.

I am glad you said purchase at the bar, because there was no sitting at the bar, because there were no seats.

Hated when they switched to Styrofoam cups!

ICE COLD TAP
AHHHHHHHHHHHHHHHHHHHHH!

Containers, Taps, Tall Boys. What else were they called?

Farrell's was one of my favorite bars. It was a great place for college kids from Brooklyn to hang out as long as we were not rowdy and noisy.

Didn't Pete Hamill hang out there?

There was a place at Park Circle that did Chinese food containers of beer.

That's the place and yes, Pete Hamill was good friends with my Uncle who took over the bar when my grandfather died.

Does the Turkey's Nest still do that? One of my husband's friends a regular there.

Pete Hamill is cool - he has the *best* New York accent. He mentions Farrell's several times in his memoir, "The Drinking Life."

Good book - read many of his works.

You could do an entire page of Farrell's memories.

you're right but who has the time, lol...

I miss that place!!

That's my middle name.

I loved the beer to go!!

Made famous by both Hamill brothers.

What made it famous was the great tap beer and you could get it to go!!

One of my best friends used to live on Vanderbilt St. (very close to Farrell's) and used to go there all the time.

Timboo's

Every Ave. had its own bars; one of the more famous was Timboo's, it's changed hands and names over the years; it was a staple on 5th Ave. Where you went and your father went and maybe your kids too, before it closed down in 2012.

Wow, I remember Timboo's well. The neighborhood bar!

First opened back in the 1940s as Loftus', by the late 1950s it had been renamed Steve's. In 1969 it was purchased by two friends who worked together, who renamed it Timboo's (a combination of their two first names) and remain owners to this day.

Went to Timboo's then my house...

Timboo's is on 5th Ave. & 11th St.

Still there.

Great place, my father went for years when Tim had it then Jimmy and Bobby had it. I miss Jimmy he was the best.

I love their family, the best people. I miss The Slope, no place like home.

Timboo's is still hangin' around...lol.

Then it became Jimboo's.

Timboos is still there. At one point it was owned by a couple.

Wow, Timboo's is closing. I'm from 11th Street and remember it when it was Loftus. That is the last of the old school bars...

The last of the last...lived up the block from there, always someone there if you needed help or just someone to talk to...so sad!! Many memories.

We still have Farrell's, but it's sad to see Timboo's is going out. All we need there now is another yuppy joint! But that's what we will probably get!

213

My father in-law must be rolling in his grave; Timboo's was his haunt--and the way the area is changing. And after a night at Timboo's, off to the diner on 9th and 5th that used to be next to Neerguards, Henry's.

Clubs We Went To

You're a little bit country; I'm a little bit rock and roll--and a little bit disco. Whatever it was, there was a club you could go to, but in the days of the 70s disco was king, the new thing. We'd all get dressed up to dance the night away to a whole new sound of the Bee Gees and we were all staying alive, and becoming endless clones of Saturday night fever-- though we had a few nite spots in Park Slope. Most of these clubs were in Bay Ridge and Bensonhurst, so lets get a round of applause for the clubs.

It's Friday; who wants to go clubbing?

Romeo & Juliet, C'est La vie, Changes/Jasmines, Fantasy Island, Scandals or any others?

Does anyone know what Romeo n Juliets name w/b4 it w/RnJ...and if so, what was it's nickname...

Night Gallery.

Don't forget PASTELS...that place has been called everything under the sun...

What was Night Gallery's nickname? Yes, I too w/a Pastels girl...in 1997 I won a contest in there to what was called, then, Legacy...

I went to all of them.

Wasn't Pastels called the Penthouse years ago?

L'Amour's- the rock capital of Brooklyn!

214

The Upstairs Lounge, I don't remember exactly where that was but It was in Bay Ridge. I also remember going to Prospect Hall dances. And a club on 4th Ave. somewhere in the 20s streets, I forget the name of it I think it had River in it lol my memory is shot!!

Port Royal!

Yes, David; the Port Royal after Ryan's or wherever LOL.

Thinking back (as much as I can anyway), that place was a death trap. Yikes.

YEP!!...one way in...one way out!! LOL!!

And up those stairs to wherever you wanted to go! (Port Royal)...

Weren't there like three levels? OMG flashbacks LOL.

Oh yea! With tables and chairs and glass covered tables on each level!! HA!

Wow the Port Royal Union St....Mr. D, Humsa at the door!

That light green awning is still up over the door I believe!! Many a wasted night into wasted dayz in that place LOL!!

Yea that was great...walking out @ 6 in the morn hitting the diner for breakfast...and then going to the flea market at the school on 7th; do you remember thoze daze?

Wasn't Romeo and Juliet...Changes?

Not to my knowledge, after R & J it became Crystal City.

Was Changes a totally different club?

I'm not recallin' that one...after Pastels, I ventured into the city n didn't hang around Bklyn anymore.

No, Jasmines became Changes.

Peppermint Lounge, Limelight, Starbucks &
Funhouse were great city spots.

Two of the biggest: Odyssey & the Palladium.

Palladium & Funhouse & Peppermint Lounge were
my favs!!

I liked Palladium, Peppermint Lounge and the Mud
Club.

Can't Forget Max's Kansas City!! Saw Blondie &
The Cramps there!! Marshall Crenshaw too I
believe!!

Saw Elvis Costello for the first time at the
Palladium! Squeeze was his opening band.

I was a DJ at Peggy Sue's in the city around the
corner from the Palladium and Oldies bar and club.

Prospect Park Carousel

This was more of a treat when we went to the Zoo:
way on the other side of the park sits an iconic place
with a thing of the past, which has stood up to the
test of time and survived close to 100 years, and is
sure to be in our kids memories like it is in ours.

The park's carousel was carved by one of the
foremost carousel designers of the time. The carousel
features 51 magnificently carved horses, a lion, a
giraffe, a deer, and two dragon-pulled chariots. I
remember riding it when I was a child. Did you?

My sisters took me here when I was a kid. I
remember everyone yelling "grab the ring" as the
man pushed a wicker basket in my face. When the
ride ended, sis asked me "Why didn't you grab the
ring?" I replied at the age of four or five "I thought
he was asking me for money...Yeah, like the basket
they pass around in church."

216

The Prospect Park's Carousel was always a childhood favorite of mine; I remember waiting on line to get on the prettiest painted horse!

I had a lifetime pass. Doesn't get much better when you're a kid!

The best "Merry-Go-Round" in the world. Never called it a carousel.

Yup Yup...My uncle was the one who'd bring me there...

Yes, sure did...

I remember waving to my dad as I rode on the horse that went up and down. The music and the beat of the drum enhanced the excitement of riding.

Loved it, and then when we were able to bring our kids there that was great; hopefully they will be able to do the same in 5 years or so.

Many times...such fond memories. :)

So true I never called it a carousel either. Merry-Go-Round.

I totally agree...Merry-Go-Round is official!

Rode on that so many times as a kid...I really miss those days.

Loved that carousel! And the cracker jacks too!!

Recall waiting on line to get on the prettiest painted horse!

WOW.... CoooLL!!

I didn't call it a carousel, to me it was a Merry-Go-Round!!

The best Merry-Go-Round in the WORLD!!

Loved that Merry go round. I think it's still there. I wonder how much they charge to ride it now.

Pool Halls

This was always a fun game of skill; some grew up in the pool halls like others loved to play sports, a lot of fun we had. 2 of these were on 5th ave one on 7th St. and one was on 11th St. When we wanted to get out of our hood, we went to Ovington Ave. in Bay Ridge, lots of great memories playing 8 ball, Chicago, straight, OK rack 'em up.

Remember Waxies Pool Hall on 5th & 7th? What a character.

Remember when the movie was filmed at the pool hall above? O'Neill's card store on 11th Street and 5th Ave....was it with Burt Reynolds? *Shamus*?

It was *Shamus* with Burt Reynolds.

I was like 10 when it was filmed. I remember everyone hanging on the corner trying to get a glimpse!

What was the pool hall called?

Biff's.

I have a photo of Burt Reynolds in his bathrobe from when they were filming that movie.

Biff's Pool Hall. The movie was *Shamus* with Burt Reynolds and Dyan Cannon. Biff had a bit part in it. They also filmed at a karate school on 5th bet. 15th & 16th; that was where Shamus lived.

Yes, they also filmed it on my block, 10th St. We still claim to see our fingers in a scene where they find a dead body under the station. Lol.

But we also used to go to 69th and Ovelton Ave. pool hall just to get out of the neighborhood.

Biff's—those old wooden floors!

218

Sanders

We had 2 movie theaters in our area; I thought the best was the Sanders; it was always a nice treat to see the movies on the big screen, it was a lot of fun and trouble at the same time, if you know what I mean.

The last movie I saw at the Sanders was *Orca*. My dad started taking us to the drive in....saw *Carrie & Burnt Offerings*...cool!!

Sanders...now that was a movie theater...not like the crap they have there now!!

True...now it's The Pavilion...

Was closed for decades!

I know, why was it closed from 1973?

Anyone know the answer?

I believe it was up for sale, but not too sure...

I think I saw *Soylent Green* there just before it closed. And the answer is (C) they were going to make co-ops?

I loved the Sanders with it's Saturday matinees...that's when it was really worth "going to the movies."

No, not co-ops, they were makin' little green crackers inside. LOL.

Matinee in the 70s was 2 for 1 movies.

As a kid I remember there were always people sneaking in the side doors when the movie was playing. You would see a bright sunny light come in the dark theater when the door opened, then the ushers would go chasing them & checking *everyone's* ticket with a bright flashlight...I must say it happened each time I went to Sanders.

219

The old name of the theater was Sanders, and after it closed, it stayed closed for many years. Plans for condos were made, but fortunately it did not happen. It was so wonderful when the Theater The Pavilion opened. Once again Park Slope had a movie house.

Oh the sneakin' at the doors in the bright light, remember doing it :). and those scary old bathrooms upstairs. :)

I saw the undertaker and his pals - a sick movie that had a funeral parlor next to a diner - you can guess what was in the hamburger?

Popcorn machine upstairs.

Saw *The Exorcist* for the first time when we did the side door; we were too young. Laughed our butts off until we got kicked out.

2 movies and a cartoon for 75 cents!

Yep...those were the days!!

It closed because the VCR was invented... "Beta Max."

James Bond movies on Saturday. *Live and Let Die*!!

The Exorcist line was around the corner.

Ya and the movie is so small NOW my T.V. is bigger, LOL.

I will never forget we just sat down in the balcony next to a bunch of boy scouts and I accidentally kicked over a GIANT Coca Cola over the edge. When the manager came up with a dripping wet guy, all he saw was a bunch of boy scouts looking at him with big innocent eyes and saying that they did not see anyone throw a soda.

I remember lots of movies there and YES, *The Exorcist* premiere stands out the most.

I saw *The Exorcist* at the Sanders.

220

So did I. Bugged my Mom for a month to let me see it. She was right. It scared the bejeezus outta me.

I saw all of my Bruce Lee movies here with my older brother. I was only eight, nine years old. My parents wouldn't let me go alone. I lived on eight street and third ave. We took the bus.

Holy shit, I saw *Enter The Dragon* at the Sanders!! Saw *Jaws* there too and I've not put a toe in the ocean since!

I am cracking up...I have never been in ocean water either since that movie lol.

The Park House Restaurant & The Sanders Theater!! I remember going to 6th Ave. between 9th & 10th Street to buy $1.00 worth of penny candy then going with a bunch of friends to see the movie *Ben*! Does anyone remember the winding stairs to the balcony? They used to creep me out!

Yea, Jim's candy store.

I remember when the price went to 75 cents and I had a fit! To get into the movies.

75 to get in; 25 for the popcorn machine upstairs.

Remember climbing up on the park house diner roof and going in through the girls bathroom?

Exorcist, Jaws quite a few--oh but partied like crazy in the br, lol.

I remember working there in '77 and seeing *Rocky* a million times.

There was nothing like The Sanders on Saturday. It was a totally interactive experience, kind of like *Rocky Horror Picture Show*! (we were ahead of our times!) The movie came in 2nd to the goings-on in the audience; if you were an adult who came to see a movie in peace on a Saturday, you were S.O.L.!

U CAN SAY THAT AGAIN!

My mother worked in the Ticket Booth of the Sanders for many years also at the RKO Prospect on 9th Street.

I saw *Mad Mad Monster Party* there—OMG, I think I was 10.

YMCA

YMCA, it's fun to stay at the YMCA; uh, I don't think so, but it was fun to play at the YMCA. We always had a ball running the tracks, playing basketball in the gym, hitting the bag, lifting weights, as well as some other activities.

Anyone remember the splash parties at the YMCA?

9th Street YMCA.

Swim, gym, pool tables, trampoline gym on Saturday, towel fights in the locker room, and the nasty pineapple orange soda from the soda machine. Paul G. in the gym & his sister Franny, and one guy Tommy D. who was the biggest guy I've ever seen that wasn't a pro ball player and his nickname was 'pinky.'

You have a great talent for recall, which includes details long forgotten by most.

You're polite and a diplomat, and I'm told an attorney, but in the parlance of the realm it's called, 'flashback ' but thanks.

I'm a little later but yeah, the rec room was quite the place to be. I remember the chlorine from the pool could be smelled in the lobby. Anyone remember Dominick and his fancy Lincoln Continental that always was parked out front?

I don't know his title but he ran things.

If he succeeded George he was the athletic director.

What about running around that track all the time...and B-Ball in the gym...

How about that soup machine that scalded your tongue?

Wow, the Y! Swimming in the chlorine - I mean pool. Smelled it through the whole building. The log cabin they had for an office--used to laugh every time I went in there. Playing bumper pool with friends while *F-Troop* was on the big old TV.

I remember Dominick...he got me started on photography. He taught me how to develop film. If it weren't for the Y I would've been hanging out on the streets doing God knows what!...oh yeah, did that too.

How is it possible that all your brain cells are still intact? Have you discovered some wonder drug that reverses the effects of our youthful actions?

Took guitar lessons at YMCA in 1970 something.

The YMCA...Wow, used to go on Saturday morning and stop at Dee Dee donuts and get a dzn. Jelly donuts to bring to the Y and have with friends. It cost 75 cents a dzn...

Remember when the guy jumped out the window at the Y and killed himself? Terrible!

Flashbacks.

Mad Dog 20/20.

Hey 8th St. guys, remember dragging the hoses out of the hallway of the Y and hooking them up to the johnny pump, and spraying up and down the block and 6th Ave., knocking everyone down?

Horse Stables

I was driving down Prospect Park South West near Park Circle today and here are 4 horses crossing the street. Seeing that took me back to when I was a young and we would go to Stables on Caton Pl and Coney Island Ave. And we would rent horses and take trail rides in Prospect Park. Does anyone remember the trail rides up in the park?

I rode many times back in the day. It cost 5 dollars back then, & that was so much fun. I always asked for the fastest horse, sometimes they stood straight up. Never fell though.

There was a wooden fence corral area just inside the 15th Street entrance I remember. I always preferred the western saddle. My friend and I would help clean up the stables and ride for free sometimes.

I loved it & my mom could always tell where I was when I came home because I smelled like the horse stables.

My cousin kept his two horses there also and had the pleasure of riding.

I enjoyed riding there also. I was not much of an equestrian. But it was fun. I can relate to the smell. My mother used to make me change my clothes in the hallway. The corral was where I spent most of my misspent youth hanging out with my friends.

Went riding there once, never again. It was my first time; they gave me a calm horse that picked up right away that I didn't know how to ride; he did what ever he wanted to do. When he came to last part of the trail he went into a full gallop & he scared the shit out of me. I held on to his neck trying to keep my balance. When he got close to the stables he slowed down to a walk. I am sure he was laughing his ass off.

Did you guys go off the trail and ride thru the baseball fields? My horse once chased after one and caught up to it until the rider kicked the horse and he took off.

OMG...I remember horseback riding my 1st and only time.

I worked at the stables & took lots of people on trail rides through the park. Still love horses and miss riding through Prospect Park. My mom always made with change in hallway before coming in the house.

Hey, it's only $37 now!

$5.00 for an hour as a kid back then. Wow.

I rode the horse a few times & it was scary but it was fun, but the last time I rode it, the horse got spooked and just started running and was about to jump over a wall...with me on it, needless to say I was shitting my pants, yelling like a girl though I was a 15 year old boy; thank God the leader of the trip was able to stop the horse before it made the jump...

Weren't those stables right across the street from a Bowling Alley?

Yes it was, the bowling alley was the old Tevans stable.

Yup. Went horseback riding in Prospect Park numerous times. One time when a bunch of us were riding, the horse that our friend was riding on started galloping so fast that he fell off the horse; we laughed so hard. Looking back at that incident now, it probably wasn't funny, but at 15 it was.

And a huge skating rink for roller skating was just around the corner also. Lots of fun there as well.

Kate Wollman Ice Skating Rink

225

Did anyone go ice skating to the Kate Wollman Rink at Prospect Park on Saturdays or Fri nights in the 60's?

Yes and Wollman's Memorial in Central Park.

Yes. I had a lot of black and blue marks on my butt to prove it.

It was fun, but it sometimes was sooooooo cold outside!!

I tried once and fell 14 times holding on to the wall!!

I am sure, falling on the ice -- black and blue butts!!

Yep. Friday nights.

Yes. I went on Fridays too!!

Yes: Friday nights, loved to ice skate even on those cold winter nights. Good memories!

I did Saturdays with my family or a group of friends. It was fun.

Do you remember, sometimes we'd be standing in line and they would say "the ice is in a wet condition; there will be no refunds?"

Every Fri night with my girlfriends, walked right through Prospect Park and thought nothing of it. :)

Many Friday nites, trying to 'pick-up.'

Yes, I did. Loved it. It was my favorite!

Yes Jahns and Ice skating rink

Did not skate a whole lot but great place to hang and pick up girls.

Yes with my older sister - I forgot about that place, lol.

Yes I did, my neighbor taught me how to skate.

I only went there maybe 2x but remember the nice times there.

Used to go every Saturday morning. Free skating from 9 - 12. Invariably we would get thrown off the ice a few times every session for playing roller derby.

Learned to ice skate in the late 1940s, don't recall the name but the rink was on Eastern Pkwy.

Friday nights to Prospect Park, not a good idea to go skating with a buzz.

I remember going there in the 50's.

Yes!! Friday night was the big social night and Saturday morning I think was free.

Remember the pompoms with bells on our skates? I went back there 2 years ago and the lockers looked like they haven't been changed since the old days.

My sister-in-law's grandmother worked there back in the day.

Used to go there all the time.

I used to go to the free sessions on Saturday mornings & then stay for the next pay session; it was probably 1965-1967 when I did this.

That was a highlight of the week during the winter. I loved going there.

As I got older, I think I liked checking out the outfits the girls were wearing more than skating, or in my case, attempting to skate.

Gold Sunday mornings 1962.

Prospect Park Ice Skating Rink, 70s for me.

I remember being frozen half to death as a little kid and then scalding my mouth on their hot chocolate.

Used to play hockey there, some days they would have games with the local teams.

You really did feel safe even 9 or 10 at night...the frozen pizza and especially the hot chocolate hit the spot.

We used to go every Friday night; one Friday night has stayed with me all these years. I was 13 or 14.

We went ice skating every year on Thanksgiving weekend...It was the start of our Saturday trips to Wollman Rink and eating at Wetson's afterward.

Prospect Park

Everyone at one time or another went to Prospect Park back then. What is the best thing you ever saw or did back in the day?

Concerts, Zoo, playing softball, fishing, the picnics under the big trees with my Mom, Dad, sis and family. The Zoo, paddle boats, the green houses, sledding in winter and the beautiful lake. Loved the place.

Loved to go ice-skating...and the zoo...

I remember the sledding during the winter snow. If the snow was bad, no school.

Loved the carousel and ice skating...

Ice skating on the lakes and sledding down those great hills.

Rollerskating in the circle.

Yes that too! Have way too many to write.

Fishing in the Paddle-boat Lake. sleigh riding Monument Hill. Playing roller hockey at the Bandshell using the garbage pails for the nets.

All of the above!! Loved the A&S Sponsored Fishing Contests in the BIG Lake!!

Everything! Back when they did not have fences everywhere. Why do they have fences to keep it natural when it was a man-made park. Gotta be the liberals.

Playing Little League baseball, exploring the park, touch football, riding my skateboard and bike.

EVERYTHING....Prospect Park is the Central Park of Brooklyn...I lived on 8th Ave. between 8th and 9th Street....so you know I know every inch of that PARK!!

Saw David Bromberg play there in the Bandshell.

When I say "apple turnover" at 9th Street playground does that ring any bells?

An "apple turnover" was a back flip off the swings. Loved those swings.

I really can't talk about it!! LOL!!

Gettin' laid count?

"That escalated quickly" LOL I am sure not only does it count but if you did not what's wrong with you? LOL

I had many picnics w/family & friends, just going for a long walk on a nice day, sledding in the winter, concerts.

All of the above!!

Fishing in the park was the best.

Wasn't a carp the laziest fish ever? That was the big deal to catch one in the little lake. You knew what you had as soon as it pulled to one side only.

Sitting under a tree & writing in my journal or just thinking were a couple things I did by myself, but then there were lots of other fun things to do with others, like picnics, going to the playground (9th-11th Streets), etc. Great times!

10-Places of Interest

- Prospect Park
- Armory
- Prospect Park Bandshell
- Holy Family Church
- Kentile
- Methodist Hospital
- Monument Hill
- Museum
- Old Building
- Pink House
- St. Thomas Aquinas Church
- YMCA
- Botanical Garden
- Williamsburgh Clock
- Prominent Places

Prospect Park

Share some of your fondest memories of Brooklyn's favorite park.

I practically grew up in Prospect Park and know it like the back of my hand!

I used to live on Parkside so the park was literally right on my block. I remember fishing for craw fish and spotting tadpoles in the lake. Who can count all the festivals they had in there? There's no park like it, not even Central Park!

Ice skating at Wollmans rink!

Funny but I'm 50 years old now and I can honestly say I've lived on all four sides of that Park in my 50 yrs of living in Brooklyn.

My kids learned to fish and Ice skate there.

We went on picnics and adventures, trekking further the older we got - through the ravine, the long meadow, all the way over to the Botanic Gardens, and what I remember as Lafayette's House, but I don't see that on the Prospect Park map anymore -- I remember it being behind the tall iron fence, probably along Flatbush Avenue.

We'd go to he horse stables down by the Parade Grounds, and then ride the horses. You didn't have to be afraid of actually knowing how to ride a horse because they were all old and had walked the path so long; you couldn't make them go a different way if you tried!

Who could forget the carousel, the Zoo, the paddle boats, or Wollman Rink? The lake, of course is the jewel of Prospect Park.

Can you imagine today a band of kids ranging from 3 to 13 being able to just go off and experience nature without adults and be relatively safe?

It sure is a great park. I agree even better than Central Park.

Do you remember going on these treks?

I remember the family treks. Those are the best memories I have of Mommy & Daddy being in love. I just don't remember there being anyone younger then me. :)

OMG...I can't begin to count the picnics we had at Prospect Park near the Band shell. We were always on the west side of the park. Every holiday we could count on the whole block coming to Prospect Park. They used to have nice concerts and all the day camps would have a trip to the park.

We had our last family reunion there.

Are you serious? That's awesome!

I have been away from Prospect Park for 34 years, but I still remember everything about it—great people, great friends, great memories.

ALL THE SUMMER COOK OUTS!

Growing up we didn't have a car so Prospect Park was our ride to the country. We used to go to the zoo a lot, and what I remember the most are the seals.

We spent a lot of time in the playgrounds there and of course there was that wonderful carousel.

As a teenager I spent a lot of time in the Wollman Rink. They used to have a free session in the morning on Saturday and a pay session in the afternoon and evening. Some Saturdays I went to all three. Like so many here I have lots of great memories of Prospect Park.

We had the park, the zoo, playground, Botanical Gardens, and suicide hill. Fished in the lake and rode my bicycle up and down the walkways.

I remember when they first built the ice skating rink. Frozen pizza and hot chocolate was the best thing during the open skate on Friday nights. And we could walk the park at night- it had to be in groups but it was safe. Can still remember the fun and the people.

I lived 2 blocks from Prospect Park, my home away from home. I always loved when the weather would get warm enough to get out. Loved walking to the public library at Grand Army Plaza.

We couldn't walk to the Grand Army Plaza- we weren't allowed. The zoo and the gardens were as far as we could walk.

Just remembered, after walking to the public library then going to the Brooklyn Museum and Brooklyn Botanic Garden...that's an oasis - thank God for the people who had the foresight of having these places here. Lots of great memories...

Those were great places-- I loved the gardens and you could get in for free sometimes. But the park was the best. It was so great having it to play in. Any season - Spring & Summer - bike riding or just running around. Winter - sledding or skating – fall, playing in the leaves.

Remember during Halloween when the headless horseman would trot by? That was fun!!

PP- it was an Oasis in the concrete of Bklyn. Who remembers the carousel & grabbing the rings?!

That park had the fattest squirrels, the squirrels down in Florida look like string beans!

I remember the carousel.

The park was my front yard.

Remember the little ponies with the cart that you used to ride on?

Armory

The Armory....The inside has been converted into a beautiful YMCA. Though there's an original YMCA just five blocks over on 9th St.

14th Street & 8th Avenue.

Did they ever fix the broken bayonet on that statue?

Mixed martial arts fighting—cage fighters, just in case some didn't know.

Many suggestions for this site, but alas, it will probably be high priced condos, because there are so few of them coming up! (Sarcasm)

Yuppie money. They're gonna get what they want eventually.

Ansonia clock factory 7th Ave. 12th 'n 13th St.

Funny this is now a co-op and its beautiful, who knew?

Back in the early 80s there was a club on the side 13th St. called the loading zone.

Wow! I remember...and even though i was only like 15...I was able to get in...

YA ITS BEAUTIFUL HERE BUT A LOT OF MONEY TO LIVE OUT HERE...

Spent my entire childhood playing in and around them.

Wow I worked there when part of it was a sewing factory in the early 70's.

Played and spray painted our names on the roofs.

I always wondered what originally was in that old building - I used to pass it every day & night going to hang out at Windsor.

Saw a clock on the lawn left out for garbage. It looked really interesting to me. Anyway, took it to a clock repair shop and asked if it was worth repairing. The guy looked at me as if I had 3 heads and said "Of course, it's an "Ansonia!"

I have one of those!!

I have an Ansonia, too. Seems they are quite the collectible.

I use to live right behind it in 1964/65 & by then it was a garment factory.

My sister and I use to sneak in through a hole in the wall adjacent to our backyard.

I remember when it was actually an Armory in the 60's. I would walk past it on the way to Prospect Park.

Wow the Armory....I lived right down the block on 15th Street.

I joined the NYNG's after basic training i was to report there twice a month.

Lived down the street from it. Remember watching a filming of a movie there once. Trying to remember what movie it was. That will be on my mind forever now.

They filmed the movie RAGTIMES on 8th Ave. and also in the armory think it was the last film James Cagney made.

Yes, Yes...I think that was it. I will be at peace today now....thanks =)

LOL no problem: it was filmed in 1981.

They also filmed parts of The Taking of Pelham 123 there.

Yes they did it was a sound stage for the command post,

I remember when I did my weekend drills a couple of us guys would go to the sub-basement in the armory motor pool, man was it creepy. They had an actual courtroom, really old looking, and a tunnel that leads to the park but of course it was closed & chained up. Just used to hang out and drink some beers and talk crap with a big lighted flashlight.

The armory also used to blow up the hot air balloons for the Macy's Thanksgiving Day parade?

235

I used to take my kids .it goes to show u how big it was.

Prospect Park Bandshell

Let's not forget the Bandshell and the kegs under the stage. Plastic red cups always bring back wonderful and interesting memories for me.

OMG! What about all the bands there especially the Singles, John, Jack, Ray, Jim, Gary, and sometimes Nick, They were first The Parkside 5.

I did a show there also.

They used to have all kinds of concerts there during the summer.

Buying taps from Farrell's and hanging out on the stage at night.

That Bandshell will bring back many good times!

That must have been a great feeling playing in the park back then.

Rarely missed a concert at the Bandshell back in the day, so many bands.

Wow! We used to take all the toilet paper out from under the shell and throw it all over the trees & it looked like it snowed mid-summer; that was a lot of fun until we were caught by Doyle.

It is such a great thing! I treasure all of my old band photos. Must have been a blast playing the park!

Holy Family Church

Anyone go to Holy Family Church on 14th St. between 4th and 5th? I was in their folk mass "band" back in the mid 70s.

I was baptized there. We used to live on that block when I was very young.

At St. Teresa of Avila, on Sterling and Classon, it was called the "Hootenanny" Mass and it was always held in the basement church...

I was baptized at St Teresa's, my grandmother lived right across the street on Sterling Pl, now that was a beautiful gold altar...

Looks like they moved the altar forward and removed the railing that was there...

I was baptized and had first communion there...

Holy Family was a tiny church. I don't remember if the folk mass was held in the basement. I know we sang at all the weddings.

Saint Saviour held their folk mass in the basement. We would sing the entire score of Godspell and some of JC Superstar.

I never thought of Holy Family Church as tiny. I was a student at the school (class of '72) and an altar boy for half those years so I knew every bit of the building. The folk masses were held in the church with the band up on the altar. On a few occasions, I know they put them up in the choir loft in the back.

We always stood on the left side on the altar (right to people facing the altar) I was the soprano. Seemed small compared to ST Sav and St Thomas.

Kentile

Who remembers the Kentile Fire?

I do, I do! LOL

I remember the Silver Cup Bread sign you could see off the BQE, I think. It now says Silver Cup Studios.

I was trying to get a picture of the Goya sign anyone remember that?

Does anyone remember the smell of roasted coffee beans wafting through the neighborhood?

We use to smell the great aroma of coffee walking to work at Kentile in the morning too!

I worked in the Coffee Piers...They were on 21st-23rd st.& 3rd ave. Millions of lbs. of coffee grounded up & you could smell it for miles, a strong but pleasant aroma. Now it's a Home Center.

Remember this, the coffee factory down on smith & 9th, they would roast out the entire area. Man did it stink!!

There was a coffee house on 3rd St. and 3rd Ave. also.

Maybe that's the one all I can remember everyday @ or around 3 o'clock they started firing it up.

I loved the smell of the coffee roasting. I think its still there. Maybe I just smell it in my memory.

Kentile was between 2nd and that bridge we had to cross. Remember it was made of wood and I use to cross it with my mom and I remember that pieces use to be missing. I don't miss that lol.

Wasn't that big old Eagle cloths sign near by as well as the Bruno truck place?

The lower Slope was more industrial area.

Methodist Hospital

Did you ever have to be taken to the emergency room at the Methodist Hospital?

Yes, I was injured one night while playing ice hockey. I needed stitches over my right eye. I was struck by the puck; when asked what happened I replied I was hit with a puck. He looked at me in shock and said, "You were hit by a truck?!!" True story.

Well I was hit by a truck; spent 21 days there didn't wake up for the first 3.

Remember the game, Don't Spill the Beans? Well, I stuck one all the way up my nose, so far that I couldn't get it out. My parents took me to the Methodist and I remember a doctor pulling it out with huge tweezers.

Went there too and was treated got bit by the German Shepard from the pharmacy on 7th between 1st and 2nd.

Wow I remember that dog.

Oh jeez, mine was a pencil eraser LMAO. That was the first time. Next up was a sprained ankle while playing basketball; my friends actually CARRIED me into the ER. The nurses were falling over themselves laughing. Third was the egg in the eye; not so fun. I became quite familiar with Methodist's ER over the years. :)

I fell on 7th St. and 4th Ave. and broke my leg and was taken to the emergency room at the Methodist Hospital...

My trip to the Methodist ER goes back to when I was just 9 years old and out in the street playing stick ball with bunch of the guys. I was standing by a parked car and my friend was a bat, he swung and hit me in my left eye. My parents put me in the car and took me to the Methodist.

Yes, I bit thru my tongue while climbing around a stoop. My mom brought me there. The wait was way too long so we went to our doctor instead.

239

Several times!! Fractured both wrists at same time, various amounts of stitches in hands, head & arm and an emergency surgical procedure.

Went there many times; it helped greatly that my mom and sister worked there, got too many stitches to count.

Between my brother and me, it seems that we had frequent flier miles in that ER.

With the 5 of us my mother was always taking one of us there. They used to question her. Idiots!

I spent more time there then I wish to remember...Then I had my children there, looks so different now.

Too many times to recall!

Several times.

My cousin was on the top landing of the stoop, I was in the aerie way and he threw a broom at me. Hit me square in the part of my lip. It split in half. Needed 5 stitches to close it. The worst part was getting the needle to numb it.

I was playing around with friends, got kicked on the left side of my jaw. Fractured it, and had it wired for 3 months.

Broke both wrists, bit thru my tongue, stitches in my knee, had my tonsils out: all cared for by the Methodists.

Yup, numerous times and almost always had to wait. Then 20 years later when I worked at The Methodist Hospital.

Went to the emergency room so much we knew the X-Ray tech.

I once stepped on a huge carpet needle (the big carved one) I hobbled over to Methodist with my mom.

My mother worked there as a nurse, and my accident prone brother one time broke his collar bone she worked a whole night shift only to turn right around and drag him there. He had so many stupid accidents that nowadays there would have the police investigating child abuse. It seemed like he was there once a month.

Was there so much had my own room.

Many times....stitches, stitches, stitches!!

Yes and remember waiting and waiting and waiting...

Let me count the ways concussion number 9, Concussion number 8, stitched, car accident, concussion number 7, stick ball bat impaled in leg, burnt face, still good looking, concussion number 5. They used to tell me if I went to sleep I wouldn't wake up...

Monument Hill.

What Is The Name Of The Monument On Monument Hill?

Who Is The Monument Dedicated To?

Is "Monument Hill" Really Its Name?

I remember sleigh riding down monument hill. The really crazy guys would sleigh down suicide hill which was the back of monument hill and had a big drop off cliff.

I Know Of A Lookout Hill, Suicide Hill & Breeze Hill. I Also Know Of A Maryland Monument.

We are also the only public park I know with a cemetery.

I always thought it was George Washington...do I win...lol

241

Quaker Friends Cemetery...

I think it was Ben Franklin up there... then when copper and caddy bumpers and hub caps were being robbed they cut his head off...remember that..

That's right the only Quaker church is located behind the Atlantic house jail.

HA! Someone named it suicide hill because of that tree you might wind up hitting going down on a sled, or getting run over by some one going down on a sled.

They stole the Copper name plate too!!

I remember havin' copper drain pipes stolen right off the side of our house too!! Thievin' Bastards!! LOL

Are u sure it was Ben Franklin?

Just remember some one walking off with a Bust on 1 of those monuments in the park and when I looked it looked like it was hack sawed off..

Just read another post there was a bust up there, maybe they hack sawed it to remove? But the eagle was robbed twice and replaced...and I also remember the sword on Lafayette's was also broken or robbed-- it was about 4 feet long; I must go down and take pics there are so many historic statues in that park.

AND DATS DAT!!

So some of my brain cells are still intact, thanks for bailing me out! I use to climb everything and that was one...and I fell off a lot of things too, which would explain a lot about me also!

Lots of memories on monument hill and the area all around it. Good job.

There used to be a "waterfall" near the 9th street baseball fields. The "waterfall" is no longer there. The "waterfall" was a pipe pumping out water among some rocks. During the hot, summer days, we would sit in front of the pipe and cool down. There is nothing like walking home in soaking wet jeans. Great Memories.

We Used To Have To Take These Stairs Up The Hill While Sleigh Riding Because The Hill Was An Ice Cube...Ah, The Best Times In Prospect Park!

I haven't thought of this spot in years.

I Hope It Brings Back Warm And Happy Childhood Memories Of Park Slope We Were All Fortunate Enough To Share...

Remember them well!! Also the sets of steps by 3rd street entrance across the road!

Brooklyn Museum

I guess no one went there much as a kid. I use to cut school and visit the museum and the botanical garden and zoo.

I use to go to museum with my Dad quite often and the botanical gardens' to eat. At Easter we use to go to gardens for their cross made of flowers which were absolutely beautiful.

A Hiding place for many of us FREE admission then!!

I used to love the early American area. It was so cool to see how it was back then. Oh and everyone was short...

Remember the Colonial style house within the Museum?

Wasn't there a movie with Robert Redford where they were robbing some diamond from the museum?

Just *Hot Rocks*.

With Robert Redford.

Robert Redford & Streisand also made a movie in your building on Prospect Park West.

Don't Forget *For Pete's Sake* in '74. Starring B. Streisand & Michael Sarazin!! Pork Belly Trading Scheme!! lol

Filmed in the Big Apt Building corner of 8th Street & PPW!!

Three places saved my life and sanity growing up...The Brooklyn Botanical Gardens, The Brooklyn Museum (especially the Period rooms :), and The Brooklyn Public Library. I have so much gratitude for them and I maintain membership even though I am far away. I love to think about children going there and maybe having the art, literature, and nature balm their souls the way it did mine.

Old Building

If I remember this was in the park next to 51?

3rd Street Park.. Or as its known J.J. Byrne Park

I know it as 3rd street Park...

It is under construction finally!! It's an open field right now with fencing and getting a whole new look!

They just renovated it, now they are redoing the playground; they put in a skateboard park.

I remember all the old men playing Bocce?

My grandfather played Bocce there & we used to watch him & his friends when we were kids I love that park!

Wow, I remember the bocce courts.

I actually went to this building for preschool. Washington stayed there during the battle of Long Island.

All the Old Italian guys playing Bocci, I would love to watch the arguments they would get into. The only words I could understand were the Italian curses they were yelling at each other.

Some battle that must have been, Washington's hanging out in South Brooklyn playing Bocce Ball and his soldiers were sun bathing out in The Hamptons!

I visited those parks recently broke my heart to see what they turned those parks into, felt like they took my childhood away.

DID you know that Wild Bill use to put on rodeo type shows in that park where the ball fields are?

Correction: Buffalo Bill.

I don't remember that. I do remember going there for the sprinklers and to play knock hockey.

So you weren't with George Washington, but you were with Buffalo Bill?

No, that too was before my time.

That building was a command center for George Washington during the war.

Pink House

Remember The PINK Brownstone In Brooklyn? At Garfield Place.

Vanessa Del Rio lived there.

Really! Did she really live there?

Yes, Remember Her In The Neighborhood. Kelly
McGilliss (Top Gun) Was Another Friend That
Lived Directly Across the Street.

Across the street from who?

Kelly McGillis lived a couple doors upon other side
of Garfield from Sol Yurick (Author who wrote THE
WARRIORS).

I don't know why, I always look for the pink house
when I walk on Garfield.

Saw it yesterday and was shocked didn't know what
to say being from such a diverse neighborhood and
SO proud of it.

Park Slope was like nowhere else in N.Y. & someone
almost tainted it.

Wow yeah I remember that house .always thought.

Ken and Barbie lived there!!!

Yea, I remember but I think its great (LIKE CT)
maybe an odd color, but the other side to that, a lot of
those buildings were losing the brownstone because
it's so soft and it was very expensive to repair, paint
was cheaper, or they just wanted to piss off the
neighbors. More likely LOL

I'm sure there are PINK houses all over the
world...but the one in PARK SLOPE, BKLYN N.Y.
USA is unique enough to get this kind of attention!!

Great place to grow up, the best!!

I think my old friend Larry Fishburne used to live
close by there with his folks.

We used to play stick ball bet.6th & 7th ave on
Garfield in the late 60's. I lived above the bakery on
7th next to Ryans.

246

Didn't Larry live on 8th Ave?

Not sure about Larry, I thought the Fishburnes' house was one of those little side streets. So long ago the memory gets hazy.

Knew Larry from back in the day.

last time I saw Larry was in Prospect park near the corral. Larry just got finished w/apocalypse now in the Philippines and we didn't believe he just finished a movie w/Marlon Brando.

Larry Fishburne Lived on Fiske Place in an Apt with his Mom until approx 1978/79 then moved to NYC & CA, in late 80's.

Used to live up the block - love that house!

It is still there.

Yea and still PINK.

No they finally were able to get a court order for the new owners to remove the pink paint.

St. Thomas Church

This is where I made my First Holy Communion. I loved this church.

First communion and confirmation.

I was baptized, 1st communion, confirmation, 2 graduations and got married there, it's SO PRETTY.

I remember going to mass and the worst part was going up to get the host, (little wafer) I was always afraid.

Ah yes, my confirmation as well! (and confession every Saturday).

Yes I remember, little dark box with slide door, forgive me father for I have sinned, let me count the ways how much time do you have?

We could also write a whole book on those Confessions.

Thanks. I bet these bring back some memories, huh?

God, yes!

I made my Communion and Confirmation at ST Thomas Aquinas Church 9th st and 4th Ave.

So many of us got married there also, such a beautiful place.

I made my Communion, Confirmation and grammar school graduation here...I actually forgot what a beautiful church it is...oh and I got married there also. Wow...many moons ago for sure...

Every Sunday the whole family dressed up and went to Sunday service.

We had to go to STA church before every ball game in little league. I guess it was to pray we would win, HA.

YMCA

Who went to the dances at the Y on Ninth Street?

Learn to swim free, Easter week...

Every Friday Night...

I think I took swimming lessons too...I remember the swimming cap ugh...

My mom sent all of us to the free swimming lessons at the Y! And we all learned to swim!

Me, every weekend, had a great time I was the one who brought the wine in, we all drank in the bathroom, LOL I hand connections

I never went dancing at that Y. I remember going to the dance hall on 15th St (I think) between 5th and 6th Ave. I'm not 100% sure. Does anybody remember what it was called?

I think you are thinking of Prospect Hall on Prospect just up from 5th Ave.

Yeah, that's it. Thanks for "refreshing" my memory. It was a lot of fun, except when I think of some of the "dress" shirts I wore, with the "ruffles" down the front and on the cuffs. UUUHHHHGGGG!!! Can't believe I thought it was "cool" at that time.

The original "Puffy Shirts"!

Not the dances but used to swim there for .25 a day.

I did we went all the time

How many of you were members of the YMCA?

I was member of the YMCA; I would go there after school as a child just about every day! I think...Just about everyone in the neighborhood learn how to swim there!!

Me!!!!!

Do you remember the hotel in the Y?

Yes, I think its still there.

I lived in the pool....

One night while I was on my way to the Y a man jumped from the top floor of the hotel and missed me by about 3 feet. Needless to say I didn't go to the Y that night; I went straight up to Muensters and had few stiff ones!

I remember that guy jumping off to Y

249

Williamsburgh Clock

My dentist as a small boy in the 60's was in the Williamsburg building.

Wow, how many memories!!

My orthodontist was there, can't remember the name though.

I remember dentist visits there too. Love shared memories.

Supposedly the tallest building in Brooklyn!!

I was up there looking out the window, gazing at the forever beautiful NY harbor on one of the most gorgeous, clear and sunny day. I could see the bridges, Governor's Island, the Statue of Liberty, and the S.I. Ferries going to and fro.

Back in the mid-80s, I read a newspaper article about there once being an observation deck right below the clock tower. Curious, I went down with my camera the next day to see. The guard I asked about it had never heard about it but was curious too so we both went up to look. In the short time up there I managed to get some really awesome photos.

During the Bicentennial, they had a great exhibit at the top of the tower, with signs with the directions of different battles of the revolution.

Lived on 4th ave and that was the clock we kept an eye on to know it was time to go home.

Those Beautifully Gold doors at the entrance.

Prominent Places

Some of the more prominent and historic attractions of park slope are:

250

The Brooklyn Music Conservatory is located on Seventh Avenue in Park Slope, Brooklyn. It offers a broad range of instruction in areas of American song.

It has both full and part-time students, and also hosts various musical programs throughout the year.

Litchfield Villa is a Italianate mansion which was once a private estate, and has since become part of Prospect Park. It also served as a great hang out for us back in the day. It is listed on the National Register of Historic Places. After years of neglect, it was renovated.

Brooklyn Botanic Garden, located near the Flatbush and Park Slope neighborhoods, sits on the edge of Prospect Park. It was founded in 1910; the garden holds over 10,000 types of plants. Its many named beautiful gardens and ponds attract many people and offer many educational events on plant science and research, community horticulture and garden publications.

Grand Army Plaza is actually the main entrance of Prospect Park, and consists of concentric oval rings arranged as streets. The plaza includes several statues and busts, the most famous being the Soldiers' and Sailors' Arch. The plaza has also been used for many events throughout the years.

The Prospect Park Zoo is located off Flatbush
Avenue on the eastern side of Prospect Park, and was
a big part of all of our lives. It was renovated in the
80s and now offers children's educational programs,
is engaged in restoration of endangered species
populations, and runs a Wildlife Theater as well as
many other programs. The zoo houses nearly 630
animals.

Remember the museum, zoo, library and botanical
gardens. Walking in the winter to the ice skating
rink. Prospect park monuments, band shelter and
park benches. I walked a lot growing up.

The picnics under the big trees with my Mom, Dad,
sis and family. The zoo, paddle boats, the green
houses, sledding in winter and the beautiful lake.
Loved the place.

The zoo and the merry-go-round!

The carousel

Saw them film an episode of The Equalizer and
Lorenzo Lamas filmed scenes from Break In there.
Park Slope has been in a lot of movies...

The Boathouse on the Lullwater of the lake in
Prospect Park is located in the eastern part
of Prospect Park; the Boathouse was restored several
times. It now houses the Audubon Center,
the Audubon Society's only urban interpretive center
in the United States. We use to love going paddle
boating on the big lake as kids.

The resulting historic preservation movement generated public pressure to save the Boathouse.

After twenty years as a visitors center and park ranger headquarters,

It was listed on the National Register of Historic Places in 1972.

The Boathouse was seen in Scorsese's movie: The Age of Innocence (1993) as the Boston park where Archer

Newland (Day-Lewis) meets Ellen.

The Brooklyn Public Library The Central Library is located at   Flatbush Avenue and Eastern Parkway on Grand Army Plaza. Brooklyn Public Library's Central Library contains over a million cataloged books, magazines, and multimedia materials...Andrew Carnegie donated $1.6 million, assisting in the development of 21 Carnegie Library branches.

The Brooklyn Museum is an art museum located on the edge of Prospect Park. The Brooklyn Museum exhibits collections that seek to embody the rich artistic heritage of world cultures. The Brooklyn Museum has been building a collection of artifacts since the beginning of the twentieth century; some of the museum's collections include Feminist Art, European art, Arts of the Pacific Islands, Arts of Africa, Egyptian, Classical, and Ancient Near Eastern Art. In 2000, the Brooklyn Museum started the Museum Apprentice Program, through which the museum hires teenagers in high school to give tours in the museum's galleries during the summer.

Park Slope Historic District is a national historic district in Park Slope, Brooklyn. The 33 block district is almost exclusively residential and is located adjacent to Prospect Park. It was listed on the National Register of Historic Places in 1980. It is roughly bordered by Prospect Park West, Berkeley Pl., 15th St., 6th, 7th and Flatbush Aves.

Prospect Park

This is where we went on hot summer nights to listen to the bands, on snowy days to go down the hills on sleds, and played in the playground when we were children, played on the baseball teams, rode our bikes around the park, roller-skated around the park, played hockey, went fishing, went to the zoo, played golf and Frisbee, just about anything you could imagine, we did in that park, especially when we got older...

Prospect Park is a 585-acre public park in the New York City borough of Brooklyn, located in Park Slope. Attractions include the Long Meadow, a 90-acre meadow, the Picnic House—which houses offices and a hall that can accommodate parties with up to 175 guests--Litchfield Villa, the Prospect Park Zoo, a large nature conservancy managed by the Wildlife Conservation Society, The Boathouse, Brooklyn's only lake—covering 60 acres and the Prospect Park Bandshell, which hosts free outdoor concerts in the summertime. The park also has sports facilities including seven baseball fields in the Long Meadow, and the Prospect Park Tennis Center, basketball courts, baseball fields, soccer fields, and the New York Pétanque Club in the Parade Ground. There is also a private Society of Friends cemetery on Quaker Hill near the ball fields.

During the American Revolution, the Park was a site of the Battle of Long Island.

New memorials were limited to the 9th Street memorial to Marquis de la Fayette (1917).

Moses built the half-million dollar Prospect Park Zoo (1935), the Prospect Park Bandshell (1939), and children's playgrounds throughout the park.

Horseback riders from Kensington stables are often seen on paths in the park. Pedal boating is open to the public on the lake. In the winter, ice skating, cross-country skiing and sledding are popular pastimes. A popular sledding hill is just inside the 10th Avenue entrance, off Prospect Park Southwest. The Bandshell hosts frequent concerts, most notably the "Celebrate Brooklyn!" Performing Arts Festival, a series of summer concerts founded in 1979 that draws performing artists from around the world.

11-Schools We Went To

- Graduation Books
  - I.S. 88
  - John Jay
- Lunch Boxes
  - P.S. 39
  - P.S. 107
  - P.S. 124

- 51's
  - School Book Covers
  - Schools We Went To
    - Slam Books
  - St. Saviour Elementary
  - St. Thomas Aquinas
    - Crossing Guards
    - Yearbooks

Graduation Books

Remember yearbook autographs? "2 in a car, 2 way kisses, 2 weeks later, Mr.& Mrs.

and "2 young to 2 go 4 boys."

Remember A. Remember B. But C that you remember me!

2 young 2 drink 4 roses. LOL

2 good 2 be forgotten.

Remember the fights. Remember the fun. Remember the homework that never got done! LOL

I have your little picture, I think it's very nice, I keep it in the basement to scare away the mice. that was one the boys liked to write.

Yours til Victor matures... he was an actor.

John & Mary sitting in a tree K I S S I N G first comes love, them comes marriage, then comes Mary with the baby carriage.

Yours til Bear Mountain has cubs.

Yours til the toilet bowls!

If in heaven we don't meet side by side we will face the heat.

IF I DON'T SEE YOU IN THIS WORLD I'LL SEE YOU IN THE NEXT AND DON'T BE LATE.

2 be 2gether 2 last 4 ever = 10der love

If all the boys lived across the sea, what a good swimmer you would be.

That I remember!

And the one you would write for people you didn't know but knew you - stay sweet...

Ashes to ashes dust to dust if it wasn't for you the boys would rust.....

On this page so pearly white it looked so good I took a bite lol

When you get married and all out of shape buy a girdle for 298.

You would fold down a corner of the page and write on that flap, "Lift This." When you lifted up that corner you would write, "Was it heavy?" Hahaha.

Sugar is sweet lemons are sour how many boys can you kiss in an hour?

ROSES ARE RED, VIOLETS ARE BLACK. YOU'D LOOK GOOD WITH A KNIFE IN YOUR BACK.

We had a kid named Fred in our class. In just about everyone's book he wrote - Drop Dead From Fred! LOL

........Was here but now she's gone. She left her name to carry on. Those who knew her, knew her well. Those who didn't can go to hell!!

YY U R. YY U B. I C U R YY 4 Me! (Get It?)

All except the yy part.

When I was sick and very ill. A bird flew on my window sill. I fed it water I gave it bread and then I squished its little head. (A Catholic school!)

It tickles me It makes me laugh that you would want my autograph.

I went to your funeral and heard the preacher say, "Here lies the shell, the nut has passed away."

When you get married and get divorced, come to my stable and marry my horse.

Here's one I got in 5th grade "Roses are red, violets are blue. I'll see you in 6th grade.

2, 4, 6, 8 how the hell did you graduate

When it rains, I think of you.....DRIP, DRIP, DRIP!

I.S. 88

The "Ally" plenty of stuff happened down there, some good some not so good.

I remember fire drills; we used to have to cross the street and look out into the highway...

Yep I remember fighting in the ally actually we use to call it rego park.

Yea I remember right adjacent to the highway.

Me n my sister's n brother use to hang out there too.

It's now called the "Butterfly Park" and owned by P.S. 10.

Man I remember walking everyday from 10th and 6th all the way to I.S. 88.

Yea I was in the annex it was closer to the park. I was a little slow OK?

I remember walking in the snow and jump starting my brothers Blue metallic Volks wagon in the winters to jump start it so he could drive me.

Who remembers the rap battles in the park by I.S. 88 Annex?

From 88 I did go to the annex for one year. anyway you put it some of us knew each from either school.

It was my elementary school before being Annex.

The Annex, I never set foot inside that building. Hung out on both sides and the back yard.

I remember their lousy basketball courts.

The annex was where they put the "bad" kids. I remember cutting class and going inside to see the dean chasing a kid through the halls with a metal pipe!

19th St & 7th Ave. There was a candy store there; I remember calling it "Congas" does anyone else recall it?

Yea, I remember the candy store Charlston Chews, I used to buy them all the time. The 67 bus stopped there...

That was the best candy store ever. I remember getting Charleston Chews and Yoo hoos from there all the time.

I remember that candy store; it was right at the bus stop, step off the bus walk in get hot chocolate and a Kaiser roll slathered with real butter... dam... lol

John Jay

WAAAAAAALLLLKKKK OOOOOOUUUUTTTT!

I need to see a picture of the "dungeon"!

It's tough to get in there these days. They redid the entire school yard recently. There are now benches to sit on, planters that will have flowers in the spring, 2 basketball hoops, the ledge is now slanted concrete (so no more going across) and you can no longer play stick ball "long ways" :-(

Wow that's sad - BTW I always get a funny look when I tell people i hung out in the "dungeon"

The School yard, complete with our Johnny Pump.

There is an old Basketball hoop hangin' on the fence.

ohhh Jungle Jay... how my parents begged me not to go...

Oh, and that garage door on 4th St. where the auto shop used to be. I remember workin' on a Bonneville (I think) that was new, but donated to us) because it was under water for weeks during some big rains in the early 70's. We did eventually get that big beast runnin'.

Does anybody remember the name of the auto shop teacher? He was this really short guy. He cracked me up so many times, because he had a "dirty mind" and just loved showing the girls where and how to find parts in the engine compartment and the under carriage, that put these girls in some "very compromising positions" Ha, Ha. He was very funny, but a pervert, non the less.

I had Mr. Nastasi. but I do remember that teacher?

He used to say the best way to find the spark plug hole was to use your middle finger. LOL

Remember The Governor, He Used to Let us Play Basketball At Night In The Gym?

51s had a dungeon also!

You know, I really can't remember and it doesn't really matter. It was a fun and easy class for me. Peace of cake since dad was a mechanic.

Slim White Haired Middle Age Italian Man, Janitor JJHS. Gem Of The Neighborhood Who Always Said Hello And Knew Everyone By Name.

I GRADUATED FROM THE STOOPS OF JOHN JAY, MY TEACHER WAS JOHN DA COP,

I remember staring at that school a lot from across the street while everyone was in school. I had that view and the one in front of the florist on 5th Street.

I attended 1975 - 1978. I remember Ms. Tobell, Mr. Bruno, and a guy teacher who used to wear very tight jeans. Smoking in the bathrooms, and walk outs.

Ah the dungeon. We set many a Christmas tree on fire down there. A friend and I once did 20 at once! It was spectacular. LOL

My Dad went there. It was Manuel Training High School back then...

Yep it was.......just the other day I was looking at old year books....amazing.

John Jay H.S. Schoolyard...Downstairs, Lower level...

Oh I know it was the darkest stairwell...and you had to go sub- basement and their were 3 classes down there...OK...LOL I could see how it was called the dungeon it's now boarded up...

The nuns at St Saviour always told us to avoid walking near JJ to avoid getting jumped. LOL, I was always afraid of you guys! What a joke! You guys are the best.

Remember the first 'head' shop across from Jay - 'Shanti'? It opened when I was still in grammar school - I got all kinds of 'Hippie' buttons in there - the only one I remember is 'Like Color TV? Try LSD'

Wow, I sorta remember about that, um, about 40 years ago! Unreal...and I remember him - very foggy though.

Lunch Boxes

What did your favorite lunch box look like?

I went home for lunch.

Awwww.. I had a pink vinyl one with a thermos. I remember that you had to be careful not to break the glass inside.

I liked my Scooooby Doooo the best! LOL YOU don't laugh!!!

LOL!

I knew it. Should have kept my mouth shut. Better yet, I should have kept that darn lunch box. It could be worth something now. LOL

HOME FOR LUNCH ALSO THE SCHOOL WAS AROUND THE CORNER.

I had superman.

Sweat Hogs from "Welcome Back Kotter"-- still have mine and I LOVE THAT LUNCH BOX! up your nose with a rubber hose!

Laugh In lunch box.

I miss them soooo much. I use to bring them to school on Wednesday's 1/2 day of school with a bologna sandwich.

I did too, you have a plastic or metal lunch box? lol...

Metal of course!! I loved Ginger snaps too!!

I had the plastic (vinyl) one. Remember those thermoses. Had to be careful not to break the glass inside.

I'm sure it was metal but I'm damned if I can remember what was on it LOL.

Didn't use one for school, anyway. We went home for lunch. But I'm sure I had one. At some point.

Went home for lunch....never had a lunch box.

I know I had a few of them too. Both metal and vinyl. Can only remember a pink vinyl though.

I remember bringing mine to P.S. 321 but then going across the street to Pino's for lunch.

I brown bagged on Wednesday.

I believe I went home for lunch everyday, but on Wednesday, can't remember that long ago.

P.S. 39

I remember the snacks at about 10 o clock we use to get to buy pretzels and milk.

At one time I think they use to have the small cereal boxes.

Yea we each use to get a chance to be the one who went around the room and handed out the milk and pretzels.

I remember the May Day dances.

Oh my god the dungeon I used to be scared leaving thru that back exit.

The Piano on the top floor?

Any one remember the Crossing guards?

What about being the Monitor?

Use to love playing in the lunch break, all different kinds of games.

We use to play dodge ball in the dungeon.

Leaving that way always scared me.

My first love was Mrs. Angelino? She was an angel.

Remember first climbing the little roofs.

P.S. 107

For anyone who attended P.S. 107,

The assembly room was on the top floor...

Ms. Massermine was the principal...

I loved the dance fests...

Even the desks were the old ink well desks.

I was in love with that music teacher, Mr. Chess, I think his name was

Yep.

P.S. 124

P.S. 124 on 4th Avenue to me.

Yes that is the school on 4th ave and 13/14 St.

I actually went to 2nd grade there. But it was a LONG time ago!

Grades 1 - 6...

And a few other blocks also....could be but lets not get technical....lol

I lived in that school yard when I was a kid. Lived right across the street on 13th.

I also lived across the street but on 4th Ave. I was always in the school yard too.

I remember the Sister telling me I see you in the schoolyard smoking cigarettes and kissing the boys! And my friend says why are you peeking out your window at the kids. And she says mind your P's and Q's LMFAO!!!!! Anyway I WAS smoking but I WAS NOT kissing boys YET lol

I think I went to school with you.

Hey do you remember we used to walk the ledge of this building? lol fun fun fun!

hehehe...& hang out on the roofs of the doorways....lol

Yup, such good times.

I remember them all fondly, what fun we used to have....what about 12th St. park...lol

I didn't know that at night the rats took over that park it was sooooo scary!

Wow !!!!...I do remember that lmfao!!!!

TOO FUNNY...I LOVE ALL THE MEMORIES!

51's

I remember 51's, had a "Bad Reputation". It was one of the first JHS's in NY to have a police patrol assigned to it (after a stabbing incident).

I was part of the "Math Team" (we competed with other schools, solving math problems) and when we visited the other schools; I was amazed how "scared" they were of us. We would walk through the hallways and the crowds of kids would just "open up" like the parting of the Red Sea. OMG we were a "Math Team" (like nerd-a-rama) not the Hell's Angels. I LOL now just thinking about it.

Can't remember name that "directly" headed the team. Mr Sullivan may have been more of an "overseer". I wish I kept those darn yearbooks.

Mr. Sullivan had the wax hand.

Another math teacher was Miss Terry Rojna, good looking girl in her late 20's, maybe early 30's.

I was on the JHS 51 math team '65-'66 & '66-'67, Miss Valentine was the coach then. She was very pretty all the boys were in love with her.

Going to 51's in the 60's is funny now but not back then civil rights black power MLK being killed there was a lot hate in that school for white boys.

You got it brother! Miss Valentine rings a bell. I was with the team '68-'69. I remember her being pretty. Did she wear glasses?

School Book Covers

How about school book covers, my mother cut up the brown paper bags from the supermarket. I don't think any of my friends had store bought book covers.

That's what we did, too. :)

Yep my mom did the same thing!! They were sturdier than the Store bought stuff lasted longer!!

Nowadays even if you get brown paper bags they are not big enough.

Paper bags at my house and some kids I remember had that thick clear plastic for their textbooks....And how about our schoolbags - long before backpacks!

Remember the blue loose leaf binder? And the rubber book strap with the metal clip on the end?

I thought I was really cool when, in 5th grade, I got an army knapsack instead of a schoolbag!!!

I became an expert on covering books with brown bags, any size lol.

back before there was a choice between paper or plastic! Brooklynites are nothing if not resourceful.

My Dad did this origami thing with the brown paper bags - no tape.

Balms brown paper bags, those ones you bought at the book store that were shiny and never stayed on and my mom also used contact paper on the workbooks

Key Food(s) bags for us...

Brown Bohack for us. :)

(And that will, of course, lead to some "Odd Couple" the movie reference LOL.)

I've got news for you; I still wrap my son's books with brown paper bags. Often, I use like an American Eagle shopping bag, they come out very nice. Recycling.

Some people used to use the Sunday comics also. And LOL at the rubber boos straps. I had one stretched way too far and when it snapped the buckle damn about broke my hand. Ouch!!

A&P bags for us.

Bohacks on 7th Ave! Mom would send me with the LIST and the shopping cart...

Those metal shopping carts with the two wheels! OMG!

Yep! And everything fit!

Yup. Four paper bags on the bottom with all the heavy stuff and then 4 bags on top with bread, meat, etc. After many years, my mother started having the groceries delivered.

I remember my Mom giving me 12 cents to get a giant loaf of Wonder Bread from Cortese's on 7th Ave bet 7th & 8th Sts. Or a dime for a loaf of Italian bread. I always ripped one of the ends off, ate it and then put the loaf back in the bag the other way before I got home. Apparently I thought no one would notice this LOL.

I did the same thing...we all though alike back then lol...

Because it was so simple! These little things made us so happy. We had to use our imaginations. It was HELL if we were trapped in the house.

Absolutely not -- only the rich kids could afford "real" book covers!!

Schools We Went To

Though we lived in Park Slope, some of us moved there and came from other schools and some of us went to other schools that were in other neighborhoods...so list your schools.

For me it was 1965 thru 1978: PS 39 Kindergarten to 5th, IS 88 6th thru 9th, John Jay HS

PS 321 1st thru 4th, PS 154 5th grade (yep sent us to the Terrace)

PS.321-k-5th, IS 88-6-9th, john jay high, 10th-12th.

PS 321.. st Thomas.. Grady...John Jay

St Saviours 1966-72 Saviours 74-75 Bishop Ford CCHS 75-79

PS 146, then moved to PS 10's during the 3rd grade..(Does anyone remember that move from PS 146 to PS 10's?), IS88's then back to PS 146 (when it became the Annex), Jay Jay HS

PS 92 , 321, 154, IS 88, Tilden HS, John Jay HS.

PS 39, Holy Family, St Thomas, Bishop Kearney, Bishop Ford,

PS77-PS321-PS 154 (5th grade)-IS88-John Jay HS

P.S.124, P.S.154 (bussed for the 5th grade), JHS 51 & John Jay

PS321, IS88, ER Murrow HS in Midwood section,

Holy Family, St. Thomas/Holy Family, Jungle Jay (against my parent's wishes)

St Francis Xavier, John Jay

PS 39 61-66 jhs51 66-70 Grady 71-74 automotive shop

PS 77 (60) STA (61-69) John Jay (69-73)

PS 39 Kindergarten, STA 1st and 2nd Grade, .PS 39 3-6 Grade...JHS 51 7th-9th Grade, Automotive HS 10th-12th....

PS 124, HOLY FAMILY 5-7, JHS 51, JOHN JAY HS

B St. Thomas 1-8, John Jay 9-12

P.S. 154 Kindergarten, Holy Name 1-8 and Bishop Ford 9-12

Holy Name of Jesus on 9th Ave. graduated in 1971 then John Jay High School from 1971-1974

PS 39 K-5, JHS 51 6,7 & 9, JJHS 10-12

HOLY FAMILY, JOHN JAY

Kindergarten, PS 39 - 1-6 grade J.H. 51 - 7 & 8 grade

St. Francis Xavier St. Saviours and Xaverian

St Saviour's then on to Brooklyn Tech

St. Saviours, John Jay

St. Thomas Aquinas, John Jay

Where are all the people from Holy Family?

Right here

Was that sign always there?? Even when I went to 7th & 8th grades in that building?

I DO NOT remember that sign! But if you're saying 85, I was already graduated for a few years.

I was out of that building (graduating 8th grade) by June 1974. So if it was after that, I'm safe. :)

I lived right across the street from here. Directly across from the convent. I went to 7th & 8th Grade in this school. 1 - 6 was on 8th Avenue & 7th Street. I did not go to that high school.

Slam Books

Do any of you remember Slam Books?

Yes Yes! They were great! Wish I remembered some of the questions passed around back then.

Somewhere I have the Slam Book. If I ever find it I think I would die laughing. Back then, it wasn't so funny. Kids are cruel!

Oh I loved the slam books!!

You're right- used to love reading them - and the fights from what was written - it wasn't private - hello what did people think slam meant?

So funny. I finally took a "closer" look & saw: Marlon Brando (young, not fat) & (not dead). LMAO

73 "I think she is conceited" (which was such an insult back then) then you look and # 73 is like one of the friends you thought you were close with It was real passive aggressive.

Exactly!

I got in major trouble at St. Francis when Bro. Patrick discovered our slam book in my hands.

Like a manual version of "internet bullying" by today's political correctness.

St. Saviors

St Saviour Elementary

Also my Alma mater graduated 8th grade 1972

Graduated 1974

That"s where I went too! 1st through 6th grade.

1st thru 6th. Sister Sean Maura was my favorite nun! (sixties)

I was scared of Sister Patricia in the fifth grade, back in the fifties.

Sister Frances Maura, (no relation to above Sister Maura) was not so nice! We were scared of her too.

Graduated 1959

1969 from the HS building...

Sister told my Dad "He'll NEVER make the Grades at Bishop Ford CCHS" Hey unholy Habit less Nun!! I graduated in 78 from Ford!!

Sister Sean Maura accused me of stealing in 3rd grade, because my parents had bought me some fancy pencils. My parents had Father O'Toole come to the house to complain. All I remember is she was sent to Africa on a mission a couple of years later

LOL...the women who shaped our lives!

Hey, despite it all, they kept us on the straight and narrow.

I got a shirt for x-mas---it says...catholic school survivor...it is so cute...loving it...

St. Thomas Aquinas

How many from STAS?

Went back and went back and taught there 20 years later!

I REMEMBER THAT BUILDING.

Graduated in 1977.

Went to St Thomas from first thru 4th grade. Then went to PS 39. The nuns used to kick the shit out of me.

ST Thomas now rents out as a public school and they had wooden boxed the holy statues that were on the building...so sad.

Do you go to the reunions? I am the one that gives out the name tags.

I was in the other class, Class of 73, I am pretty sure you were in my kindergarten class at P.S 39, Miss Ryan was the teacher.

I went to kindergarten in PS 124...Miss Costa was the school teacher..

St. Thomas for the entire 8 years!

273

1st and 2nd grade only.

Yep me too. 8 years, graduated in 1970. Then my girls went there later on in the years.

I went to STAS for 8 years also....they didn't have kindergarten back then, so we went to public schools for that.

I went to PS 39 on 6th ave & 8th st for Kindergarten.

I went to Holy Family but used to go to dances at St. Thomas Aquinas. Right down the block from Duffy's Funeral Parlor.

Class of '83.

I went to St. Thomas for 8 years - graduated in 1969.

I went to STA for the 1st and 2nd grade, then PS 39's for 3-6 grade and on to JHS 51's. I played little League and was an Alter Boy at STA.

Remember those dances. Went all the time.

I went to public school it was more fun lol

That's why I only went to STA for 2 years; the nun's kicked my ass. So I went to PS 39 and when I got to JHS 51's

Went to St. Thomas for 1st and 2nd grade....Nuns put Bobby Pins in my hair because they said it was too long. I didn't miss Catholic School.

I went there and graduated in '75.

Graduated in '74.

Graduated in 1976.

Does anyone remember Mr Giordano class of 73?

"Sir the cow sir, she walks she talks, the lactic fluid extracted from the female of the bovine species is highly prolific to the nth degree sir."

Your right, it was always LET ME HOLD A NICKLE. That school was bad back then and when MLK got shot all hell broke loose. We ran for our lives.

When MLK died they broke a bunch of windows & the school was closed for days.

I wasn't a student, but I spent a lot of time there for Girl Scout meeting & events.

Class of 1970. Great memories.

8 years and I remember the mean nuns and basement. I got in trouble everyday cause I wore a t shirt and shorts under my uniform. As soon as I left the building the uniform came off.

I went to Religious Instructions there, before I made my communion.

You're right, I went 2 STA 4 5 years and was always sick my mom took me out and put me in 39; I loved that school but we had 2 give an Aunts address...

No Longer St. Thomas Aquinas School. It Is a Public School Now.

That's a shame.

Wow; really? Is the church still there? I was baptized in St. Thomas Aquinas, but went to school @ St. Saviour's. How sad.

Church Is Still A Church Though...

I was at the church 2 weeks ago as beautiful as ever....

I went to St Thomas what memories

The crucifixes around the school are all covered over now.

As are the religious statues. See them boxed up in wood

No more baskets of cheer raffles. No more bazaars.
A tragedy.

I went to St Thomas and I also got married there.
Wonderful memories.

No more "Night at the Races"...

There was the old convent for the nuns @ St Thomas
Aquinas before they moved to the professional
building next to Duffy's funeral home.

I remember going to Christmas party's there.

Was that the place they converted to an orphanage at
one time?

Wasn't that a Home for kids? Still is?

Yes, I went to summer camp there, there was a nun
who was an amazing basketball player, I still see her
taking a jump shot with her habit on.

It was the Sisters of St Joseph convent before the
new convent across the street was purchased for $1.

Yea it was Sister Geraldine I was there all the time.
Went to summer camp then became a counselor at
summer camp. Not an orphanage a home for
runaways.

Crossing Guards

Anyone an AAA school crossing guard? Wearing
that nifty white vinyl belt thingy with your badge
prominently displayed?

I was one at PS 39 in the Mid 60's, my post was
across from the school by the Library.

I think he carried the time over from AAA school
guard to the Job...Lol

I hate to admit it but so was I. PS 107. It had perks. You got to leave 15 minutes earlier and come in 15 minutes later.

Yep, I was one too @ Saint Saviours School 7th Street & 8th ave, we had a crossing guard on every corner while Mrs Garcia (who was there for a very long time!!) directed traffic!!

We had a Green/Silver badge (Sargent) & a Blue/Silver one (Captain) they gave us ranks to make us feel important & keep our interest I guess!! LOL great time!!

Oh yeah got to report peeps to Principal if they didn't obey your crossing instrux!! too ;-))

I think I was one once. Some kids had the ones with the red or green on them I guess they were the bosses lol.

I was... at P.S.39 around 78/79.

Crossing guard at P.S. 39, 6th ave and 7th street, 64 to 66.

Yearbooks

I went the same years 7th, 8th and 9th and then graduated from John Jay in 74.....

Really? Are you in the Year Book? I still have mine.

Which yearbooks do you have?? Did you also go to John Jay?

I have my yearbook for John Jay Class of '74. I don't remember ever keeping anything from JHS 51, and I even was in the "printing club". Yea, spent many after school hours printing (on mimeograph machines even. Ink ALL over me).

I am going to get my John Jay yearbook out. I did have yearbooks from 51's they were soft cover I have to look.

Those rubber things to hold the notebooks were covered with names, too. Also, the little space between the toe lines on the pro Keds. I still have a spalding ball with me all summer. You never know when you can pick up a game of handball or kings.

I know I have a year book, and it's in prime condition except that I hated my pictures and cut it out. So whoever was "behind me" on that page is gone also.

Isn't that funny about nobody liking their pics. Never figured that one out. Remember also the Keds and bands. Remember being cool about the multi-colored sports socks & multiple, different colored laces?

7th, 8th and 9th grade, '69, '70, '71, respectively. What about you?

Blue canvas loose leaf binder wrote all your friends name (who loved who) all over it and the rubber strap for our books. ....NO schoolbags or backpacks back then.

Man I thought those rubber straps were cool then, but the writing of names, Nawh, that had to be a "chick' thing.

Yeah..... I guess it was a "girl" thing.

Mostly done during class...

What year did you go to JHS 51?

I cherish my yearbook. Best school years and memories for me.

Too funny back then we all thought we were the shit now we look at our year books and go daamnnnnnnnnnnnn lol.

278

12-Stores We Remember

- 5 & Dime
- Brooklyn Aquarium
- Butcher Stores
- Candies and Stores
- Chinese Laundry
- Dixon's Bike Shop
- Funeral Homes
- Germain's
- Hardware Store
- Ice Cream Parlors
- Johns Bargain Store
- Kresge's
- Laundromat
- McCrory's, Woolworth's, Downtown
- Pat Kenny's
- OTB
- Pops & Al's
- Sam's Work Clothes And Stagenhagen
- S & H Stamps
- Soundtrack
- Sepe's
- Tony's Record Store
- Stores
- Shoes
- Sneaker Circus
- Places Left

5 & Dime

They were all special for something. The Kresge's sold an ice cream sandwich with a block of Neapolitan ice cream between two warm toasted waffles. It was absolute heaven. Think it was 35 cents.

Like wining a free banana split, or the grill cheese, or pickles, or cotton candy

Woolworth's had a terrific lunch counter with a great grilled cheese and lime Rickey.

Woolworth's five and dime; they had counters that went on for miles filled with toys and things you could buy for 25 cents and up, it was truly a wonderland of fabulous things for practically no money

My favorite was the Woolworth's, You could get a bag of hot salted roasted red Spanish peanuts, A hoagie sandwich, or a bag of popcorn, Or just sit at the lunch counter and order a sandwich or soda or a lunch meal.

Oh yeah they did sell small tropical fish in the basement. And you could also buy Oilcloth tablecloths for your kitchen table.

Remember when we all used to use those to cover our kitchen tables when we were growing up. So easy to clean and you did not have to change the table cloth and launder it after every meal,

Just wipe it down with a sponge or rag. And they came in many patterns and colors.

When I learned to sew, it was there that I would spend hours selecting just the right patterns from the Simplicity and McCall's books in the fabric department.

Woolworth's was also the source for turtles and goldfish, and Tangee Natural lipstick, as well as nylon stockings, hair curlers, white gloves, ribbons, clear nail polish, Windsong perfume...in short, all the necessities of life for a teenager. It was also the site of the best soda fountain in town.

Brooklyn Aquarium

Who remembers the pet store on 9th street between 5th and 6th, just down the street from the YMCA? Growing up we got all our tropical fish and supplies there. Sadly, it's gone now.

Brooklyn Aquarium

Thanks for the name brain froze

And every Easter they had all those baby chicks in the window, we had a full grown Rooster the only one that survived

I remember the chicks - we always wanted one!

I bought a Gerbil there in 1971.....Damn cat ate him!

OMG I forgot all about that pet shop. My dad bought us a chick and a duck for Easter one year and they shit all over the house. My mom told him to bring them back!!! Thanks for the memories.

I used to go to that pet shop and we used to get 10 guppies for a dime/ they always died like within a week.

Yea I can't Count how many Toilet bowl funerals we had.

We used to get turtles there too.

My mom bought a dog there for my sister's birthday! I remember us all walking home and being so excited.

Bought many hamsters in there had to fool my little sis every time Ben (the hamster)died we had to get another one that looked almost like it, till the one time we happened to get a female and it had babies, that one was a little hard to explain...LOL

I bought the cutest and sweetest black calico cat there.

I remember the Pet Store. I had a friend that worked there.

Yeah...brings back a lot of memories! At this age I need help remembering.

I remember buying Large Turtles, Chameleons, Salamanders there they had a great selection!!

Had that huge window looked like a big cage all the bird in there.

I use to get the mice for my snakes there all the Lizards and exotic pets before some of them became illegal.

I bought a duck there once, called it Suzy duck. I use to take her to the park with me once in awhile and she would keep up as we walked and played in the grass with her, I think I over fed her though? She had this big neck then one day she died. :(

Butcher Stores

Who was ur fav butcher in Park Slope

Emhardt's & Pergola's.

Don't remember the name, but it was on 7th Avenue right off of 1st. It was full of saw dust and we used to skate around while our mothers would chat and wait for their meat to be cut.

Tony's on 5th ave bet.7th and 8th. Right next to Leopold's.

I remember mom would say 1 pound chuck chop lol

There was a butcher on 5th ave we used to go to. Somewhere between 1st and 3rd. forgot the name. Remember the saw dust and moving it around with my feet.

Don't remember the name but it was right next to The Roost on 7th Ave & 8th St. The saw dust was the best. I used to get it from them when I needed it for class projects LOL. Pretty sure it's not there any more.

Where was Emhardt's & Pergola's?

When I was kid my mom went to Eddie the Butcher. He was on 5 ave bet. 11 and 12 street, next store to the shoemaker.

7th ave between 10th and 11th street. Sal and his Dad run the place!

Between 7th st and 8th st on 5th - John the butcher.

When I was a little girl my Mom went to the butchers on 7th Ave, between 5th and 6th St. He always gave the kids a thick piece of bologna to eat while our Mom shopped. As I got older my Mom then started going to Pergola's and they became her favorite butcher shop.

Day of the Neighborhood Butcher is sorely missed In Park Slope!!

On 6th ave 10th st. & Franks on 7th ave.

10 street and 7th ave..

I also remember my mom would bring us to the butchers across the street and we would play with the wood chips on the floor.

Butcher shop bet 7th & 8th st closed down pretty recently.

The Westin, butcher shop!! I remember the saw dusted floors too!! Nancy the crossing guard from STA worked there!!

That was about 10 years ago.

Really it was that long ago?? Doesn't seem like it.

Seemed as though we were playing with that saw dust for hours. They must have been slow as ...

There was a butcher on nearly every corner. We all usually went to whichever one was closest to where we lived. This is probably no longer the case in many places. How sad.

Ralph's was the name of that butcher I believe.

I worked for Pergolas as a delivery boy; my worst night mare was a 5 story walk-up with 4 bags of meat.

I also made chop meat and cut steaks on the band saw.

Liberty Meat Market on 10th street & 7th ave.

Mom used to go to the butcher on Pres. St bet. 5th & 4th Ave. for meat and somewhere in Carroll Gardens for poultry & goat, which was "butchered" while you waited.

Did anyone go to Tony and Pete 6th ave btw 10th and 11st. lol

Yes lived across the street and use to also ask for bones that had meat on them so we could barbeque them in our little hide away club house down on 8th street.

SAM'S ON 23-24TH STREET N 5TH AVE OR DANNY'S ON 5TH AVE DON'T REMEMBER THE STREET LIKE BETWEEN 21ST AND 22ND ST MAYBE.

I thought Sam's was on 4th Avenue. I was always afraid of Danny when I was a little kid.

Ben's pork store on fifth between President and Caroll omg

Definitely the meat market on 5th Ave between 7th & 8th Street ... not only the sawdust all over the floor but I'd always get a slice of bologna.

The Great Western butcher on 5th ave & 8th. St.

Sam must have died after I moved, I don't remember that. I miss all those stores on 4th Avenue. Charlie's Deli & Leo's Candy Store.

Candy Stores

Probably the biggest part of the whole book and the best part of our child hood was all that candy. And it's also probably the reason for all our teeth problems today. I'm sure most would agree if not all. But how could something that taste so good be so bad, but we didn't care, we just scrimped and saved, and begged and did chores, and fished for coins in the subways grating, just to get a few cents for some of the most delicious candies, no matter what it was, it was all good MMMMMMMMMMM

Do you remember Danny's on Garfield and 7th?

I'll call the Cops boy!

I LOVED THIS PLACE!

soooo coool!!

Check out Friends of Danny's candy store FB group. Tons of great memories. "GET OUT OF MY WAY BOY!!!!"

HEYYYYYYYY BOOOOYYYYYYYY!!

Loved reading all of those memories. Made me laugh and smile so much!

One memory that stands out - the soda refrigerator that shocked you when you touched it!

It's AMMONIA Time, He'd pour it over the radiator to make your eyes tear so you would leave the store...Sick!

BEST SIGN in Danny's Window "NOTARY PUBIC" misspelled! It hung for years!! LMFAO!!

That's cause there was always a huge puddle of water in from of box in winter!! LOL

In his later years he'd just throw it on floor & sidewalk!!

Loved the 2 phone booths in the back.

Much "Heavy Petting took place in those booths!! LOL!!

What a thing to say to YOUNG INNOCENT Impressionable Youths!! LMFAO!!

Yeah right, innocent!!!!

HEH!! HEH!! ;-)))

Awesome. I first played asteroids there.. First real video game.

He used to charge through the store, "OUTTA MY WAY BOY!"

He had to guard his prized "penny Candy" makin' sure everyone paid for every piece!! LOL

Absolutely. We'd all crowd around the glass doors of the case rummaging through the gummy fish and licorice with our bare hands. No spatulas in those days! Loved walking out of there with a brown paper bag full of my favorite candies!

AND NO ONE GOT SICK!! LOL!! In the later 70's he would love to tell us " GO TO RYANS/COACH & Drink yaselves ta death or go to movies & watch them kill the girlz (Slasher movies) Movies JUST GET DA FUCK OUTTA MY STORE"

Smoking in the Old Phone Booths...

Making phone calls from those phone booths and the one outside across the street. Remember the "you have five cents credit toward overtime" recording. And then when you hung up the phone it would ring and the operator would personally ask you to deposit the five cents.

Sorry folks I'm at it again. Your favorite penny candy from the Penny Candy Store. For me it was the Banana flavored peanut shaped marshmallow.

Button candy or the liquid-filled wax "bottles" LOL. OK pixie straws were really good too. Oh jeez don't get me started LMAO.

The Wax candies, those "sugar buttons" on a paper roll (I think I ate more paper than candy LOL),

Those small wax "coke bottles" with sugar, sugar, sugar, a little water with color die #99 Black!, corn syrup, corn syrup, and another "touch" of sugar. Who the heck needed those little bottles of 5-minute junk?

Also those "necklace" candies that you "nibbled" during the day, 'til your neck was so sticky that your mother couldn't separate herself from your neck when she hugged you.

Wax lips and wax buck teeth.

Squirrel Nut zippers.

Right there with you. Bonamo taffy!

Mary Jane

The wafer "flying saucers" that tasted like toilet paper, but you ate them because there were those little sugar balls inside them.

Cracker Jacks

Oh, the taffy! If I were to eat them now, I would lose all the "metal" in my teeth. Even the "Charleston Chew" bars.

Charlston Chew, freeze'em and crack'em.

How about the rock candy?

Arty (of "Arties Toy & Candy Store" on 5th between Union and Sackett) I "blame" you for all this. I think I'm starting to lose all my teeth.

Milk Duds, Sugar Babies, Pixie stix, Bubblegum Hot dogs

Bit-o-honey, Marshmellow "Cheeps", Frenchies

What about PEZ and the great dispensers

The fake chalky candy cigarettes with the red tips -- and i wonder why I started smoking when I was a teenager, lol.

Seriously though, my favorite -- Goldenberg Peanut Chews,

The best Shoelaces

Do you mean those long, multi-colored licorice (spelling?) type chewy candy?

Yes and no, shoelaces were licorice, but long red very thin strings that you usually wound up into a circle like and chewed away....

Those candy necklaces that made your neck sticky.

Yeah the licorice shoe laces ..Red was my favorite :)

Twizzlers still taste the same.

Jawbreakers in small, medium, large and what the hell were they thinking size!

Mary Janes..........looooooooove'd them!

Jawbreaker size? Who knows? They made for a good "babysitter", for one who would not "shut up", just POP one in the mouth (size relative to mouth size) LOL

Atomic Fireballs were awesome, still are.

Lest we forget the wax Pan Flutes,

Bazooka Bubble Gum!

Grape, Cherry or Original Bazooka?

Original first, then grape. Cherry was not a favorite of mine.

One Bazooka Joe comic that I remember "Doc, every time I drink Hot Chocolate I get a sharp pain in my eye"...Docs response "take the spoon out of the cup"

Bazooka Joe comics save a bazillion and you can get X-ray glasses that absolutely didn't work! LOL

OOOPS MARYJANES ALWAYS AND STILL MY FAVORITE ALTHOUGH NOW THEY PULL MY FALSE TEETH OUT HAHAHAHAHAHAHA

One more, a one liner......."I had a dream I was eating a large marshmallow......When I woke up my pillow was gone!"

Coconut Watermelon......almost forgot about them.

I loved the coconut watermelon slices.

Squirrel nuts, peanut chews, bit o honey, oh the list goes on for me lol

Candy dots on the paper.....wax bottles filled with a juice or whatever it was.....

What was the name of that taffy that came on a long strip of paper. Brightly colored Green or Pink or Orange with White? Did they even have a name?

Chocolate "Gold" covered coins.

Nothing like walking into the store with a whole quarter in your pocket and acting like you owned the store. I would like 7 bazooka bub...wait, wait make that 9 ooh wait.

Wax soda bottles??

The Marathon bar.

Wax harmonicas.

You know what's weird; most of the candy was not wrapped. One of my faves, Swedish fish, not wrapped, they are now!

Remember those well but never bought them.

Bubble Gum cigars. If you were real careful you could use the band as ring.

Bonomo Turkish Taffy

Red Hots

"Good n Plenty"......

Malted Milk Balls aka Whoppers

The fake ice cream cones wafers

Mahan Italian ices in the yellow cup with a wooden spoon loved flipping it to get to the bottom.... chocolate was the best

Candy is Dandy..........Liquor is Quicker!

I don't know what you call them, but they were caramel wrapped in some kind of white stuff, and I remember little Reeses peanut butter cups.

Marino's Italian ices! THE Best!

Ice hands down! I liked the lemon.

I remember lollipops were on a paper roll also.

Candy Hearts ......for your first love!

Tootsie roll yummy

Charms from the bubble gum machines................and if you had enough made a bracelet or necklace with a string

The cool prizes in the Cracker Jacks boxes.

I remember making bracelets out of double mint gum wrappers. You had to carefully fold them in to small squares and interlock them.

My sister made a photo album out of gum wrappers. lol

What a feat!

Ice cubes & jelly rolls Ann & Franks candy store 12th st. & 6th ave.

Remember those flying saucer candies with the little candy beads inside the saucer was a wafer like thing that melted in your mouth...

How could we forget Brooklyn's own, Now and Later's.

I call them Annihilators, because they totally destroy your teeth.

The Now n Later factory was down on 3rd avenue and 34th street. We would go in there after playing hockey get handfuls from the rejects barrels!!!

I remember the candy store in Coney Island next to Nathan's...one of the candies I liked were cocoanut flavored watermelon slices.

The candy store in Coney Island is still there. I liked the little candy coated different color chocolate balls wrapped in cellophane that they sold in the candy store by 88's on 19th ST.

You can get the flying saucers in the Poconos! They were like Communion Wafers.

Yeah, one of my favs. Like I said before, I usually ate more paper than candy. But it was gooood!!!

WOW Loved those!! Used to get a Danny's Candy store on 7th & Garfield!!

The name is on the tip of my tongue. The candy store (& toys) on 5th Ave. bet Union & Berkeley?? Artie's??? Help!

I think there was another Dots candy in a box, but I think these were called Dots too.

Why did we like those so much?? The Dots in the box could pull your teeth out they were so chewy.

Yeah Dots DEF!! ;-) Italian Candy I believe!!

I remember them well. They were too much work to chew!

I think they were also called Candy Buttons.

Yes I rang in my head when ya said!!

They still have Dots in Disney world in Florida and several other candies.

This was one of my favorite candies growing up. I have recently seen them in a candy store in PA and unfortunately, like everything else, they are not the same.....

I saw those peanuts everywhere, but personally I hated them.

Yeah, Candy buttons is what I remember them as.

Jim's Candy store on 6thave between 9th & 10th street
First stop every morning to get my sugar fix!

Do you remember Violets? They were square, in a
roll like life savers, and they made your whole mouth
purple, and it smelled like,......over-powering violet
make-up powder. LMAO

Violets used to love them!! Such an odd taste I got
addicted & O'D on em!! LOL!! Haven't seen em in a
while!!

I think they made you dump purple too. LMAO

I loved them too. Some people told me they taste
like soap. Not to me, I would eat the whole roll.

I think you got more paper than dot from this strip--
but we ate it anyway didn't we? lol

That's what it was called button candy?

Omg I use to love them!!!!!

Remember the candy necklaces candy was on an
elastic string

I remember having my own slobber, all over my
neck and chest from eatin' those stupid necklaces.
But boy were they good.

What a sugar rush we had in those days. I think our
parents were so glad that we played so much outside.
Otherwise we would have been bouncing off the
walls. I think maybe that I "vibrated" in my sleep.

Does anyone remember the orange wax harmonicas?
I loved how they smelled - they were Halloween
candy, and wax Lips

I loved all those wax things. Remember the Lips?

What was this from? Marsh, marsh, marshmallows
are funny. They're good for your tummy.
Marshmallows are funny.

Eclair, that's what we called it. Remember when we had Hoffman seltzer deliveries, and the bottles had those pressure valves to create the white foam?

Prettiest girl I ever saw was drinking Hoffmans through a straw...

Ah, the Egg Cream."A classic drink that actually uses neither egg nor cream! This is an old NYC drink from back in the days of soda and milkshake shops. This always reminds me of Sunday mornings with my father."

Choc egg cream yummy..........

8th St And 4th ave Johns candy store penny candies and egg creams. My cousin used to work there. We would stop on our way to the movies on a sat, have and egg cream and a bag of penny candy. Give him a quarter and get change to go to movies. Those where the days.

Chinese Laundry

Though most of us did our own laundry in the house of and the laundry mat some had to get their cloths done by the pros

Does anyone remember the Chinese laundry on Garfield Pl a few doors down from Danny's candy? That familiar laundry starch smell when you first walked in.

The Chinese laundry had a minah bird that would whistle the "wolf call" at all the women who walked by and it spoke with a Chinese accent. It often said "Ha are youuuuu"

The answer it was LEW WAH Laundry!!

I am impressed that you remembered it!! LOL ;-)

OMG, you remember the name! It's coming back to me now. I used to pick up my family's shirts there and remember that overwhelming smell. It was a tiny place. It was there in the 60's. Wonder when they closed.

My father got his shirts done at "Personal Process" cleaners on 3rd St. and 7th Ave but my mother had a few Irish lace tablecloths that she would have cleaned at Lew Wah only!

This may not be politically correct, but it's true. When I moved from 8th street to Garfield I took shirts in there to be cleaned---I didn't mind that overwhelming smell because they did such a good job. I asked the very old woman in LEW WAH's "when will the shirts be ready for pick up?" and she yelled, "TUN-NAY". I was confused and said, " 'scuse me--- but when did you say the shirts will be ready?" and she became very annoyed and screamed "TUN-NAY!" I felt a little bad I upset the old woman, but I was quick to learn --I went back each week the day after Monday and my shirts were ready.

That's not so bad My old man would come home from work & say " ya take my shirts to the"CHINAMAN"?? LOL I still call Chinese laundries the CHINAMAN cause of that!! Could say worse things I guess!!;-)

Hate to say it, but my father used the other "word", not out of malice, but it was just commonly used by his generation. I remember the shirts would be neatly wrapped in brown paper and white string. And if you didn't have your ticket, it was very hard to get your shirts. Yes it was true...(don't say it...you know what expression I mean)!

LOL NO TICKY NO SHIRTY!! LOL couldn't
RESIST!! Everything is still same today!! I go to the
one between Union & Prez only thing that changed
of course is THE PRICE!! NO SURPRISE THERE!
LOL!!

Dixon's Bike Shop

Dixon's was there as long as any store left in the
slope and still is to this day

Well the fact was if we needed to fix a tire most of us
would get the patch kits and do it our self, but also
the fact show that if Dixon's is still around more than
half of us probably, didn't do it our self

We bought our bike to him to get it repaired more
when we got the ten speeds English racers.....shifting
gears the prelude to the first car, we use to ride down
to Coney Island

I got my first bike from Dixon's

Dixon's was right next to the fire department

Who remembers the parties on top of "Dixon's Bike
Shop"? My sister had her sweet 16 there?

What about the brothers and his wife who worked
there with Mr. D..great guy..

Always had great bikes and old bike for that matter
hanging on the racks inside

We use to rent bikes from him and go for a ride in
Prospect Park

I used to hang out there with Mr D and work there
with Mr Dixon and his kids I learned a lot about
fixing all types of bike

Loved all the old bikes hanging around the shop.

That big Yellow mural on the wall on Union St, with the old fashion bike, how can you forget that?

The mural is still there to this day!

Funeral Homes

One of the facts of life and also the saddest was the trips to the funeral parlors we had to make when your young most of the funerals were your great grandparents, grand parents, some times moms and dads, but it really hit home when it was one of our friends, or brothers and sisters, as I am sure most of us attended at least 2 or more of those who died to young, some accidental , car crashes , drugs, fights as well as Aids, these were the saddest times of our lives

Duffy's funeral home 9th street and 4th avenue

Last time I saw my Dad. Bittersweet Memories!

Your not from Park Slope, unless you get laid out in Duffy's...

Wasn't there another funeral home on 7th ave near Lincoln Pl? For some reason the name "Thomas" comes to mind...

There was a Funeral Home named McCaddin's on Sterling place 1st block off Flatbush!! My MOM, DAD & BROTHER all were waked there!! It is no longer there!!....

My whole family has been laid out in Duffy's.

Whatever happened to the Edward Dunn Funeral home that I believe was on 7th Ave.?

Dun's closed about 10 yrs ago...maybe more.

Dunn's was on 7th Ave between 7th & 8th st (closer to 7th st I think)

Does anyone remember a funeral home at Carroll or Garfield and 5th avenue yrs ago?

I think it was Russo's. I believe the name is still there in stone.

I remember Russo's. Always gave the creeps passing by there as a kid.

My Dad worked in Duffy's !

Russo was the name and there was always an elderly woman with a white french poodle on the roof near the driveway. We used to play buck-buck there and kings across the street.

What about Adeos funeral home on corner of 7th st 4th ave. They always had the basement doors open and we all used to sneak down the stairs to see the bodies

I remember Russos was a really creepy place that always looked like it held a lot of secrets,

Lyman's Funeral Parlor on the corner of 13th Street and 4th Avenue. Went to my first wake there

I really hate Duffy's-- so much heartache associated with that place.

Germain's

According to Steven Germain (great grandson of the store's founding fathers), Germain's was opened in 1898 and closed in the mid 1960's.

In a 1938 Brooklyn Eagle Newspaper, Germain's was referred to 5th Avenue's Greatest Shopping Center...but can't find any photos

Christmas memories of Santa

There was also a Key Food inside Germain's in the back, along with the one on 14th Street.

If I'm not mistaken it was also Bohacks at one time after Germain's.

Key Food was on the corner of 14th Street & 5th Avenue, there was also a Key Food in the back of Germain's on the corner of 15th Street & 5th Avenue.

Back then there were 2 toy stores, Kresge's on 10th St, Germain's on 15th St & John's Bargain Store on 8th St & they all had toys galore !!...it was great to be a kid in Park Slope!!!....lol

I remember Germain's, my mother used have our holiday picture with Santa taken their, we would then pick out one toy to buy, I usually picked Aurora monster models, my mother used to say that anything you needed you would be able to find on 5 avenue, the avenue was always busy but it was magical during the holidays

Mom was right, not only could you find ANYTHING you needed but, when you went to the "avenue" you saw EVERYBODY & their mother....lol...a normal hour trek up there ended up being 3-4 hours....lol...

That may be true. Lol!

Germain's OMG wow that was a memba moment!

THEY ALSO HAD A PET SHOP IN THE BASEMENT AT ONE TIME IN GERMAIN'S...

Loved to go there with mom & never knew what we would find.

Loved the basement part of the store.

The only pet shop I remember was on 9ᵗʰ St.

GERMAIN'S BASEMENT HAD ONE BACK IN
THE LATE 60s...I'M AN OLD TIMER...LOL!

Germain's basement had the pet shop & house wares
& hardware, curtains & bedding.

Hardware Stores

As a kid, I had lots of hobbies and one was fixing
things...or should I say, taking things apart and trying
to put them back together again and be missing a few
screws. Well, that lead me into doing construction
and becoming a jack-of-all-trades and a master of
most, but you couldn't be a master if you didn't have
the place to get what you needed to do the repair or
replacement.

I have taken so many things apart in my time in Park
Slope, and I would like to fix them rather than
replace them; that was the trick to being the best
handyman: when you took things apart, you would
know what made them tick and what was broken
inside...and anyone who knows me to this day knows
I know just about how to fix anything...and again the
best hardware store was Leopoldi's, they packed into
that little store probably what Home Depot has in it
today, just on a very small scale. That's why they
were my first place whenever I was doing any repair;
if they didn't have it there they didn't have it
anywhere.

I found this article about Leopoldi's Hardware store
in Park Slope. Joe Leopoldi, Sr. used to own the
candy store on 5th St. and 6th Ave.: "The Place."

Wow, that had me in tears; it's terrific that they're
still going strong. Many more years to them & may
they be able to hand it down to their kids. :)

300

Congrats To You All, Leopoldi's: Your Family Store
Is Truly the Best Around!!

"Hey, Pete, do you have a?" were always my first
words...and they did always have it, some where in
there, on the wall in the draws, under the counter in
the bin.

Wow they are still there a real nuts and bolt store
always had what I needed.

Wow! Now this kicks up some shit.

The best HARDWARE STORE.

I can still remember the smell in the hardware store
also...

What a great family...

My dad sent me the newspaper article. Wow...I was
always going to this store as a kid on errands for this
or that. What was the black guy's name who used to
make keys! Great store/great folks!

Louie! Yeah it was Louie....always had a cigar in his
mouth!!

I remember Louie too...Never without the cigar!

Oh yea Louie...small guy looked like Sammy Davis
Jr ha!

I like Leopoldi's Store they are always so helpful. So
much nicer than the big stores.

Great store..... I was in there not too long ago. It's the
old kind of store that has everything you need. Not
many stores like that around anymore.

Great memories of what stores use to be
like...another one like it was Forman's on 13th and
5th.

Another great store.

There was also another hardware with everything in it on 10th street and 5th Ave. in the early 70's.

Speaking of hardware stores, does anyone remember Henny's Wonder Store, corner of 7th st and 7th ave, right across from Santos deli? He used to sell those metal ring whistles and you could buy nails screws, anything by the bag full.

Wait; don't forget about Tarzian on 7th ave down near First St.

And yet another hardware store was right on Flatbush ave and 5th ave, everyone must remember Pintchik's for everything including wallpapers, and Bergen tile across the street. Now Barclays center is right across the street.

Ice Cream Parlors

Next to the Pizzeria which was more of a winter hangout there was the Ice cream parlors, I'm sure they couldn't wait for the summer months for all the little kiddies to spend their Quarters in their store, especially on those hot summer days, even though we had the ice cream truck this was a cool place to hangout (Literally).

I seem to remember an ice cream parlor that was located on 8th Ave somewhere in the teen streets, homemade ice cream you could take home in those old school white containers. Does anyone remember the name?

Actually, it may have been Häagen-Dazs when the first store opened on 7th Ave lower down though, near 2nd Street. Yum!

I remember an a TO-GO Italian ICE place in Windsor Terrace up by Holy Name!! Nothin' on 8th Ave!!

Can not recall...I do remember the one down by Union St & 7th Ave though. That was like an old time ice cream shop....can't remember the name. Even had the red and white stripes decorated in the shop etc....

The Häagen-Dazs was on 7th and 1st.

I think it was on 8th between either 11th and 12th or 13th and 14th.

Thanks, was starting to think I was imagining it.

What was the name of the Ice Cream Parlor on 7th ave and 5 street?

Yes it was...I remember the Jukebox right in the middle...

It was Pat Kenny's.

When I was young, I thought it was Pat and Kenny's. I didn't really know anybody with two first names.

We used to play "Kings" against Pat Kenny's wall.

It was Pat Kenny's he had a sister also and I am pretty sure they live on top of the ice cream parlor.

Pat made the best Cherry Cokes in the neighborhood. Would always go there after a night of B Ball at John Jay.

There was an old school ice cream parlor on 7th and 8th 9th St...

I remember a candy store/fountain on 7th Ave bet 8th & 9th Sts. Woman named Ann owned/operate it. In cahoots with everyone's parents, she absolutely positively would NOT sell us candy before lunch LOL. I don't recall the name of that shop.

They filmed a few scenes from "The Lords of Flatbush" at the store on 12th st.

Yes and if I remember correctly it was in the movie "the Lords of Flatbush"... I loved that place when I was little.

Beat me to it! LOL

It was Ehrich's. The ice cream parlor was named Ehrich's.

It was Herman's. Filmed *The Lords Of Flatbush* there & had the best tuna sandwiches ever.

11th-12th street and 8th ave.

My Friend lived across the street from Herman's. She was a extra in the Lords of Flatbush. She had to walk in front of the store and have the guys give her cat calls. She was also in a scene inside the store both scenes were cut.

Thanks Guys!

The Carvel store 7th ave n Carroll Street, boy I miss all that free ice cream!!

I loved that Carvel Store.

Oh just the memories makes me re live the excitement of going in there and getting an ice cream cone, I remember the refrigerator smell, It's so nice when something is that buried in your memory.

I loved the Carvel store, except for the time I fell down the stupid open cellar door. Spent many a summer evening there with my friends.

OMG, I used to work there.

My Dad would take me and my brother there when we were kids.

I loved that place.

OMG, lived around the corner on Carroll bet 7 & 8th...that store is so prominent in my childhood memories! Cones were 35 cents and since the counters were so high they could never see me waiting so I'd tap my quarter and dime over my head on the counter top to get the attention of whoever was working! Ah, soft chocolate on a wafer cone never tasted so good...

Oh my God!! This was home!!

OMG the memories I have of this place. Lived on Carroll bet 7&8 from 1970-1979. 35 cents bought you a cone. I loved this place.

So miss those parfaits where you took off the top and put it on the bottom to stand up. I actually bought my wedding flowers from the florist that bought it afterwards. The door made me very nostalgic.

One of my favorite places to be....

I worked there.

Wasn't there a Carvel or maybe a Dairy Queen on 7th Ave (8th & 9th)?

There was also the Dairy Queen on 5th ave and 8th st used to love the shakes in there also the flying saucers ice cream sandwiches then nick bought the subway on the corner also.

That was "Dairy Joy" on 7th between 8th n 9th.

There was a Dairy Queen on 5 ave bet 8th and 9th st...

Best ice cream cake in the world.

This was a big part of my childhood!

I remembered as soon as you mentioned it. It's funny how the mind works!!

Carvel - flying saucers - fudgie the whale cakes - the owner would give us extra sprinkles even on my flying saucer! - loved that store.

Mister Misty's brain freeze.

The Chocolate Thick Shake Float!

With an extra scoop of chocolate thrown in for good measure.

I remember it well.

I loved going there! My favorite, marshmallow syrup over vanilla with sprinkles. Beats Häagen-Dazs any day.

Oh...the things the boyz who worked there used to do to the food items there...frightening...you know who you are, and you know what you did...naughty ones.

I know the NAMES & THE PERPS!! YA WOULDNT BE SURPRISED!! LMAO!!

I hope you never had the orange drink!

Dairy Queen on 5th Avenue between 7th & 8th or 8th & 9th?

Who's on first xxx lol?

John's Bargain Store

This wasn't our store of choice; this was our mom's store. This is one of the places we were dragged, when there wasn't anyone to watch us, or mom just wanted to torture us, LOL, but it was a little fun with some of the fringe benefits.

JOHN'S BARGAIN STORES

Holy cow. I would have NEVER remembered this. Thanks

I will always remember the one on Flatbush Ave right by the old Plaza Theater!! Eventually became a Stationary store!!

What street???? You're making my tired brain work

I thought it was on 5th ave and 10th street

There were two John's Bargain stores on 5th ave. The other one was near 14th st, by Germain's I believe.

I think one of them was on 8th street and 5th ave???

What prices!!!!

I certainly could use some 5 cent men's socks for my husband! LOL

That joint was Mecca for my mother.....

My Mom loved this place, especially with 8 kids...LOL

Kresge's was on 10th & 5th ave.

What a great place that was - five floors of stuff

Classic Brooklyn. All over, Everywhere. There were Hundreds of these stores. Mom loved them too.

Funny how all of our moms shopped at "John's", and we all ranked on each other for it! Where'd you get them sneakers "John's Bargains??? Yeah!!! My mom was in line right behind your mom!!! Go figure???

There was no shame in shopping at "Johns"...but it sure was a good zinger during a rank session!!!

Called them" Rejects. They make your feet feel fine. Rejects. They cost a Dollar Ninety Nine". LMAO !

Really, If you didn't sport "Pro Keds", Chuck Taylor "Converse", "Pumas" or "Adidas", You got snapped on. If you came from a big family, you might get snapped on for those "Hand Me Downs" you were wearing. LOL !

Don't let all them Chuck Taylor, Puma, Adidas,
Converse, Pro Keds wearing kids fool ya...they were
wearin' something from John's.!!!

Everything else...LOL

Yep that's right!!!

Remember the other store on 5th ave & 11th? Had
bins of cloths everywhere. Some called it the Junk
store....Corner store?

At least you got older brother hand me downs. My
mom tried telling me that dungarees were dungarees,
and it didn't matter that they were my sisters. YEAH
RIGHT mom I'm young not stupid!

10th street and 5th avenue across from Kresge's?
Right on the corner.

You could find anything from a blender to a Leather
Bomber Jacket in that place.

Surplus City.

Kresge's

How many remember Kresge's on 5th with the
luncheonette counter?

Pop the balloon for your price to pay for a banana
split.

First time I won anything popped a balloon and got a
Banana Split for a penny.

My mom would always get the Chow Mein
sandwich.

Loved the grilled cheese.

THAT WAS ONE OF THE SATURDAY STROLL 5TH AVENUE STORES LOL...LUNCH AT EITHER KRESGE'S - GERMAIN'S - LENNY PIZZA LOL - LOVE THEM ALL AND IF YOU WERE REALLY GOOD WE WENT TO LOFT'S CANDY STORE NEXT TO KRESGE'S.........

They sold Barton's chocolates in there and my Dad always told me they were just for us :)

Egg Creams at Kresge's! The best!!

I agree the best egg creams EVER!!!!

My Mother was the waitress behind the counter for years.

I used to love to go there as a treat and pop the balloon to see how much of a discount you would get for a banana split!!

I ONCE GOT A BANANA SPLIT FOR 1 CENT I THOUGHT I HIT THE JACKPOT LOL...AND MY AUNT ONLY HAD TO PAY 1 PENNY..SOME THINGS YOU NEVER FORGET.. THIS IS ONE OF THE MANY GREAT MEMORIES I HAD GROWING UP

PS EVERYONE IN KRESGE'S WAS CHEERING THAT WAS A LOT OF FUN NEVER FORGET IT...................

It was on 5th ave and I think 11th street. It was a 5 and dime, as we used to call those bargain stores.

Kresge's was on the corner of 10th Street & 5th Avenue, where Rite Aid is now.

Yep, you are right.

Kresge's on 10th St. and 5th was called The 5 & 10 cents store. I remember popping the balloons there and winning a banana split.

Thanks for the memories of Kresge's. Remembering the lunch counter? And the balloons you picked for a "surprise" ice cream sundae? And I think there was ALWAYS a parakeet loose and flying around the store....

Kresge and Woolworth were on the same side of 5th Ave. and across from each other on 10th St. My Mom used to treat me to a chow mein sandwich and root beer at Kresge's. I believe Kresge's went out of business before Woolworth's. We used to shop in both 5 & 10s as they were called back then.

I loved those stores... I mean, where else could you buy a needle and thread, vanilla coke and a parakeet in one place!

Wow break the balloon loved that never got the 1 cent price.

In the 40s, 50s and 60s Kresge's and Woolworth were both on the corner of 10th St. and 5th Avenue across from each other. I don't remember what replaced Kresge's but I remember Grey Shell (a discount store) replaced Woolworth's.

I thought Woolworth went out and Kresge's took over. The Grey Shell was on the same side street but across the street. I remember eating at the little counter in the Woolworth and having French fries and Hamburgers.

Kresge and Woolworth were on the same side of 5th Ave. and across from each other on 10th St. My Mom used to treat me to a Chow Mein sandwich and root beer at Kresge's. I believe Kresge's went out of business before Woolworth's. We used to shop in both 5 & 10s as they were called back then.

I can still remember the smell of the old wooden floors when you first walked into the store.

Didn't they call it the 5 and dime store too?

310

We called it the "5 and 10"

Oh that's right 5 and 10 store and I used to get a Chow Mein sandwich on a hamburger roll at the food counter...it was my favorite as a kid.

My mom got all my school supplies at Kresge's and we would eat hamburger and fries at Woolworth's with am occasional Sundae when there was money for it.

Kresge's!! LOL

In 1977 Kresge's officially changed its name to Kmart

Mom worked behind the food counter, used to love to go there and break a balloon to see how much I would have to pay for an ice cream Sundae.

The Laundromat

The Quiet Passing of a Park Slope Landmark

The Launder Center at the corner of 7th Avenue and 8th Street closed in 2008. It is not surprising that its passing was barely noticed: it was no grand edifice or marble monument, which is how people normally think of historic landmarks. Also, there are few people still around Park Slope who remember the day in 1947 that the Launder Center opened. It was in that time after World War II when factories were still re-gearing for domestic consumption and washing machines were a precious commodity. That first day of business, people waiting to get into the launderette lined up all the way down 8th Street to the library.

I recall a photo hung in the laundry mat, of the couple that had owned the laundry mat & the property where the Carriage House is as well!

They still own the Carriage House.

I lived on 9th between 7th and 8th and went there with my father to do the laundry.

We had to walk all the way from the park side near the big lake to the one on 14th st and 8th ave that place is still there today.

Wow I remember that one it still looks the same as it did 40 years ago

Drove by there on my last visit to the slope its still there

There was also the one next to the bakery near John Jay... that's been there forever, not that I used it I never went to school land hung out in front of it

There are a few on 5th ave also one on 10th street. I think one they are laundry mats they just change hands . So much work goes into them and everyone needs to do laundry...

One of the older Laundry mats is still on 13th st and 8th ave I think?

McCrory's-Woolworth's-Downtown

Though these store were based in another neighborhood these are still considered a park slope memory, we either went downtown shopping with mom for presents, mostly around Christmas time or holidays, or went just to take a shopping trip downtown had a lot more fringe benefits than 5th ave ..That's for sure.

Who remembers McCrory's 5 & 10 in Downtown Brooklyn?

I remember they would make fresh potato chips and popcorn.

I do, I went in there all the time.

I used to love watching their product demonstrations. I guess that's where TV infomercials got their idea. "But wait, there's more."

A lot of the infomercial pitchmen got their shtick from the boardwalk pitchmen of Atlantic City. That's according to Ed McMahon, who got his start that way.

Mmmmmm! Chow Mein in Taki cups!

Waffle and ice cream sandwiches at their counter.

Mom used to bring us down there to see the baby chicks at Easter time.

Fulton Street really went down the tubes.

My mother worked in that building and I often meet her at lunch time to do some shopping and then have a quick lunch together before she had to be back at work.

When it went down the tubes it was painful. It is a memory that I cherish.

My first job as a teenager! (1972)

It's a shame that Dollar Stores have replaced our five and dimes... The Five and Tens had so much more personality!.

It's a sign of the times!!!!!!!!!!!!!!!!!!

So sad to see it go with all the other 5 & 10. Who remembers WOOLWORTH? The last one I remember was still open in the '70's and saw it close down, was in Sunset Park bet. 53rd and 54th streets. I believe it is now a Foot Locker store...

I loved shopping in Woolworth's! I could spend a few hours in there...looking around. I remember the wooden floors and the way it sounded when they creaked when you walked around the store...

I forgot all about it....thanks

313

I loved their sundaes, burgers and fries. I also spent a lot of time in the photo booths with friends, making silly faces and then waiting for the black and whites to be developed and dispensed. I still have many of them :)

How about May's dept store.

My aunt worked at Mays.

Mother bought a lot of my clothes there. When I was older and went to A&S she thought I was spending too much.

Loved May's!

Orbach's was downtown as well. Got my ears pierced there when I was 12.

I remember when it opened!

Went there every Fri with my mom. Still have large ice tea glasses she bought me. We would get there ice cream. She would get strawberry syrup and I would get choc.

I remember going to McCrory's with my mom and they had the most delicious custard ice cream with chocolate or strawberry syrup.

I used to go there all the time with my mom and sister. We'd always stop for a Chow Mein sandwich (on a hamburger bun). They put rice, Chow Mein and Chinese noodles on it. Who would have thunk it??? Loved them!

Wasn't it McCrory's that had a lunch counter that made banana splits and you popped a balloon that was strung overhead to see how much you paid for it?

Always stopped at McCrory's for a knish or chow mein sandwich with my mother after shopping for clothes at Mays & shoes at Miles, National, etc. We stopped going to downtown Brooklyn when Kings Plaza opened.

I don't think my Mom went downtown....she was more a city girl. She loved Manhattan

Yes, McCrory's was part of the "downtown experience" Those were the days. I forgot about the Chow Mein sandwich!

My mom worked there in the 60's

Loved McCrory's My grandmother used to take me there. Also loved May's. I remember a blue dress I got from there.

Downtown Brooklyn was part of my life. Usually we would take the bus from Park Slope. Along with McCrory's, we would stop at Mays, A & S and a more expensive place - Martins, I think - mostly just to look around. There were chandeliers and a woman wearing white gloves ran the elevator announcing each floor. I can still see it in my mind.

My grandma and her sister always took us downtown Brooklyn, and we started by having cream cheese on Datenut Bread and Hot Chocolate at Chock full of Nuts. So simple, but those days were so great.....remembering the Chow Mein sandwich...

Ice cream waffle sandwiches - Yummm

THE GOOD OLD DAYS.

Went there every Saturday on Fulton Street!

Sure do, used to go school shopping downtown.

That was my ultimate favorite Chow Mein on a bun.

I would sit at the counter having an ice cream waffle sandwich, feeling so grown up!!!!!

315

All time fav was the Waffles and Ice cream.

Livingston Street....

We would take the GG train 2 stops from Carroll Street and come up the stairs right into McCrory's. I remember the smell of popcorn hitting you as you entered.

Levi Ice cream and hot waffles. At home I warm up Eggos and make an ice cream sandwich. Every time I do so, I think of McCrory's downtown. I know it is not the same but the warm Eggos and ice cream melting... yummy.

I loved their cheeseburgers.

Now that's a memory. I worked there during my senior year in high school in the front food area. I made pizza, waffles and ice cream and pretzels.

You are sooo right. I remember, my mom taking me & my sister to McCrory's, for the fresh, hot waffles & ice-cream that melted as soon as you put it in your mouth!!! YUMMMMO

I almost forgot about this store. I do remember it. We shopped there often.

1 of the best 5 & dime stores other than Woolworth's, yes the ice cream & waffles classic, the balloon pop, the tons of candy on display, and yes, the exit to Hoyt-Schermerhorn St. subway station, I remember the photo booth where you can get your picture taken sitting down with the curtain closed, too much fun :)

Yes I remember whenever mom said we are going to the 5 and dime I knew we were McCrory's bound.

Yes, yes, yes..... I still often talk about those waffles now. They were the BEST and so were the franks at the stands on the corners downtown.

Who remembers Nedicks Orange soda and Hotdogs?

Lord yes!!! My daughter looks at me like I am crazy when I talk about them.

Hey, who remembers the Duffield Movie theater downtown? I spent many a day cutting school in there!

Fulton st as far back as I can remember, had Mays dept store, Korvettes, A & S, Woolworth's and so much more

So great at Christmas time especially A & S windows

Waffle Ice Cream Sandwiches and Soft Pretzels...always a treat

Remember the aroma when you walked in!! I was working there when I was 16 - and for years my mom took the pictures of kids with Santa at Christmas!

I remember learning how to sew in shop class and buying patterns from the basement at McCrory's. So many fabrics and patterns to choose from!

The lunch counter with my grandmother. Grilled cheese with a grape drink served in those paper cups in the plastic holder.

I forgot about grape drink lol

Those small funnel shaped paper cups... Which just triggered a memory of the Sno Cone machines - ice and sugar coloring...

COOOOLLL!! Loved em!!

My favorite was the Scharoltte Rouche deserts. Does anyone remember the white carton filled with cake and whipped cream?

They had a nut counter where they would roast whatever nuts you picked out...I loved the salted pecans all toasty warm!

I loved to go to McCrory's. We'd shop at A&S and Roman's for my mother (lol) and sometimes May's. Then we'd have the hot dogs at the Papaya King-type place and maybe a knish...and finish off at McCrory's for the ice cream and waffle.

I remember it served on a piece of white cardboard. And, you're right about the smell....it was like a sweet buttery smell. Wow! Thanks for the memory.

OH YEAH! McCrory's and Woolworth's. The smells were amazing!! And it was magical during the Christmas season! How about May's, the big dept store?

I remember going with my family in the early 60's to see the Christmas Display at A&S. Loved the Hot Dogs at Nedicks. Does anybody remember the Old Horn & Hardart's? On Fulton Street.

Horn-Hardart aka automat my mom took me there when I was 6 expected me to be impressed that u can put quarter in slot & get food; I looked at her like eh so what, lol

I remember the automat almost forgot about it, also McCrory's use to go to lunch counter and the banana split could get from 1 cent-49cents whatever the price was in balloon that the waitress popped

McCrory's was absolutely amazing especially around the holidays. Many happy childhood memories going there with Mom & Dad and checking out the toy/comic book section with my brother. They don't make them like that anymore. Same with Woolworth's.

Wow McCrory's, Mays, Korvettes great times. Remember the automat. You put your money in and you open the door and get a sandwich or whatever food you choose. That was such fun as a kid

Yes the ice cream & waffles classic, the balloon pop,

318

The tons of candy on display, and yes, the exit to Hoyt-Schermerhorn St. subway station, I remember the photo booth where you can get your picture taken sitting down with the curtain closed, lol, too much fun :)

Everyone has a story about Downtown Brooklyn hope this refreshed yours.

Pat Kenny's

When I was a kid my mom worked there. I would eat lunch there every day. I thought I was hot stuff because all the high school kids would always talk to me.

My older sister would take me there when she was watching me for my Mom, and I thought who I was.

Also, it was fun, and the music was always playing, I use to get vanilla cokes...oh did I love the sweetness of that soda...

Jukebox 3 for a quarter - cherry coke or a lime ricky I lived around the corner on 6th street.

Those were the days my friend we thought they never end...now I am singing in front of the puter...check me out...LOL

Pat Kenny made his own ice cream for 10 cents a cone 1 penny for sprinkles.

We use to get ice cream almost every night right before superman came on. He use to call me Little Miss Chocolate that was the only flavor I liked.

We lived on 5th Street 5 houses down from

7th Avenue. Till this day best ice cream in the world!

There was also an ice cream parlor on 7th ave, between 3rd & 4th st that made there own ice cream

Also...Lindroths, not too sure of spelling, and their ice cream was also great...they sold the store

I was the soda jerk, old name back than, when I was in high school. Great place also

I didn't know that Kenny's ice cream was home made back then. Now look at the price of it...

My favorite from Pat Kenny's was butter pecan - and for 2 cents more you got a sugar cone...priceless lol...

At Easter time the whole glass case along the side wall was full with chocolate bunnies, and oval choc eggs with pictures inside. All the bunnies were decorated so beautiful, you really don't see stuff like that today.

Pat Kenny's had a fountain on the left as you walked in and seating in the back right?

The counter was all down the left side the grill was in the front; the back had the tables and the jute box in the right hand corner. On the right before you got to the tables there was the ever present phone booth

I had a few kisses in that phone booth - OMG - now you made me laugh

OH BUT THEY WERE GREAT KISSES NOW EVERYBODY KNOWS OUR SECRET LOL....WELL IF YOU CAN'T SPILL THE BEANS. HA

Isn't it funny the things you remember :)))

Pat Kenny was the nicest, all the store owners treated us nice, and like the saying "It takes a village".

Yes I do remember. He was such a nice man wish I could go back there it was a nice place do u remember the guy who had the monkey he use 2 dress her up & go 2 Pat Kenny's?

OTB

Who has GOOD memories of OTB LOL

My mom n dad lol. . .couldn't get them out of there

12 street and 5th Avenue OTB closed. It is now going to be a Key Food supermarket.

Wow, Key Food its going to be small...

My dad would send me to the OTB off of 7th ave & Flatbush with money and a note and the guy would place the bets and send me back with the tickets

Oh so many memories, waiting for the racing form the night before @ the plaza street news stand, going to OTB around noon then all of us would gather around a radio and listen to the stretch calls of the races on news 88 AM, on the stoop on Garfield

Many trips to various OTB's on Triple crown days!!
;-)

Never got into that. I love horses, and always watch the "Big" races looking for the next Triple Crown winner, but I never made a single bet. Just not my "Thing". I have nothing against betting on the ponies though.

OTB - full of smoke - lol

I remember volunteering at a convalescent home, and we were collecting for something, and this little nun, who always wore a habit decided to go in to OTB and ask everyone on the line. The sight of her standing on line amongst all the bleary eyed men makes me laugh to this day! It was worth her while, she got lots of money.

My brother used to 'play the horses'. One day he asked me to pick a name of a horse from the newspaper. I chose "Impressive Prince". He bet on him and won!!!

COOL!! I remember playin da ponies!! LOL!! I still
do too!! Belmont & Monmouth mainly!!;-)

Let me know if you need a winner, I'll pick one for
ya!

Does anyone remember what was on 12st and 5th
ave before OTB

I remember the Deli next door to the OTB

Dawson's Deli

I was in Brooklyn today and took a ride along 5 Ave.
I see they opened up a Key Food on 12 street and 5
Ave, where Vim's and the OTB was.

I believe it was Vims appliance store

Vim's an Appliance store was in that spot before
OTB

Wow I remember VIM's from a loooong time ago.
"Vim's for Value".

Vim's.....I remember it so well.

Pops and Al's Toy Stores

Next to the candy store this was the place where we
would spend a lot of money but what we got out of it,
are most of the memories we cherish today, most of
our childhood fun was centered around a simple toy
of game, like a spaldeen, or a top which would give
us hours of fun and lot of different games, these were
2 of our favorites, one on 5th and one on 7th ave, and
depending on where your were playing you knew
which one was closer and which one had just what
you needed

For all you sports fans. "Pops" was the place to go . .
. if Jack was feeling extra generous . . . "No tax" for
you.

Nice piece of local history in tha Slope.

I walked by there several years ago and I looked in the window, said to who i was with "I wonder if Pops is still around" Just then he stepped out of the doorway and answered me, he even remembered me. It had been at least 20 years since I had been in there. He was a great guy.

WOW...that store was the best.....I was there when he closed down....got all my sports stuff there.....he was history!!

Wow Pops I got all my sports stuff there hockey sticks skates pads gloves. we even got our team jerseys there. Pops was the best. It was always so dark in there though.

Probably because he had so much stuff hanging all over the store it blocked out the lights, def one of those old fashion stores that had everything.

This place was great.

OMG I LIVE RIGHT AROUND THE BLOCK ON 6TH STREET SO I WAS THERE EVERY DAY FOR WHAT EVER REASON.... THOSE WERE THE DAYS LOL.

Omg...I remember him like it was yesterday...all the 6th street boys got all their hockey stuff from him.

WE USE TO CALL HIM POPS.

Wow that was such along time ago. Time goes by so fast ... we had great times down on 6th st that is for sure and we still do when we get together. Everything just seems to look smaller..lol lol lol

Pops once told us a story that Art Modell was his 1st partner in the sporting Goods Biz& actually owned part of Pops store for awhile!!

LOVED THE GUY.

I loved going there with my father and my brother for our baseball equipment!

I loved that place, it was a sports palace. It was the only place that would re-lace your old baseball glove. I must have been in the store everyday when I was a kid!

It was the Modell's of the slope, he had everything.

I remember pops used to go there for our spaldines and stick ball bats lost a lot of ball on 8th st.

HOLY SMOKES, I WAS THERE EVERY SAT!

Lady with the blonde bouffant going on!

I got my Davey Cash baseball glove there in 1977!!!!!!! GREAT!!!!!

I loved two blocks from levines, wish I had a penny for every spalding we bought there, that wound up on roofs we could not access no matter how we tried.

Hockey skates with the steel wheels ... hockey sticks ... My first baseball glove!! WOW, what a great memory! 13th street between 4th and 5th.

He had anything and everything, if he didn't have it he got it

Bought many bats and clinchers from him! And gloves.

Got my first real deal catchers mitt there. A Mizuno. At that time nobody ever heard of that brand. So instead they made fun of it. Breaking my chops my cousin.

Pops always had the high end stuff.

Al's Toyland. My best memory of Al's Toyland is when I had my Tonsils removed my Dad bought me the "Batmobile" and "The Black Beauty" H.O. Aurora cars from Al's.

324

I found out about ten years or so ago that if I still had the Bat mobile in original packaging and good shape it would be worth 2 grand.

Al's was always a place that a kid can go and "Dream"!

They gave my parents "lay away" on toys - didn't realize it then - thought I was in a dream world - they'd let you look for a long time & never made it like it wasn't about Santa.

Who remembers those old light wooden planes that have the rubber band propellers? Man the simple things made us so happy back then didn't it my friends..............

I still love them.

Those balsa wood planes! They were great!

Loved to by models and paint to paint them from Al's.

I Bought a Styrofoam one from a model shop and it has a remote control and flies like a dream. I want one. Balsa wood is great, but remote control, wow!

We ran to Al's and did the test bounce of the Spaldeens before our stick ball games

Always had a spaldine ball with us everywhere we went.

Hey what about Sepes toy store 5th ave between 10 and 11th street

And the toy store on 13th and 5th next to J & Michaels.

Sam's Work Cloths and Stagenhagen

Remember Sam's Work Clothes, We all went there.

I bought everything from Sam's Work Clothes on 16th & 5th...

Good quality clothes at decent prices. What more could you ask for, unless you were a fashionista!!!

How bout the pawn shop next door ...sold a watch or two back then

Yea wasn't that called stegan hagens? Doubt if i spelled it right. Bought a watch or two from there back then :> ha

Pawned a few things there in my time.

Once upon a time, there existed a two-storefront-wide pawn shop named Stavenhage...

You mean stole a few watches lol

I not saying anything lol lol

You mentioned Staven Hagen ....I remember looking in the windows especially around the Holidays with my Parents ....me and my brother were into music ....and one store front window had all the musical stuff.....and the other window ...would have the poor wedding rings sold ...because of broken relationships or to pay their bills ....kind of like now.....so sad!

S and H Stamps

Remember S & H green stamps and the store on Flatbush Ave where you could redeem them for appliances and other stuff?

Remember it well. Mom was a Green Stamp Queen. It's amazing what you were able to get from their catalog.

MY MOM TOO!! CAN YOU SAY VACUUM CLEANERS!! LMAO!! GOOD ONE!!

326

I just remember she had lots of them in the glove compartment in the car.

Yeah, like free toasters for opening a new bank account. Like with 7 kids, she would open new accounts of $25.00 for each of us and get enough small appliances to "fully stock" a kitchen. Ha, Ha!!!

Plaid stamps too from the A&P... loved putting then in the books for my mother and grandmother...what made us happy.....

I think my mother still has something she got with green stamps! Didn't they give out stamps at the gas stations too?

I think they gave out plaid stamps at the gas station also. I remember the Esso on 5th and 4th ave had them, and yes hence the name Esso not Exxon .

Yeah, they did, but we didn't have a car.

I remember going to the store to redeem the books with my mother and she picked out an ashtray on a stand...fancy fancy

Stamps I remember them well and what a catalog!

I remember the endless lines to redeem the books with my mom. Had to go somewhere on Flatbush AVE!! HATED IT!! LMAO!! ;-0!!

I couldn't remember where it was thanks....I remember those lines too....

Do any of you remember your mom's going to the movies and getting free dishes-bowls or plates my mom still has those. Gas Stations use to give out glasses to. What about Welches Grape Jelly and the jar was actually a glass. We had a bunch of those with the Flintstones on them

I remember exactly what you're tawkin about!! Especially the Jelly & Gas Stations Glasses!! How about the detergents that would stash Dish TOWELS in their detergent boxes!! As kids we would yank them out & detergent all over the place!! LOL ;-)

I also remember cutting the boxes of Corn Flakes for the flaps or the bar codes. You'd mail them in to get some kind of item - Tony the Tiger mugs or bowls I think.

I got my first Instamatic Kodak Camera from saving the labels from paper towels. It used the cube flashbulbs. Remember those?

OMG, absolutely.

You could always tell right away when the bulbs were blown out.

Soundtrack Records

Does anyone remember a Record store on 7th between President and Carroll; the owner was a guy, black curly hair? I would ask him and he would order me records so I didn't have to take the train to Discomat.

Though not the oldest records store in the Slope, Soundtrack had a bigger store as well as a bigger selection, and kept the music up to date.

I used to DJ and bought most of my records from there.

Sure, I remember that store! I used to live in there!

Yeah, always ordered my albums there. Later moved to 9th and 7th.

Also sold more than records.

I remember that store, too.

328

If I remember correctly... that was "Tom"...worked there with him...Tom's brother opened soundtrack on 9th...but that was movies.

That was his brother Vic, who ran Soundtrack on 9th and 7th ave.

The guy that worked there passed away. Everyone knew him at both stores.

He worked both stores but was always in the Carroll St. store.

I worked at soundtrack on 9th St. too, didn't I?

Sepes

Does anyone remember Sepe's toys on 5th ave between 10th and 11th street. I used to work there in the early 70's.

Was Irwin the boss there (in Sepe's)?

Yes, he was.

I worked there from 1970 - 1980 on and off.

Yes, I also lived 3 doors down from it.

I don't remember; it has been a long time.

Yes...go a lot there for my kids...they even held those cabbage patch dolls for us reg. moms when they were hot and you had to stand in line for them...loved them.

And how about Abels for baby furniture and stuff? I think they were on the corner of 14th st & 5th ave.

My favorite store on the planet.

Remember Sepe's, but wasn't there another toy store as well on 5th ave?

Platt's toy store I think.

That was it. They were on 5th ave between 12th and 13th street.

My Parents shopped at Platts, they had the Holiday Lay Away Plan, with 5 Kids my Parents always managed to get us that special gift, And my parents sacrificed giving each other a gift in order to make the holidays special for the kids.

OMG my parents shop there as well, and did the holiday lay-away as well.

Always went there. Did all my Christmas shopping on the avenue... Why schlep all the way downtown? And there was parking too.

I got my first Barbie doll there! *LOL*

Loved Sepes! I remember going there with my mom in 1969 and she bought me a banana curl Skipper! Weird how we remember specific things, especially from the good old Brooklyn days.

Tony's Records Store

You know Tony's if you were a record collector or were just passing by and started to browse and wound up spending hours there just looking through old LPS and 45, and probably wound up selling him your old records also, he had so much packed into that little space.

I used to work here and buy all my records here, I remember Tony's.

Park Slope on 5th ave between 8th and 9th street, spent plenty of time looking through lots of great albums, since the 70s maybe longer...

Tony's record store on 5th ave and 9th st! The first time I was in there I was like 9 yrs old buying 45's! I still have his old business card. :)

The landlord wanted him out at one time, but every1 fought for him to stay!

You could find just about any record in that place if you looked.

I bought all my 45s there as well as the needles for my record player...oh, and the little plastic things you put in the middle of the 45s so they could play on your record player!!

I remember buying all my records there...thank god he is still there.

This record-shop still exists...

Tony's record shop; saw Tony a few months ago and he is still going strong.

Tony's Record Shop has been there for so long. I think it's the only record store around now. You'd think he'd retire, because if he was so much older than me, and I'm 67 now.... imagine how old he is!

Vinyl records are a big thing again the place is always packed.

Bought many a 45 there, still have most of them.

R u kidding me that record store is still there ... Amazing.

Still no heat either, LOL.

Stores

Over the course of 20 years or so, there have been so many stores in the slope some lasted a few years some 5 years and very few 10 years besides the few iconic one that are still there, this is the best of our memories and our favorites that stand out in our minds still.

I got one Kresge's: 10th & 5th, remember the counter?
YOU CAN GET EGG CREAMS FOR 35 CENTS,
HOLY SHIT WAS THAT A STEP BACK!

They became Kmart. Miss the old "five and ten."

Who stole the horse?

My mom worked there for many years, until the last
day, before she started in the Methodist Hospital,
xoxo

That was good, what horse, lol?

Everyday after school I had to go there and wait for
my mom to get off of work; I would do my
homework @ the sandwich counter....I was pretty
much raised in there. :) xoxo

Did u ever win a banana split from balloon, lol?

My mom & grandmother used to shop there all the
time. "Come on, we're going to the five & ten!" And
if we were really good (LOL) we'd get to go to
Sepe's, the toy store that used to be on 9th St. just
below 5th Ave. What great memories!!

Many years ago Sepe's was on 8 St below 5th ave.

The lady made me one almost everyday after
school....I wouldn't have been allowed to win
anything cause mom worked there...I had my "perks"
@ the sandwich counter...xoxo...my fondest memory,
from that store, was when they had their company
Xmas party and closed the store for the
evening....they literally decorated it like the North
Pole....her boss would have me sitting w/Santa,
greeting all the guests n their families...I loved it, and
the beautiful sparkly dresses...xoxo

To win the Ice Cream Sundae: You had to pick a
balloon, then inside was a piece of paper with the
price of the Sundae. It ranged from free to 39 cents...

If someone has a sketch artist, I can picture it in my mind!!

I can picture the chicken chow mien sandwiches lol.

According to Steven Germain (great-grandson of the store's founding fathers), Germain's was opened in 1898 and closed in the mid 1960's.

In a 1938 Brooklyn Eagle Newspaper, Germain's was referred to as 5th Avenue's Greatest Shopping Center...

OMG! My dad took me to see Santa at Germain's. What was the name of the store on 10 st and 5th ave...

OR SEE AN OLD LADY TAKE HER TEETH OUT AND CLEAN THEM IN HER COKE---JUST ENOUGH TO MAKE MY COUSIN SCREAM---IT WAS SO FREAKY...LOL!

Wow!! My first job was working at the counter after school and all day Sat. made $1.81 per hr plus tips. Managed to kick in $20 a week to my mom!!

I would come by for the grilled cheese, one slice of pickle and a couple of crinkle cut potato chips on a paper plate.

That was our best seller!! ha ha.

I REMEMBER the drawing contests they had, I won one year and was so honored to have my crayola masterpiece hanging over the front counters (that I barely peeked over on tippy toes) & can even remember the aisle where they had the fake Barbie dolls on a shelf just in my little arms reach.

Is the army navy store still on the corner?

Yes it is.

The Army, Navy Store has been on 5th Ave & 8th St. the longest! & The Leopoldi's Hardware as well on 5th btwn 7th & 8th St!!

Wow!! I think I remember every store on that ave, even Danielle's florist somehow...HA.

I also remember my mom would bring us to the butcher's across the street and we would play with the wood chips on the floor.

Butcher shop bet 7th & 8th Sts closed down pretty recently.

Hey, I believe Henry's is still there...on 5th that's where my dad proposed to my mom....best egg creams, hands down.

Henry's gone.

For the past 15 years it's been called Daisy's Diner.

Wow, that was like a landmark, how bout Neerguards?

Neerguards is still there!

The bank that was across the street is now a gym!

What about that clothing store in between Henry's diner and the newsstand, they sold expensive suits and the latest clothes for men; I bought some clothes there and my first Members Only jacket.

What was name of the jewelry store on 5th ave near 11th St.?

Garry's Jewelry.

No it was across the st. lol

Albert's.

It was called J&D...

Clock that ran backward.

The side wall was painted Peter Mac style and the hot dog vendor used to be on the corner and we used to play off the point there.

Pete was the hot dog guy.

One of the guys from the neighborhood painted that wall. If I remember right his name was John, can't remember his last name. I think he was from 12 or 13 St...

Brunell the "Deli' on 5th between 11th and 10th...

How about the camera store on 5th avenue between 10th and 11th street? I think the name of the store was Rolaids; that's where we took our film to be developed.

You get Rolaids at Falks Drug Store. And you get your film developed at Rolee's Camera Store...lol!

Black and White took 2 days and color took a week.

I lived right next door to The Savino's who owned Savino Oil Company on the corner of 6th street and 4th Avenue.

I REMEMBER SAVINO'S HE WAS OUR OIL MAN.

I do remember JD men's clothing store. I liked to shop there because it wasn't very expensive and I had three brothers to buy gifts for.

I remember Max Blatt Furs; no one ever went in there.

Remember Pioneer food store on President and 7th that turned into Citibank?

And that old pharmacy on Lincoln and 7th with the black and white tiles that no one ever went into? I once went in there to buy a piece of rock-candy and everything was coated with dust. But there was a pharmacist in back in a starched white uniform with buttons up the side. Weird.

Do you mean the bodega? The man who worked there was so nice. Do you remember Max Blatt across the street, I loved that neon sign.

I remember that place they made great egg creams. There was also a deli between Carroll and President on the same side of the avenue; I would go there for a hero before school.

Does anyone remember the candy store on the corner of President and 7th across from the bank? There was a guy who worked there with granny sunglasses. They had a counter for fountain drinks and a phone booth.

Yup he earned his name "Greasy Jack" from that grill.

I remember greasy Jack's. Middle of the block, counter and stools, knishes are what I remember (w/mustard). That grill! I don't think he ever cleaned it off. That's where the flavor is!

Does anyone remember greasy Jacks? He was two doors down from Danny's, I think the sushi take out window is there now. He sold hamburgers and fries and had a cotton candy machine.

Danny's. Now that's Park Slope. What memories!!!

He had the best assortment of penny candies ever...I remember my dad sending me down to Danny's on Sunday morning to get the paper for him...He'd give me a dollar to get what I wanted and I'd always come home with a little brown paper bag full of penny candies. :-)

Don't forget the bakery across the street from Danny's...I used to get off the 67 bus and get a fresh jelly doughnut before crossing over to Danny's to pick up the latest comic books.

Yo, who out there from the slope knows or remembers a cat from Dean St (I think) that used ride his bike goin' up 5th ave and Poppin' wheelies when he would pass Garfield st? We would be standing on 1st and start yelling at him to pop one.

336

I think that was Joe from the bakery. He did that every day. He owned the bakery on 2nd street. And fifth ave.

But he was the one on the bike every day in the early evening   straight up fifth, watched him all the time.

That was the guy from the bakery on second street back in the day.

Williamsburg Savings bank building is now called One Hanson Place, but we Brooklyners call it 'THE CLOCK TOWER.'

That was my clock every morning; used to wake up to it before going to school--who needed an alarm clock when all u had to do was look out ur window? Lol.

Fifth ave collision.

OMG all the Collision Shops and the Races to get to the accident stop; be the first to get the tow!

And put oil on the roads to create accidents.

If you called it in to them and they got the tow, they would give you 25 bucks.

Between Carroll and President street, Nick's pizza...or where u can get the best cold cuts: Ben's pork store on fifth between President and Carroll...omg I'm getting sentimental here!

If I could go back in time...this is beautiful, Park Slope...thanks for the walk down memory lane when life was so much easier.

Does anyone remember this place on 7th st between 3rd and 4th? Had the weird looking cars.

Something's tugging at the back of my brain on this, but I can't seem to pull it forward...that sign is so familiar, though.

337

The French Citroen Car Company.

I remember I hung out down there for some good times.

I think they sold the Avanti there, also.

I lived right across the street from that Citroen sign...that was a weird looking French car...all the workers were french...one of owners was named Jacques...they all spoke french.

We grew up on 9th st btwn 2/3rd avenue. Memories.

That's where I grew up; do you remember the shoe repair store or grandma little store on 9th st?

Yes I do. I was born on 9th st near 2nd avenue. Are you talking about the store on 9th street between 2/3 ave? Tom's grocery was on 11th st and Mary's grocery was between 10/11 st.

On third avenue lol.

It was right across the street from Mrs D'Oreigos, not sure of the spelling.

Hey you guys...I was raised on 9th Street between 2nd and 3rd Avenue...I lived there from birth till 1969.

Do you remember "Mom's?" The candy store on the other side of the street? Or Vito's candy store, next to the Liquor store on 3rd Avenue?

Corner on 3rd Ave?

I loved going in there as a kid.

Yes I do. How about the ice cream parlor?

Or the old-fashioned candy store on 8th and 4th ave across the street from STA.

Tom's grocery on 11th St? Was that on the corner on 3rd Ave?

338

I remember the Army Navy store on Flatbush--I would save my babysitting money for weeks to buy painter's pants---also Canal Jeans---I loved that store...

Triangle that was the name of the Army/Navy store on Flatbush.

I remember the Triangle store well. Not only did I get my carpenter pants there, but my chinos! Beige chinos mostly. Crisp, brand new with the crease in the front. And don't forget the brown carpenter shoes, with the lace going up the front to the ankle.

I do remember a German Deli next to the Chinese laundry on 7th bet 5th & 6th.

We went to a deli on 4th street and 6th avenue for a sandwich and the other Jewish deli on 5th street and 6th ave (Dave and Molly).

I remember the hobby store on 5th & Sherman. What was the name of the hobby shop? It was around 15th street? Was it a toy store also?

Was it Bliss or something like that? My brother would remember because he used to get his plane sets there. Anyone remember Testers Glue? That stuff made ya dizzy. Al's Toy Store was on 7th St. & 8th Ave.

I think you are right. Al's used to be closer on 7th between 3rd and 4th before he moved to 3rd Street. Remember Mur's on the corner of 4th Street and Seventh Avenue? It later became Irv's. Got all school supplies there.

That hobby and toy store was called Ginsburg, and then it turned into Martin Paints.

I was thinking of something else. If you were coming from 20th street it was on the right side of 5th avenue. I think it may have been a toy store. I know Able's the baby furniture store was maybe not too far...maybe I am crazy, but I do remember a toy store with bikes in it also...(on 5th maybe in the teens or closer to 9th street) On the tip of my tongue...lol.

Platts on 11th Street? Sepe's on 8th street and 5th. Able's was on the corner of 13th Street.

The other place with bikes & toys was Platt's. Yes Sepe's and I forgot about Platts, WOW.

Platts...yes, Able's was right near Lady Fair, where I worked, on the opposite side of 5th avenue.

Sad to see another long-time business gone. McGovern's Florist on 25th Street.

They sold it to Greenwood Cemetery; it will be a visitor's center. From what I understand the building will be preserved and be turned into a historical center. My dad worked at Greenwood for 35 years. I remember this florist well!

As do I. I loved the smell of flowers in there. Hey Fred, what was the name of the florist on 5th Ave, between 8th and 9th streets?

Me too. :(

I think it was Connors?

Blooms!! 431 5th ave.

That's It. Thanks!!

It was on 5th avenue for as far back as I can remember; if you went in and asked for $1.00 or $2.00 worth of flowers they would always ask who the flowers were for...and always gave you a beautiful bunch with a ribbon...

My mom worked there.

I got my prom corsage at Daniel's.

I remember 2 ladies, 1 with short gray hair and the other with brown hair both very nice always helped me pick out just the right flowers.

Was Daniel's on 5th Ave & 8th St? That's where we got most of our flowers, whatever that place was. LOVED the smell when you walked in the door. Still love that 'florist' smell.

Hasn't this place been closed for awhile?

Thanks, guys. I forgot the name was Daniel's.

Daniel's was closer to 9th St, but there was also Dousmane's closer to 8th St.

Dousmane's was between Blimpie's and Dairy Queen?

I thought that was Daniel's. I don't remember there being two florists on the same block.

I am a little cloudy on that but I think you are right. It was also a little pricier than Daniel's. Daniel's would give a kid some little something for even a quarter!

Daniel's florist could afford to give it away cheaper; they owned so much real estate in the slope. Many buildings along PPW.

Oh no! That has been part of the landscape my whole life.

Wow, I worked there back in 1982.

Does anyone remember Royal Farms? It was on 9th, between 5th & 6th.

OMG there were 2 supermarkets on that street. The A&P was closer to the YMCA, and honestly I didn't remember that the other was Royal Farms! Thanks!

You're welcome. That's right I forgot about the A & P and the Y. Thank you!! I wanna go home sooo bad.

Who remembers the supermarket DILBERTS on 5th and 10th--and a few doors down by the newsstand was the butcher?

I think the butcher was Marcal Brothers. They got in trouble for selling horse meat.

Dilberts was on the corner of 5th between President an Union across from bank on Union. Up Union off 5th was another grocery store named Spinners. Right next to the bank.

Dilberts...that's where my mom shopped. Also Ebinger's bakery.

That was my neck of the woods. Who remembers Artie's toy store on 5th between Berkley and Union, right next to the fruit and veggie store across from Finklestein's Hardware?

The butcher shop was right next door to the newsstand and then the Diner was on the other side of it; trust me I was there every Saturday morning with my mom, she would call up and order her meats, go shopping in Dilberts then pick up her meats for the week...

Used to frequent the Diner with my hubby back in the 1970s.

My friends and I would go to Artie's to buy model airplanes.

It was the Newsstand, Butcher and Fruit Stand, Diner, Drug store, A and M Clothing, Henry's and Dilberts...

Who remembers Carl the shoemaker on 5th Avenue between 11th and 12th? And there was also a shoemaker named Walter above 5th Avenue on 11th Street.

342

At one time there were many shoemakers in Brooklyn. It was the thing to get new heels or soles on your shoes. I don't remember anyone throwing away a pair of shoes like we do today.

Every time we would walk by Carl the Shoemaker, he called us in and asked us to go buy him coffee. And yes there was Walter and Louie the Barber.

And Joe the barber on 5th and 13 street.

No, Joe the Barber was on 5 ave near 12 street. Next store to the hole in the wall candy store. Years later he moved over to 13 street.

Yes! My family shopped there plus I used to run errands for elderly neighbors from my block so I used to go there all the time. I remember it well.

I still remember my parents shopping there on Fridays and waiting with my sister in the car while they shopped then coming home to watch Brady Bunch and Partridge Family and making forts and cars out of the boxes they brought the groceries home in.

Oh and as a side note. It was where the movie theater was at one time. I spoke to one of the managers of C TOWN and he said that the balcony area of the theater is still intact with seats and all. It has no electricity though.

What was that little store on 12th St & 5th (it was either on the corner or just off the corner), they had school supplies & basically anything you needed...there might have been another one by 15th-16th st somewhere.

They were the best days of my life & I hold those memories very close to my heart.

My family moved to Bay Ridge. But my happiest memories were growing up in Park Slope and reading about everyone else's memories.

It was Meyer's.

YESSSSS!!!!!!...that's it; thank you so much, that
has been bugging me for some time now...lol.

Did a lot of Christmas shopping there with a couple
of dollars, lol.

A few doors down was Whelan's Drug Store, cards
gifts and lunch boxes.

There was also Falk's drug store on 5th avenue and
12 street next to J & D's.

There was another gift shop on 9th St btw 5th & 6th Ave
but can't remember the name. Shopped in both stores
often. Miss stores like that. Seemed like "back in the day"
there were sooo many great
Stores on "the avenue" as my family called it. Lol.

But not too much anymore. :(

On 9th St? You mean that little gift shop between the
tuxedo shop and Royal Farms/Consumer Foods?
(The child mannequin in the tux store window used
to freak me out.) I used to buy stuff in there
occasionally.

Does anybody remember the pastry shop on 5th ave
called Bonocore? They made delicious cookies with
the chocolate swirl on top--they were delicious!
What about Lily's bakery on 7th ave? She made the
best Cannoli!

Who remembers Smilen Brothers fruits and Veggie
place on the corner of 11th and 5th before O'Neill's
card store? Now I'm dating myself.

Next to them it was Erwins Childrens clothing store
and then National Shoes.

I remember National's. There was also Bootery and Thom McCann shoe stores. Always got my shoes from there. Also remember a children's clothing store called Blossoms. It was around 11th st and kinda pricey but if you walked over to 13th st to Peanuts..JACKPOT!! Lol. Oh the memories.

Who in the neighborhood didn't know O'Neill's?! It was the GO TO STORE...especially when we were young...need a card for Mom, Dad, Aunt, Uncle, ANYTHING...Ya Went to O'Neill's.

Got my Communion dress from Blossoms. My Mom used to go to Smilen Bros for fruits and veggies. There was also a food market called Einhorn's, across from J. Michael's furniture store.

I also remember Erwin's, National Shoes, Kresge, Woolworth and other stores just like it was yesterday. I loved growing up in Park Slope.

Anyone remember the Palace meat market on 5th ave., between 14 and 15th?

You have to fit Mile's Shoes, Belmont's Men's Shop and Lofts Candy. Along that block with Smilen Brothers, National Shoes, Erwin's and Kresge's...And yes one more place, it was upstairs from Lofts Candy. I don't remember the name of the place they sold loans...

Oh, how the hell did we forget Biff's Pool Room upstairs from Smilen Brothers?

Regal's Bowling; it was downstairs.

Blossoms, O'Neills, Buster Brown....they and the people that worked there were such a part of all of our lives and milestones...it's so sad that the kids growing up there now don't have that.

Who else loved Myer's? 12th & 5th Ave. They also had another store on 16th & 5th ave; 5th ave was the shopping mecca at one time. I worked at Forman's hardware on 5th ave betwn 13 th & 14th street. I worked there for 27 years...

Wasn't Martin Paints on the corner of 14th?

Yes, martins paint was on 5th ave. Btwn 14 th &15 th on5th ave...

I worked in the hardware store btwn 13th n 14 th on 6th ave. It was called Forman's hardware. I worked there for 27 years...

I agree with you John. Fifth Avenue had anything and everything you could possibly want when going shopping...

So many changes you would be lucky if you could find 6 stores still there from the 70's.

I remember Nicky & Mary's Greek diner on 5th Ave btwn 14th & 15 (I think) could have been btwn 13th & 14th. Does anyone remember that?

Yes!!!....Was it next to the liquor store, a lil hole in the wall?

What was the name of the deli on 13th and 5th? And Joe's Pizza across the street towards 14th.

Glasgow's?

When I lived there it was Morty's.

Anyone remember this....11th street above 5th... the hair shack?

I vaguely recall it!!

Yes! Even though I rarely ever got (or get) my hair cut!

LOL!!! I have had a haircut or 5 done there.

I remember that place. Also, Hair Concern on 7th between 1st and 2nd (I think).

I remember. Wow I do remember, of course I never went there.

My mom thought she was a hairdresser along with a nurse, doctor, cook, seamstress, and everything in between

Gleason's deli on 11th and 5th

Those were surely the Wonder years...now a days a kid gets a bad hair cut they're killing their parent or in therapy for years. Crazy world.

Does anyone remember Blossoms on 5th ave and 11th street?

Yes. I got my Communion dress there. And on special occasions, a new dress.

Omg that store had all the nice clothes for kids. My sister-in-law bought my daughter her christening set there, beautiful clothes. Do you remember Lady Fair? I got all my maternity clothes there!

You're right about Blossoms in that they did have beautiful clothes. I remember Lady Fair and also Cushman's Bakery next to Lofts.

Does anyone remember the children's store, Punch & Judy, on 7th Ave near Garfield?

It was always jam-packed with clothes, you could hardly walk.

All of that sounds like we walked in the same footsteps back then - what great memories.

Lady fair, I can still remember the ladies that worked there.

Me too, do you remember G and G the clothes store on the corner?

What about when Burger King was on 10th street &
5th?

I worked in that Burger King too.

My mom used to get my clothes @ ERWINS on 5 th
ave when I was a kid...

My Buffy sweatshirt came from Erwins.

My mom also used to get my clothes at Erwins but as
I got older I started to shop at Miracle Corner and
Something Else. After all, I had to have a new outfit
to sport at Charlie Browns every Friday night lol.

I think we raised a few elbows there together as
well...wink wink. lol

Who remembers J&D's on 12th and 5th??? My
brothers used to hang out on the corner there and no
one can forget about Pete's Dirty water DOGS on the
corner also.

The hotdog man in front of Grey shell store.

Wow the Grey shell store.

I think the German deli was called Bonson's, and
then eventually became Hanson's. The original hot
dog man on 14th & 5th was Pete the hot dog guy, he
was before the Greek guy.

J MICHAELS: funny that you mentioned that
name...my mother shopped in there; I remember she
sent me to get 2 plastic orange nightstand lamps...lol
$3.00! OMG now I can laugh about it.

When I was little at first I sneaked to 13th street to
the deli on the corner and would go to J. Michaels
store front and look in the windows.

Remember a doughnut shop on 9th street just below
5th Ave that made fresh doughnuts every day all day
long? That's all they did was make doughnuts.

Was it next to the newspaper stand on the corner?

It was called Dee Dee Donuts and it shut down a couple of years ago.

They were great the donuts were always fresh from just being made.

Best glazed donuts...OMG!

the smallest shop in the world with the best French crullers.

I love the homemade donuts in the diner on 7th ave and 9th st. They're so good!

They have the real cream donuts with a lot of cream and the real crullers when I buy a dozen donuts I don't go to dunkin'; I go to that diner!

DEE DEE donuts!! Best donuts around!! I miss them. The Dunkin on 5th Ave off 9th st isn't that great.

Remember it? I think I still have some fat cells left from the donuts!

Remember Nationals & Miles shoes.

Shoes

We all needed something to walk around in. Those who went to Catholic schools wore shoes most of the day while those in public wore sneakers.

Who remembers Mr. Gutters shoe store on 7th near 14th Street... getting my Pete Maravich's.

Gutters was around 12th St and 7th Avenue. It was a messy place but they had brand name shoes...and I guess cheap.

Remember the man with the ladder? Always went there with my mother and brothers for new shoes.

OMG, when u said the ladder it all came back to me. Yes now I remember getting my saddle shoes there. Thanks.

What saddle shoes??? I remember going to a store with and old man who probably was not really old. lol

That's where my Mom took us for shoes. I forgot about Gutters!

We went there all the time, especially because we lived on 7th bet. 12th and 13th. Another freakin' blast from the past!

Gutters! Of course we all got our shoes in there. I remember his yellow sun shield on the windows. He used to go in the back and have a "nip" in between customers.

Lol. Loved that old man and his shoes!

OMG I forgot that. Those yellow sun shields. I would have never remembered that. Lol

I remember a shoe store with the guy on the ladder, but I can't remember if it was on 5th ave.

We always went to the shoe store on 5th Avenue & 19th Street. It was called the Shoe Box.

I remember the shoe store on 19th & 5th. Wow, we're going way back... very early 60s...I would give anything to be back there and then. At least we can say we once had those days. We are all so blessed with these memories.

Yes shoe box...I forgot about that one.

I don't think anyone mentioned those stores. Thanks for the memories. I don't think any shoe stores sit and fit people for shoes.

BUYING CONVERSE ON 1ST ST FROM THE OUTLET.

The sneaker factory below 6th?

I got my Chuck Taylor high tops from the Square Store on 8th st & 5th ave across the street from Blimpies and Dairy Queen.

Square Stores is still there, and the Blimpies is now a Subway.

Guttermann's. Stained glass above the door is still there. He was a retired cop. Had vintage shoes and his police hat on the upper shelves. All our mothers took us there before start of school.

Gutters was the best. He would tell you what shoes you were getting and that was it. He always had that police hat on the table in the back and a bottle of booze there also.

Many pairs of shoes from Gutters with my grandfather.

The newspaper store on Eight street just up from eighth ave, next to Sonak Deli. My first job at 11, putting together Sunday papers.

Tom McCan and the other shoe store, I forget the name.

Buster Brown shoes.

Wasn't there a Florsheim's on 5th, across from J. Michael's?

Yea there was, and there was a Fabco somewhere over there, then peanuts.

There was a hosiery store between 13 and 14 street; she had a giant dog in there and next to her was a tiny hole in the wall pizza joint.

National was another shoe store.

NATIONAL SOLD TOM MCAIN SHOES, RIGHT? OR WAS TOM MCAINS NEXT TO IT? I DON'T REMEMBER.

Chucka Boots!!! LOL! I remember everybody HAD
to have a pair!

Sneaker Circus

Back in the day, there was a place were the poor kid
could feel a little bit better about himself, just by the
status that still stands true today--and that is the street
cred you earned just by having a real pair of Pro
Keds.

My mom even brought me a pair of the black
Chinese slippers with the rubber bottom that was the
same color as an eraser on a #2 pencil. LOL

OMG the Chinese slippers. I use to pretend I was
Bruce Lee with those things on...lmao

Man if you bought rejects from here...the ranking
was on!! Had to be the real pro Keds.

Holy crap: Now that brings back memories!

And jelly slippers and flop flops, they were called
jelly beans I think.

That's old skool.

I miss that place. And my jelly sandals...lol

Lmao that was the spot.

Omg my mom used to buy us the jelly sandals in
every color.

The green and yellow boots...lol sanitation boots.

I remember feeling extra cute and special in those
damn things. I would never take them off. Jumped in
rain puddles in those things.

I hated the green rubber snow boots with the yellow
soles and laces that Mom would buy.

Those looked like some reject fireman boots. lmao

Hahaaaa. Ditto, regarding the rubber boots with the metal buckles.

I had the 1.99 special from the bin when you had to find a matching right and left one in the right size.

If u knew your mom was taking u to the basement part of it...U were fudged lmao, nothing but plastic bottoms lol.

Remember my mom getting me 69ners Mark 5's.

Was mark 5s a park slope thing? bc when I bring it up to friends they look @ me like I'm nuts.

How about converse with two stars and everybody knew you went to the factory for them, lmao.

I used to go there and get my rejects out the box in the basement. With a ten dollar coupon

Oh and forget about having pro Keds we got pro cons from the factory lol.

LOVE THE SNEAKER FACTORY!!! WE WOULD GO ON A SATURDAY AFTERNOON WHEN DADDY WAS HOME FROM WORK, CUZ OBVIOUSLY HE WAS THE ONE WITH THE MONEY HA HA HA.

Places Left

OK SO WHAT IS LEFT STANDING IN PARK SLOPE? SEEMS LIKE EVERYTHING IS GONE?

What about Rays dry cleaners on 9th between 5th & 6th? Then you have the library 0n 6th ave & 9th street.

Many years ago it was called S & S Cleaners. It was next to the YMCA.

Tip top gift store...on 5th ave btw 8th and 9th st. Square stores on the corner of 8th st and 5th ave is also still there.

Library is closed for renovations (closed for a year already), S&S is still there.

Neergaards? Smith's Tavern (Smitty's)?

Neergaards has a second floor as well now that is a cool toy store! Smith's still there but they removed booths.

Smitty's was my dad's watering hole...

WHATEVER HAPPENED TO MARTIN'S PAINT NEAR GERMAIN'S? LOL.

Martin's Paint went out of business back in the 90's.

Wow, Martin's Paint has been out of business for years...

What about the newsstand on 9th and 5th ave.?

I SO MISS TAKING THE KIDS TO THE BROOKLYN MUSEUM AND TO MANHATTAN, BRINGING THEM TO THE CIRCLE LINE, TO ELLIS ISLAND, BATTERY PARK ON THE WEEKENDS...FOR ALL KINDS OF CULTURAL STUFF....WELL THE KIDS ARE ALL GROWN UP AND NOTHING LEFT IN PARK SLOPE....SIGH.

YMCA is still on 9st and an extension was opened on 14th Street and 8th ave - big running track, basketball courts, workout classes and free weights.

Is that where the armory was?

Yes, the Armory is on 8th Avenue between 14th & 15th Streets.

Yes, they took over 80% of the space, renovated it looks great, and left 20% for the women's shelter.

What about Angelo's giving everyone the exact same haircut for 40 years!

7th Ave & N 4th St!! Haven't gone there in 20 yrs, he cuts hair the way he wants to cut it!! LOL!!

Yes, 7th ave n 4 street....my dad's barber for many years.

I remember when it was on the other side of the street where the felafel place is or was. Is it still there?

Yep!! Angelo & his brother, still cutting!!

Felafel place still there too!!

Wow, Vito and Ang still going strong LOL!

Felafel still there, wow...I used to love that place, with the little spinach squares, and the gyros? With the fresh lamb on the burner? My dad still goes there....hehe. :)

Souvalaki N Shish Kabobs!! YUM!! Keep that NASTY TAHINI sauce (Chickpea sauce--tastes like paint!!) away from my pitas LOL!!

I used to get a haircut there as a child, it looked like he put a bowl on your head and cut around it...Always hated it! BTW, his glasses are so thick (Coke Bottle Bottoms) he almost took my ear off once...Ooops!

I used to go the barber's on 11th St and 8th ave and then eventually to Mary's Hair Salon - above Herzog's...She got all of our Hippie Pony Tails!...

Tahini is made from sesame, not chick peas. Felafel is made from chick peas and so is humus. Get your facts right.

SHADDUP SHADDING UP CHEF RABBITT!! ;-))
Still nasty N tastes like PAINT!! ECKKKK!! LOL!!

Wife and I took our son there for his first haircut...caught it on video... cried most of the way through. But the lollipops helped.

LOL!! Still tastes like PAINT!! I like my Souvlaki & Shish Kebabs w NO sauce!! Nice N dry!! AAAAAHHH YUMMY!! Lettuce provides all the moisture ya need!!

No I have a craving for Souvlaki N Shish Kebabs!! LOL!!

And of course Tony's records and Leopoldi Hardware.

Well another one bites the dust: as of this writing the Triangle sporting good store on 5th ave and Flatbush has been sold. This is all due to the expansion and growth of the downtown Brooklyn area and the new NY Nets arena they have built.

WOW!! So SAD to hear about this almost 100 yrs in BIZ N being squeezed out by Bigger Sporting Good Corps!! All things must come to an end I guess but hate seeing local ICONS like this forced to close!! Part of the allure was climbing those rickety old steps to search for fav sneaks or boots or sports gear!! Hope the building has LANDMARK STATUS, at least: a GREAT piece of architecture, it will be missed!!

13-Things We Did

    – Arcades

    – Birthday Parties

    – Ice Skating

    – Johnny Pump

    – Roller Skate

    – Tar Beach

- TV Shows
- Paddle Boats
- Block Parties
- Water Balloon Fights

Arcades

Finally, let's get to some entertainment...now if you had lots of quarters, you could play Pinball and tilt the machine...or if you had finesse you could beat the Pinball machine...or play the new Joust or Asteroids...and win a free pie, or other foods if you beat the highest score...I did that all over, even went to other neighborhoods to beat their high score, just for the thrill of victory and the taste of the PIZ!

Luv it!

Pacman!

Air hockey was almost as dangerous as darts in a bar, LOL.

AIR HOCKEY!! YEAH BABEE! & the occasional crunched/bruised finger!! LOL, or head shot, ouch. Snooky's Style...

Spent too many hours and quarters, LOL, sitting in front of that thing. :)

Coach Inn too!! Coach had the original Pong/tennis I believe!!

Man, I spent loads of singles on that machine when they had it at the 24 hour store around the corner of 1st street and 7th ave, and also won back a few bucks when I had a winning streak going on.

Still have my Atari, brother!! Plus games.

Just bought one at a yard sale the kids look at it strange when they see the tennis with 2 lines (paddles) and 1 white blip (ball). LOL

PONG! That was the greatest game LOL.

Those two little lines that where it all started.

If you go to the Museum of Moving Image in Astoria you can still play one that works plus some other arcade games like Asteroids. My kids had a blast.

Wow!!! Looked like it was from a nuclear submarine lol.

I had one of these. But it all started with "Pong" and I was hooked. LOL.

I just played this game again today. Wow, it's been years since I've even seen this game at all. BTW, it's still awesome!

Hyperspace...

I totally forgot that feature.

Have it on my phone now, we've come a long way baby!

Asteroids? Y'all must be whipper snappers! It was pinball and then, years later, Space Invaders, for my generation. God, Space Invaders was so exciting when it was the only game in town.

I still look around at arcades for the Phoenix game.

Man, I used to rock that pinball machine like Tommy and spent lots of quarters to prove it, learned the tilt function and how not to set it off.

And Smiley's had a video game...was it Asteroids?

Yes, lol I was always there. A lot of us hung out there. I remember that "night rider" racing game they had. Many showed up just for that. Their chicken n ribs were def. good. I know; I made them. lol :D

Smiley's had that race driving game where you could select your own courses. Also Millipede. I go to this museum on Pier 39 in SF called the museum de' mechanique; they have coin operated games dating back to the early 1900s. It's really cool.

As far as the video games go: Star Castle, Asteroids, Pacman and Space Invaders...we used to get thrown out of the stores because we would put one quarter in and switch players for hours. No profit.

Birthday Parties

Who remembers their birthday parties? Cake, ice cream a little candy....pin the tail on the donkey...and when we were older spin the bottle...a birthday corsage with gum or life savers and birthday punches and one for good ouch...Look what the kids have today for their birthdays...

I do...I do...

Me too, these kids today have no clue what it is to enjoy growing up in a world of yesterday years...

One punch for good luck ouch...

Even had some birthday parties up in the park.

Birthday Parties were great then. Now...I don't need any "reminders."

Musical chairs and a pinch to grow an inch.

Oh darn. I forgot about the pinch move. I remember it now, and still "feel" some of them. LOL

How can we forget the great pin the tail on the Donkey?

I loved the night before my birthday party -- putting all the favor bags together, making sure the decorations were just right - so exciting! Yeah, what a change 40+ years later LMAO.

Now a sweet sixteen party cost 10,000 dollars...lol.

OMG musical chairs that was so much fun lots of bumps and bruises to trying to get the chair...LOL.

So many fun games we played at the Birthday Parties.

Ice Skating

Remember the Kate Wollman skating rink?

So I tried ice skating once. Nearly broke my ankle. Decided it was probably more fun to watch little rugrats skate rings around (and knock over) others. I was right. It was LOL.

Someday I'll tell you about my attempt to skate. But not today. ;)

Still ice skate every winter but the rink was closed last winter because they are building a new one.

I am so in awe of people who can ice skate. I was never quite able to get it.

I wanted to get those skates with the training blades, but figured I'd look like even more of an idiot than I did.

I spent so many hours skating on that ice. I loved it so much and got to the point where I could skate backwards and do a figure 8 (not professionally of course).

As I recall A&S used to run contests every year...

I ice skate, like Ralph Kramden roller skates!

Thank you, for a minute there, I was all alone LOL.

Great memories at that rink. I remember skating backwards but never learned the figure 8.

What was nice was holding hands with a boy and skating around.

Remember that rink well--playing ice hockey, at times watching my brother play on the hockey teams. Too bad it was all the way on the other side of the park.

I remember after the ice skating was done the Hot Chocolate and the long walk back home to 10th street, with the skates tied together hanging over my shoulders.

Johnny Pump

Good old Johnny Pump!!! Lots of fun!!! :)

I remember once we had a "bathtub" someone threw out and we all pulled it over to the " johnny pump" and filled it and one of the best block parties there ever was...(including the "adult" fight" that followed!!

Had one in front of my house on 10 st., lots of fun in the summer.

Just hated when the boys would grab u and bring u into it and the others would cup his hands so it would come out real hard at u then u would go flying across the street ugh!!!!!!!

I remember we would often start a car wash and charge a quarter per car. In the end we would go to Maxis and buy penny candy.

I still call it that and no one knows what I'm talking about. Not even my husband and he's from Queens.

The boys used to throw me into the johnny pump and any time they did I would get really mad. My clothes were soaked but more importantly, my hair got wet! Lol.

The tin cans would get the best height on the water...you could flood someone's basement across the street if you weren't careful...and hold on to that can...if you were in its trajectory... it could sting!

<~~~~~~~IN ITS TRAJECTORY ONCE! ;(

Years ago I'm walking down 3rd street, and I say to my son--he was like 5 yrs old, he's 19 now--so I said " Its right there, right next to the " johnny pump!" And he said, "What's a johnny pump" I died laughing. I forgot it's a hydrant now!

Johnny pump!!

25 years and I still "catch" myself calling them Johnny pumps. Get strange looks and statements like "so you give 'em names up north?" LOL.

I didn't know Johnny pump was local! We don't have many here so I haven't been called out on it. It cracks me up, and people here find that very strange and say "in line." Someone once asked me after I said it if I was from the East Coast.

Oh the endless hot summer nights playing in the johnny pump, and the long days.

I love jumping over the Johnny pump!!!!

You described our summer vacations. Turned on the "johnny pump" on the very hot days.

How could I forget trying to get that damn thing off with an old rusty wrench, but somehow we always managed to get one of them off. Then Doyle would come around and scream at us, lol.

The Best Times in Park Slope!!

The OLD Park Slope.

Always had the johnny pump going on 7th Ave and 20th St...Even washing cars as they passed...made a few dollars for soda and chips afterwards.

362

When I first moved away, a friend and I were parking and I said you're too close to the Johnny Pump you cant park here...she got out of the car looking for the johnny pump saying where is it I said right there dumb____...she said that's a johnny pump? I've always called them a fire hydrant in a long drawl, welcome to the south.

Cops would shut it off and it would be back on before they even turned the corner.

Get a faggy sprinkler cap they would tell us--only about 1/3 water would come out!!

Scrape the cans on the concrete until the tin bottom fell off. Turn the Johnny Pump on full blast & send that waterfall 30 ft. in the air...Priceless on a 90 degree day with 90 percent humidity LOL!

Hot fun in the summer time.

The pump was the greatest opportunity 24/7...and close to home!!

So...many kids on my block. All summer long the johnny pump was on...We lined the towels up on the sidewalk & chased each other with our water filled milk cartons...Good times to reflect upon!

Hey-I always wondered where "Johnny Pump" came from: answer...the firemen on the day were called Johnnys...and of course...miss it so much!

You could turn them on with a coat hanger and a stick!

Then there were the unsuspecting victims who would casually drive past the open pump with the windows open, well you know the rest hit and run...HA...

Roller Skating

Did all my skating in the park and around the park on the road, it was great, took you right round the whole park.

Played roller derby and hockey in the Bandshell; you needed a perfect surface for these skates to work; remember the metal wheels?

Went there every Fri and Sat night.

Must have been awesome.

I still love roller skating, I went a few years ago, and I still got it. lol

Loved roller skating...went to Park Circle many times.

Roller skated at the Bandshell.

Went to Sheepshead Bay to roller skate once in a while.

"Rock Skate Roll Bounce."

Roller skating that was another summer everyday thing.

I used to love to jump things with my roller skates, pick up enough speed and fly over the barrels and crash into the car and bleed all over the floor, what fun that was...

Tar Beach

How many of us have done this at one time? Somewhere in Brooklyn?

Tanning on Tar Beach. It was sooo hot.

With the reflectors and baby oil at that...

YES I have a photo of me the summer of '86 on Tar Beach...just behind my shoulders in the photo are the Twin Towers. Kinda bittersweet.

364

And the baby oil with iodine.

And the skin cancer that follows 30 years later!

WHILE LISTENING TO THE SONGS, UP ON
THE ROOF... LOL.

Tar beach, yeah! Oh yeah!

Bring a blanket and a radio...up on the roof! During
the day, it felt like you were a million miles away
from everything up there, and at night you could
almost touch the stars!

Every weekend!!!!! Tar beach!!!

Do you mean sunbathe on the roof, or spy on girls
sunbathing on the roof? LOL.

I can't tell you how many times I've taken pictures of
girls sunbathing on rooftops.

The question should have been, how many *haven't*
done this!

Wayyyyy too many times for me...very relaxing and
u felt somewhat secluded.

Good thing we didn't have long summers, otherwise
we would all look like the seniors on Miami Beach!

All leathery!

Yes and I used baby oil and iodine to get a tan.

Every summer - just hooked up my skylight to open
so I can do it again! Brooklyn never changes
underneath!

Yeah but the damn tar would stick to me!! Looked
like a leopard all summer!!

Ah tar beach! I cant remember who it was but they
went up on the roof, lathered themselves with
vegetable oil and then laid down on foil, need i say
anything else?

I did it when I was living in Park Slope, Boro Park, etc. I always had the baby oil, iodine, and the sun visor.

Yes tar beach.....visited many times...

Tar beach with a sun visor frying (baby oil sometimes with hydrogen peroxide mixed in). What were we thinking!

Tar beach, baby.

I remember people making those things themselves, out of cardboard and aluminum foil!

Did it all the time, now dealing with skin cancer!!

See, that's because you didn't wear eye shadow & lipstick like she did.

Us too, but we knew we were looking cute at the time though, shhesh if only we knew, my sister still does this...crazy.

Thinking? We were kids. We were never thinking! LOL

I always thought those people were from Mars when I was a kid walking around the big lawn at Prospect Park.

Every 4th of July and when I couldn't go to the beach...tar beach was the spot with baby oil!

Lmao! What about 1/2 bottle of baby oil and 1/2 bottle of coca cola? That mixture gives u a Hawaiian tan...I still do that lmao!

TV Shows

I am a die hard *3 Stooges* fan!

Love the *3 stooges*. Remember Sunday mornings on channel 11 they were on then after it was *Abbott and Costello*?

We can't leave out the *Little Rascals* on channel 5 now!

Weekday afternoons, *Officer Joe Bolton.*

I loved Abbott n Costello watched it all the time!

I don't know how old you guys are but I use to watch *Winkie dink.*

I'm 45 and i remember *Winkie dink.*

I loved that show, drawing on the TV and I forgot to put the screen on it, my mom got pissed.

Land chiller with the 6 fingers.

Lmao we ain't had it like that I used my fingers lol.

They still show chiller on cable.

I see it sometimes, man I miss those old shows not so much winkie dink...lol.

Speed Racer, Gigantor, Rocky and Bullwinkle.

Tell me about it, I sit back many times wishing I can go back lol.

Captain Kangaroo Bob McCalister Bozo.

I can never get into speed racer but *Gigantor* was the shit loved that show.

How bout *Wonderama*?

I went to the filming of that show.... when Neil Sedaka was playing on it.

Oh man i know the name lmao but can't spell it .his partner was drop a long.

droop a long.

Bing bing bing.. That rabbit, was his name Rickashy.

Yea that's it.

U can watch a lot of these shows on youtube.

I do watch on youtube, it's freaking great.

Can't spell it but I will try. rick a sy.

LMAO THAT'S BETTER THEN WHAT I WAS GOING TO PUT. LOL.

ABC's Wide World of Sports: Spanning the globe to bring you the constant variety of sport! The thrill of victory, and the agony of defeat! The human drama of...

I always hoped the "agony of defeat" guy at least got a lot of money for showing this week after week.

The amazing part if I remember the story correctly is that guy wasn't seriously injured. HTH did that happen?

I liked how they once interviewed the guy he goes right over (guy crouching down with camera in hand) right before the Skier takes the deepest fall!!

My favorite part "the human drama" Vasily Alexeev setting a world record for the clean jerk. I think it was 560 pounds.

Don't forget those Timex Commercials that aired during Wide World of Sports.

1971 Timex Torture Test Commercial with John Cameron Swayze.

Yea, I think he left his nuts on the ground. LOL

One of my very TOP TV shows of the 60's!! Loved Emma Peel & John Steed the classic *English Gent*!! *The Avengers* (1967) -

One of my Favs, *F-Troop*.

I loved this, "I Spy", "The Man From U.N.C.L.E.", "Wild Wild West", oh so many great shows from that time!

Don't forget It Takes a Thief, Burkes Law, Honey West, 77 Sunset Strip!! Mission Impossible, Hawaii Five-0!!

Anyone remember the Prisoner?

Yes and Secret Agent Man.

Patrick Mcnee.

Diana Riggs, the sexiest woman on TV in black leather, and then cat woman.

Eartha Kitt & Julie Newmar!! Loved em both!!

Remember the Osmonds, Jackson 5 and the Beatles cartoons

Get Smart.

Favorite show -- especially The Cone of Silence AHAHAHA!!!

Loved this show too!

Just remembered Agent 99 and 86!

Would you believe a troop of cub scouts, and a???

Mel Brooks and Buck Henry, two of the funniest guys wrote for this show.

Mel Brooks created this show. And when you look back you realize "Of COURSE he did; who ELSE could have been responsible?" LOL.

I was just remembering -- Agent 13. That was the guy who showed up in like garbage cans et al -- the oddest places LOL.

What was the robot's name?

Hymie. Played by Dick Gautier (it's the last credit as the video ends).

And how many of us used to do that "dropping down" thing in every phone booth we passed when we were kids??? (Hand waving frantically.)

I'm sure I did.... LOL

Missed it...byyy that much!!!

My sister loved this show...

Kojak - A Bald Police detective with a Fiery Righteous Attitude Battles crime in His City.

Mom loved this & I'd watch it with her sometimes. He was fun.

Who loves you BABY! Loved him!

Love, American Style's TV theme song.

Love American style for youuuu and me! I always loved this theme song...I think it was by the Cowsills who sang "the rain the park and other things" which I also love.

That was a great show!

LOVE AMERICAN STYLE TRUER THAN THE RED WHITE N BLUE!!

That Girl, Love the "retro" fashions!

Flying Nun Theme Song.

The Newlywed Game.

Brady Bunch.

This program messed a lot of us up, Mike Brady never screamed, the kids never got hit. He never shouted " Cause I said so that's why,"

Hogan's Heroes.

Don't do the crime, if you can't do the time.

Baretta- A streetwise undercover cop. Tony Baretta, often using disguises with the help of Stoolie to solve crime...

Was getting ready to watch this the night the lights went out in New York lol...I was pissed.

"You can take that to da Bank!!"

Never liked this one. He always irritated me. Maybe I knew...

I liked him...when he was a Little Rascal.

My Dad's favorite show...

Father Knows Best TV Theme.

Father did always know best till mom started burning her bra!

Mission Impossible - Original Intro.

We will disavow any knowledge of your actions.

The Bionic Dog.

Max, The Bionic Dog, saving the day.

Loved the "Tiger Paw" sound effect!

Mod Squad intro.

Mary Hartman, Mary Hartman.

Charlie's Angels.

Manixx.

Welcome Back Kotter.

I along with every other Brooklyn goyl hoped to see Vinnie walking down 5th avenue.

Gilligan, Skipper, Ginger, Mary Ann, The Professor, The Millionaires, worldly Calvionists stranded on a island without their ungodly toys, they will have to do...

OK OK I'll say it again...if they could build a $&%Y& radio, why couldn't they fix the damn boat?? LOL.

Wonder Woman.

Perry Mason.

The Streets of San Francisco.

This was a BIG favorite show...

The incredible Hulk.

"Don't make me angry, you won't like me when I'm angry."

Loved Lou Ferrigno.

I liked the 6 million dollar man...Imagine today...order online what you'd like to be for 6 million dollars...pick an arm...2 legs and what else to be upgraded in you....lol....free shipping!!

Don't forget about 'The Bionic Woman'

The Rockford Files.

Night Stalker with Kochack?

Loved this show as well as the Bionic Woman & Wonder Woman, but there was a show called A Man from Atlantis. I fell in love with Patrick Duffy!!

I do....Re-MA-kable!

Officer Joe and Captain Jack.

WPIX broadcasting "Back then" was the best!! Loved the chicks in the Magic Garden!! HEE HEE!!

You still love them.

Of course I do!! Just as I do YOU and all my FRIENDS!! ;-))

Loved the "Superman" reruns. I was in my 20s before I knew that some episodes were in color. Did'ja ever notice how the bad guys would shoot bullets at him and they would bounce off him and he'd give them the look like "Don't these guys ever learn?" but when the bad guy would THROW the gun at him, he'd duck?

The last 4 seasons were in color, only the 1st 2 seasons were B&W. I love the color episodes cause you can see SWEAT stains on his uniform!! LMAO!!

Beachcomber Bill, Officer Joe Bolton, Captain Jack, Chuck McAnn and all the cartoons: Magilla Gorilla, Wally Gator, Mushmouse, Popeye and all the rest. Great Memories.

Was Claude Kirshner, a guy dressed as a ringmaster, on PIX? He was on a local station, and after the last cartoon, he would sign off with " And now it's time for most of you to go to bed."

Oh wow, Beachcomber Bill forgot about him!!

Ignatz the Brick throwing mouse!! LOL.

I wonder what it says about me... I remember each and every show!

We have TOTAL recall!

Paddle Boats

What good memories we had riding the Paddle Boats in Prospect Park, lol.

Watchin'? Yes! Paddling? Hell no! Tired, strained legs and very heavy breathing! Give me a row boat any day!!!

Back in the day, the denizens of the Monument and Hippie Hill used that lake as the "Ole' Swimin' Hole!"

I heard of a "few" drownings there. Rumor has it that though small in surface area, there is an extremely deep hole below.

Never rode the paddle boats but had a horse escape the stables and run into the lake so we could not catch him, and the park ranger thought he had a great idea and paddled out to him only to have him sink the boat and the ranger in the lake; wish I had a camera.

THIS WAS BACK IN THE 70'S AND I BELIEVE HIS FOOT GOT WRAPPED UP IN THE CORAL AT THE BOTTOM OF THE LAKE. NOBODY COULD PULL HIM UP. BUT ENOUGH OF THE SAD THINGS. I HAD A LOT OF FUN THERE WITH FRIENDS BACK IN THE DAY.

Yes, I remember hearing about that drowning.

Spend the day nice picnic, do a little fishing and go on the paddle boats, loved those memories.

Block Parties

Miss my Brooklyn Block parties!

Same here.

So much fun...cleaning up once all cars were cleared off and the streets were blocked. Everyone eating together.....all the grills out front...what great memories.

Yup.

Me too. I'm not in Bklyn anymore, but I don't think they even do them anymore. It's a shame, they brought people together.

Block parties = street fairs.

We had the best block parties on 14th St bet 5th & 6th.

I certainly miss DJin them as well.

Sure miss the block parties, back in the day you knew everyone from your block, we were all one big family, I live in California now, I don't know the family that lives in the house to my left, I've never seen them, living on this block for 9 years, can you believe that!!

We sure did! Johneey pump, BBQ, stick ball games, music, some times fireworks and best of all no cars!! The street was ours.

Mine were on 11th St.

Totally the best times ever...

Loved that they were for 2 days also...even as a kid the nights were my favorite...once the DJ got there I was even happier.

16th st bet. 8th n 9th ave...BEST BLOCK PARTIES EVER!! Remember someone threw out a tub, n the "grown ups" filled it with water from "the johnny pump" n we played for hours!!

WOW...see we know how to have good times in Brooklyn.

We had a couple of really big block parties; Blocked off the street, no one gets in till we were done.

We did the same thing strung up Christmas lights. eat eat eat...Banner went between the things to block off the streets.

We hired a DJ, and rented rides like the "Whip" for the kids...and the party went literally all night!!!

Same here...my BF and I were just talking about the Whip, would come to the block parties and we'd ride over and over, good times for sure. One of the exciting things when much younger.

8th street bet. 5th and 6th ave had some of the best block parties and stick ball games, 4th of July block parties were the best.

We had some great block parties.

THE best block parties. We had the same band every year and they were awesome!

So did we, Live Bands, DJ, even my own band played at our block parties!!

Ours were great too.

Remember the 5 and 7th ave fair back in the 70s and 80s?

I remember in the 70's, didn't 7th ave shut down? Also loved our 8th st block parties.

Yep that's when the fair was the best. Went from Atlantic Ave to like 17th St. The city started making it shorter. Not as exciting as when I was younger but still go anyway.

You said it it used to be like 30 blocks (the 5 ave fair) then each year it got shorter and shorter.

Its like a 5 block 5 ave fair now. What a joke, and I bet the yuppies ask for a bike lane as well.

The Bands in front of John Jay.

If you noticed the fair is where u see people u don't see all winter long. Lol.

<u>Water Balloon Fights</u>

Water Balloon Fights!!!

Don't kids do that any more?

Most kids today don't go outside!

Those were the good days. Back before technology had us by the throat. Back when I got home from school I did my homework and went to play with this thing called a stick, and it was in a magical place called outside. Now kids just sit on a computer and phones.

To many balloons using a faucet...better to use a hose nozzle, which also doubled as a back-up weapon in case of an attack during refueling!

This result was a standard happening on my spigot!

That's awesome! Such cheap amazing fun! We didn't need no stinkin' video games (Ataris) or X- boxs or anything like that! Metal trash can lids made great shields when you were playing war, and my dad made us stilts out of 2x4's and we walked up and down our long driveway! Good times!

And those big bad water balloons put no one's eye out. We didn't wear pads on our elbows or knees, we played outside, built "forts," ate mud, rode bikes without helmets, had friendships w/o texting....AND WE LIVED...only to give birth to a bunch of spoiled kids who have no idea what I'm talking about.

Water Balloon Fights turn you into a kid again....no matter what your age!!

What about that ass whopping u get after the water bill comes? Priceless.

Remember those big thick balloons that came with a rubber band that you punched? We used to fill them with water, stand in a circle and toss it to see who it would break on.

I must still b a kid cause we still do that !!

We used to fill laundry baskets and buckets with water balloons. Some will bust as you get the count up. So much fun.

We'd also have water tracking from the bathroom through the house to the front porch. Loved it.

Water balloons, big ones, water tasted good back then.

I drank from the hose too.

Kids can't fill or throw water balloons because they would have to put down their BlackBerry or some sort of electronic gizmo they all have. They don't even associate with anyone in their presence. Were we poor or did our parents care?

We once had a neighborhood water fight that was truly EPIC!!! Water balloons, squirt bottles, water hoses connected to faucets DOWN THE STREET... Best days ever!!

Oh yeah, we had a great time blasting our kids with them and water pistols. Neighbors went nuts with all the screaming. lol

Loved those simpler days playing under the streetlights all summer long.

Hahahahahahaha hell yea I remember that.

14-Things We Wore

- Dungarees

- Jeans

- Earth Shoes and Stuff

- Sneakers

- Jewelry

Dungarees

Here's a question....How many of you still call your denim pants "DUNGAREES" and not jeans? People make fun of me all the time b/c I still say dungarees. I mean really--they're dungarees and a dungaree jacket--OK let the teasing begin!!!

You are exactly right.

I remember in JHS "Hygiene Class" (Yea, you heard right) they showed us a picture of what a drug addict looked like. They "pointed out" that they would be wearing dungarees!!! LOL

I call em dungarees sometimes. Some habits are hard to break.

I just can't bring myself to say "jeans" -- can't do it -- especially "jean jacket" -- I'm sorry, but that's just WRONG!!!

I was the one painting all the band album covers on everyone's dungaree jackets back in the day.

Those words "ain't" coming out of my mouth, lol.

I still call them dungarees...the boys make fun of me every time!!! What, is he still livin' in the '70's??? LOL.

My old man took pride in sayin' "I neva owned a pair of Dungarees" Old Codger called em Denims!! LOL!!

I say both. Old habits are hard to break. Dungarees.

When we were growing up in PS -- only the hicks from outta town called them jeans and then it was "blue jeans"...SO THERE!!!

Shit, I still say knapsack too -- I didn't realize that went outta style as well ... Oh well . it'll always be a knapsack to me, just like dungarees, lol.

OK getting back to DUNGAREES: no I don't call them that but I do say Johnny pump, pocketbook, and aerie way!!

Isn't it really Pockabook!! LOL!! ;-)

LOL. I don't say Pockabook anymore. I now call it a bag. My friend's 17 year old calls it a purse, which sounded 'old' to me. She must get that from her mother.

Down here in South Jersey they think I'm strange because I IRON my DUNGEREES!!

I think you're strange for doing that LOL. Of course, I gave up ironing some years ago. Too Damn Hot here in hell. :)

Well I have to be honest I don't iron my dungarees all the time but I still do it sometimes. Old habits are hard to break!

With the crease.

Yes exactly!!! Its all about the crease!

Yes, ironed dungarees with a crease, and Gibson white shoe polish for the sneakers!

Dungarees not Jeans.

My sister still creates a crease in her dungarees for herself and her husband. Scary.

I think I wore mine a bit too tight, that would explain my Bee Gees Falsetto.

Jeans

Why was it that when u took these jeans off, ur legs looked like they belonged to a smurf lol lol. The dye used to run and when u washed it u had better have it separated from the other loads of wash....

That's so funny, but true. Just sweating or getting caught in the rain. Amazed the first time it happened.

Working...playing...day or nite...thanks for the laugh!

My Jordache jeans with a pair of candies!

Classic Jordache Jeans commercial from 1979!!

The Jordache look.

I was a fan of Lee's. My American arse could not, would not go into those french style jeans. Not to mention they would look silly with my tried and true Lee jacket. Nonetheless they really did a nice job for women.

Jordache jeans and matching Jordache sweater, made me think I was all that.

Yes Candies were the way to go.

Sergio Valentes and Faded Glory's is the one I couldn't think of

How bout the Vidal Sassoon jeans...

WITH THE CREASES SPRAYED WITH STARCH.

Starch, the magic stuff!

After a while you had the white line down the middle, after ironing them so much.

Jordaches are back...wonder if they make em in my size though. Ha.

Earth Shoes and Shoes

Who remembers EARTH SHOES?! The most comfortable shoes ever!!!

They were ugly but oh so comfortable.

I wear a blue suede earth shoe (w/platform) lol!
Xoxo

I had the light brown suede ones. There were many imitations. But the best were the authentic ones.

I had a couple of pairs of these. Can't remember the colors but I also lived in clogs. Uh, never mind; still do, LOL.

Still got clogs too! Remember the Dr. Scholl's wooden sandals?

I had the red ones, but to me, they were never comfortable.

Couldn't wear them; so uncomfortable. Never bought any because of that. Oh jeez and then those Candies things came out - UGH.

Espadrilles & "buffalo" sandals, remember those?

Espadrilles were great. I had those. I had a pair of Candies, but only wore them a few times. They were killers on the feet. I remember Buffalo shoes but forgot what they looked like.

Remember Chinese slippers?

Yes, I do remember them. Don't remember if I had a pair; I must have though.

They were really cheap and cute shoes! I remember buying them at the five and dime store on 5th avenue and 9th street.

I don't remember them, but we wore moccasins and they were great.

I loved my Frye boots.

Remember Marshmallows?

LOVED my Fryes. :) They're so expensive now. Were they that expensive back then? LOL!!

Had to buy Fryes on 39th st near the piers at Frankles.

Remember all the work that went into keeping those Frye boots clean, polishing them?

Thanks for letting me off the hook---we can't be held accountable for our fashion crimes back then. :)

I had earth shoes. They were so comfortable.

Fryes were really expensive back then and I'm sure they still are. I used to spend all of my money from part-times jobs on clothes and shoes.

I remember dancing with my Marshmellow shoes.

If I could get them today I would. I lived in them!

Probably the best shoes I ever owned -- that and Dr. Scholl's sandals in the summer and Frye boots in the winter!!!!

Remember Desert Boots?

Marshmallow shoes were the most comfortable.

Loved my marshmellows.

I had Capezio's, very hip in the 80's clubs, I bought them in the village.

If you were a hippie like me -- we wore earth shoes, clogs and Jesus sandals (lol)!!!

I had earth shoes in the 70's. I was a half breed; I liked Rock and Disco. Went to clubs and concerts. Lol.

YO...hey what about those 4 inch high heels us guys used to wear, what's a matter no one wanna admit to that now?

All of you Kiss fans.

Sneakers

How about the Converse factory on Lincoln Place between 5th and 6th avenues? You could get converse sneakers for almost half the price; just had a couple of flaws in them, but no one could tell.

Mark V sneakers, the bootleg version of blue suede Pumas. You got them in the bin at Lincoln Place. If you were lucky enough, they were attached by an impenetrable plastic tie. If not you had to go bin diving for two of the same size.

I remember bin diving for the second sneaker and you held on the first one for dear life and hoped that someone else did not have the match.

PF FLYERS Run Faster Jump Higher with P.F. Flyers!! LOL I forget who their Lil kid spokesman was though!! He had a name in the commercials!!

His name was Swifty Flyer. I won't take credit for knowing that, I cheated.

We got ALL our sneakers there when we were growing up! Oh and I found a pair of woman's PF Flyers, low top, original green label in the back, more like deck shoes, some years ago. Most comfortable sneakers ever. Wore them out. Can't find them anymore. :(

I could usually tell. I remember buying white Pro-Keds with a glue stain on the side.

Never had PF's got my Converse's on Lincoln. Could never afford the genuines.

Joe Swifty!

Do you remember this Sneaker factory jingle? "Rejects, they make your feet feel fine, Rejects, they cost a $1.99."

Rejects, they make ur feet feel fine, even cheaper...they cost a nickel and a dime!

They leave you behind.

I couldn't afford Keds, lol.

I remember the place on Lincoln. The place smelled like rubber before you even walked in the door. Now I have that jingle running through my head. Lol.

384

Thanks a lot, I too have that jingle in my head now...but its worth it thanks for the memories. ;)

How about the Pro Keds 69ers with the 3 lines running along the base of the sneaker?

Sorry guys, not me. It was those 99 cent Skippy's from the factory on Lincoln for me. I'm old enough to not be that proud anymore.

KEDS!!!!! LOVE MY KEDS!!!!!!

Remember getting Nucons and Procons down at the Factory?

A few years ago I found a liquidation factory and bought about 4 pair of Keds, they lasted me for a few years.

Jewelry

Need a Christ head, Horn, Rope chain?

Didn't we all have one of those growing up?

I Still Have Mine My Mom Gave Me For Communion...

Had all of them; got a Christ head three years ago for Xmas. Every time I wear it someone comments on my old school bling.

I still have the same jewelry; my daughter used to borrow it all the time.

Yea same here; wore the rope earring also.

Know what else came to mind? The Italian hand on the chain with the two fingers, that either ward off the devil or mean, well I can't say it here but the letters are F... U, or a hand motion under tha chin.

My bracelet was bought at Garry's jewelry store on 5th...

I still have mine.

Ditto!!

I have the exact same one...

I still have mine too from 1983!

My bracelet was bought at Garry's jewelry store on 5ᵗʰ...

Mine too!! I got it for my birthday in June 1983, it has 11 diamonds. I told my son about them for his GF and he looked at me like I had six heads...lol.

They will be back in style again...I still wear mine once in awhile!!

That was a big purchase for a guy way back then....

I still have mine (in pieces) with jade pearls.

I still have mine!

I thought yours got tossed in the trash.

I was not allowed to accept gifts like that from boys....as per my father....so what does my mom do.....buys me one....I was mortified!! Lol! Xoxo

Not sure if that's better or worse than never getting one. Yes, that would be me -- never got one LOL.

Ha I still have mine!

I still have mine too!!! Some things you just can't throw or give away!!!!

Mine came from Gary's too.

And ID bracelets for guys, remember the silver ones...

I have one on now... :)

15 -Toys We Played With

- Cap Rockets
- Bikes
- Bubble Straws
- Click Clacks
- Etch-A-Sketch
- Paddleball
- Pet Rock
- Spaldeen
- Toys
- Yo Yo's
- Tops

Cap Rockets

Anybody remember one of my favorite toys? One of those rockets and a box of caps and you were all set.

Yes, def!! I had a few myself!! Cool!!

I loved them.

We just used to play with the caps. Scraped them with a nail to get that spark!

Remember water rockets? You filled them up with water and then pumped pressure into them until they TOOK OFF! Such fun!

Oh, I loved both of them. Got me started into "Estes" Rocketry!!!

These would be "Outlawed" today. OOOH, waaay toooo Dangerous. LOL Like Lawn Darts. Just get out of the way STUPID!!!

I forgot about these. What memories.

ooooooooooooooohhh damn!!!!! I had those!!!! Now ill show my kids and I bet they'll start laughing,

And the cap guns to go along with them... those were fun days.

I see them every so often and buy one just because...there might be a neighborhood kid that needs to know how to have fun without a "gameboy"...

They were great. I had totally forgotten about them.

Also had totally forgotten about them....Wow! The memories...

Loved playing with those.

Had not thought about them for yrs. Thanks for the memory.

I haven't thought about these in years as well. They were fun. Loved the smell.

The best thing was taking a roll of caps and hitting the caps with a rock. I completely forgot about those cap rockets. I also had in my arsenal a tin cap gun.

Bought them at the candy store.

Thanks for the reminder.

You could put three or four caps in them for a bigger bang!

We used to stuff these full as possible! What great simple fun.

Had a lot of fun with those!

Wow, loved them.

OMG..I remember those.

Wow, now that's a great memory. I also remember the smell after the caps went off.

Who remembers taking rocks and rubbing them on paper gun caps and watching the flames come out from them? The smell was awesome!

Did it all the time. We actually made a game out of it by throwing rocks and seeing who got the most to go off.

Were we trying to get high on that smell? I remember it too.

Yup.

Bikes

For a young kid, you weren't cool unless you had a fun bike. But most importantly, it had to make noise. Also, as we grew up the bikes got bigger and we were able to go further...Banana seats and English racers.

Stingray bikes with the banana seats and slicks on the back to leave skid marks.

And let's not forget the cards in the wheels for sound affect.

We could have made a lot of money with all those ruined baseball cards. Had we known .lol.

I'd like to put an old Topps Baseball card in the spokes of my bike with one of my mothers clothes pins and ride around the block, imagining I was on a motorcycle cruising down some highway like I used to do as a kid. Back then our imaginations were our best possession.

And what about the streamers from the ends of the handlebars!

Sting Ray Bike...This bike looked awesome.

Schwinn Sting Ray! Yeah baby!

The wide monkey bar handle grips.

Mine was stolen when I was a teen, about 14. Ran in to get a soda, and when I came out it was gone forever. I never even told my parents as I was afraid they'd yell at me for being a fool for leaving it unattended.

That was your bike? Sorry but I did get a lot of use out of it if its any consolation.

I also had a siren on my bike. I would pull the chain and it would rub against the rim to spin the siren.

The longest ride for me was riding down Ocean ave to the Brighton beach. Loved the bike trail could ride for blocks with no hands...

The Banana seats were good for giving a friend a ride. I didn't like to put anyone on the handlebars because you couldn't see where the hell you were going.

Remember the basket in the front ha ha ha ha...

No basket. I was way too cool for the basket.

On the smaller bikes you would ride a friend on your handlebars and one on the back.

Yea and when we got older you could try to seat 4 on English racer. One on the handle bars, one on the crossbar, one on the seat, and another on the back.. And he could stand on the wheel nuts.

I used to zip all over Brooklyn on my bike. If I only had that energy now.

Gotta get some balloons and tie them on the wheel frame so they rub against the spokes...sounds like a motorcycle...now you're cruisin'!

I played Evel Kenevel a lot jumping over garbage cans and trashing a lot of bikes...

Spent lots of time down the old sani looking for bike parts to make choppers...

What about riding around Prospect Park...or riding down suicide hill on a bike.

I remember the long sissy bar that you attached to the back of the bike too....it came up real high.

We did many crazy and dangerous things in our youth and most of them were done with the bicycle.

Riding around all day was a great adventure just to get out of the neighborhood and visiting other crowds.

Sometimes we got jumped for our bikes a lot of times in Prospect Park.

Yes the bike was our first form of independent transportation.

I use to ride all the way down to Coney Island. Ocean Ave way, sometimes no hands for blocks at a time till I fell! HA.

Yea riding on the handlebars.

Remember all the types of handle bars.

Then the baskets to deliver the papers in the morn.

What about the pegs that screwed onto the back axles so your friend can hitch a ride and not have to sit on your seat?

Remember when we use to pimp our rides adding extra forks on the front to turn them into choppers?

Guys I use to love to rob your bikes I was too lazy to make my own and we were poor. Sorry.

What about all the different types of lights and horns and bells...oh forgot the reflector so we didn't get run over at night.

Then came the banana seat bikes with the low back or the high back like a real chopper.

I use to ride to the 69th st pier to fish and also to Shore Rd, and ride the trail for miles under the Verrazano.

Popping Wheelies all day.

Riding all through Prospect Park, all the hills and all the bumps and bruises those hill would bring when you fell.

I ran into quite a few cars in my days.

And I, my friend, have been run into by a few cars-- and once I was following one down 6th st; he was going fast and so was I; he hit the brake and I went flying over him, and I live today to tell the story.

I know everyone's hero at the time was Evel Knievel. I used to set up the garbage cans and try to jump just a little bit more and more each time.

The worst: when you got a flat and had to go through all that to try and fix it.

Bubble Straws

Do you remember Bubble Plastic...

Plastic Bubbles? The stuff that came in a tube w/a straw to blow the bubbles?

The answer is YES! Loved the smell of them & loved chewing on them, after the bubble was deflated!

Yes Plastic Bubble.

I remember it well. Squeezing the stuff out of the tube and twisting it around the tip of the 'blow' tube just right to get it to work.

Surely do...putting the plastic on the tip of the straw or tube and blowing the bubbles; wow, blast from the past.

I loved the way they smelled too, probably toxic?!

Wow, almost forgot these. Never allowed today. Looked it up, it was liquid plastic dissolved in acetone. That's what made it smell so good (at least to me). I guess we survived.

Same with model airplane glue. No restriction on purchasing it back then, and now it is a different formula.

Click Clacks

Yes - my son has them - almost hit myself in the head showing him how to use them LMAO.

Sure those weren't Nunn-chuks!!?? LOL ;-)

That was funny.

Blue. Balls?...Never mind.

I own a set of these, but they're new.

Yep! Remember the little "chips" that flew off the "cheap" ones. Very noisy at times.

I AM THE QUEEN CLIK CLAKER.

Didn't these things get banned cause too many kids were losing eyes & cracking others Skulls!! LOL, guess that was an URBAN LEGEND!!

They were banned at PS 307...

My wife still has her original Clik-Claks.

I never had a problem with clicking......clacking not so much........8>)

Great set of weapons...never left home with out em lol lol lol!

393

Oh my God!!! Who's got the blue balls???

I wanted them so bad when I was a kid my mom said I would take my eye out lol.

You bet!!

Etch-A-Sketch

Definitely remember. Also remember that the Etch-A-Sketch didn't "like" being "mishandled." They weren't very sturdy.

You would know what I mean if you remember your fingers/hands/your lap, made you look like you were the Tin Man from the Wizard of Oz. Silver EVERYWHERE.

And you left a "trail" (door knobs/doors, windows, other toys, books, footprints...you name it) where ever you went. LOL.

What was that stuff, was it real lead?

Paddle Ball

Oh yeah. I just loved bouncing that ball between the paddle and my face. Or if the rubber string wrapped around my neck, the back of my head. I loved stompin' them into the sidewalk, and I was really good at throwing them over the roof too. Ah...the memories.

Someone made a joke once, You get this toy as a gift, you play with it a while, then the rubber band breaks and you break something in the house, then the same person who gave you the gift is hitting you with the paddle.

Pet Rock

Get a pet rock....sold millions of them.

I had one of these too.

Never got one. R U kiddin' me. Get real!

My old childhood friend......lol!!!!!

I have one of those I created; It was my pet Rockman had it since '77 sits on my desk...

I can't believe the creator became a millionaire because of this idea.

I didn't have 1 I had the one called Rock Concert.

I remember those ... I think I had one LOL.

Yes, I remember these! Adorable...

OMG- i just took my stuff out of storage - dusted this off it's on my dresser right now - wow!

OH I HAD ONE OF THOSE!

Oh my, I have one of those... :)

We had a huge pet rock on 5th st. We stole it from one of those entrances going into Prospect Park.

And no pooper scooping. :)

33 years and never ever stepped in it once. :) But I did drop him on his head a few times...but he's like me, we both have a head as hard as a rock. :> <:

I'm sorry to hear that you have so few friends. LOL.

It may be my only friend, but it stuck by me thru thick and thin!

Spaldeens

Spaldeens

pink and supple.

strong and bouncy.

like its users!

Street Spaldings. Kinda tricky. But that's how it's spelled.

You spelled it just like we all said it....to this day only people from Park Slope know what I'm talking about when I say Spaldeen.

It's true, nobody I know ever collected on the chips call!

Remember how they split? I remember putting one on my neck, pressed it down and it gave me a fake hickey. I had explaining to do!!! OM, the memories!

Or putting it on your elbow and straightening it out.

They actually use a similar technique in acupuncture!

LOL...I forgot all about that.

A kid from Brooklyn probably came up with that idea!! LMAO!!

Cross the avenues on 10th st and 6th tracking them down and snagging them.

Those sky high pops were hard to keep track of, coming down at ya they would waver from side to side.

Interesting that we all learned how to hit that "Spaldeen" straight when playing stick ball. You would get a lot of shit for putting one up on a roof. Wow, to go back to those days, again! In a heartbeat!

Big for us was roofing a "Spaldeen" from home plate on the 14th street side of PS 124's schoolyard over 219 - 13th street - that was a 5 story apartment building ... that was some shot!! We called it an "Automatic." Nobody caught shit for putting one over that roof. We were in awe!! I think I saw that only two or three times.

The best was being able to hit it into the 39's School yard on 8th and 6th.

Did that more than a few times.

We were able to play so many games with one ball, off the point, Kings, hit the stick (with a Popsicle stick or dime), asses up, slap ball, hand ball.

We all knew it said spalding on the ball. But somehow "spaldeen" just fit. I remember taking a half a spaldeen when it split and putting it on my elbow to see if it would stay on when I bent my arm down. Ouch! I was never without my spaldeen. Does anyone remember how much they cost at Danny's?

Spaldeeeens!!! Hand ball, or roofing!

As long as the spaldeen didn't get roofed...You could play all day!!

Very nice! How I remember how a new, tight spaldeen was all you needed for an entire day's fun. No duds allowed!

You had to squeeze a few to get a good one, lol.

Did you know you can still buy them? I'm holding one right now, that I bought just this morn.

Did you test them all for the highest bounce?

"No duds allowed!"

ALWAYS had to TEST for BOUNCABILITY!!

Had to bounce a few of them, to make sure you got the best one...

As for testing you would grab a few out of the batch, hold them both at the same height and drop them, that would be repeated a few times, where the highest bouncer would make the sale.

Hated those sponge balls. Couldn't play stick ball with them.

397

Yeah, they were lousy!

All of those spaldeens rolling into the sewers before we had time to catch them!

Most Ended Up On Roofs...I Loved Going Up & Finding A Few Free GOOD ones!

We always roofed them on 13th street atop the Ansonia clock factory, but went up to get them. I also sell these at my store.

And that's when we had to take the sewer covers off and hold some one by the feet and hope they didn't slip, and that someone was usually 98 LB ME!

LOL! What we'd do for a spaldeen!

That's funny I picked up a new spaldine when I was back in The Slope this past March. They look exactly the same. I squeezed a few to make sure it was a good one. Didn't want to bring back a "dud" home. Don't tell anyone, but they made for a good "cheat sheet" during exams. You wrote the answer & past the ball while the teacher wasn't looking. I was good. Never got caught. Ha, Ha !

A Wooden Broom Stick, A Spaldini & 10 Kids=A Stick ball Game. Priceless Times In Bklyn.

Probably the best thing kids of our generation ever had and used. Cheap, fun and could play all day with one. The most versatile toy ever. I've used a spaldeen to play dozens of games. Remember when everyone chipped in to play stick ball?

Everyone took a turn looking over the ball. Like it was a piece of gold. The most fun for under a buck. Now I'll spend hundreds of dollars on my kids stuff and they will never know the joy or simplicity of a Spaldeen and what could be done with one. Its sad when I think of it.

The best! I wish my kids could have experienced what I did growing up in Brooklyn. There was nothing else like it! I loved my Spaldeen(s) too! I wonder how many I bought in all those years as a kid!

Hit em too hard & they would split (probably cause Danny's would let them BAKE in window!!)

Loved checking the rooftops occasionally, used to find some really good ones.

They were also good for hand ball.

This was a staple in my toy box!

Stoop ball, Kings, Poison Ball, stick ball. This was the all sport ball. Not uncommon to be standing there bored shooting hoops with it either.

What could keep you busy for hours on end? How many different games could you play?

Endless handball games...

Remember the line of 5 people playing kings against the wall.

Toys

I could play the card game War for hours on the beach.

The best "toys" we had as kids were the appliance boxes and the absolute best of those were the refrigerator boxes. We made everything out of them - - clubhouses, slides, tunnels ..... whatever. It was great!

Frig boxes, great clubhouses. Help up in the rain pretty good too. Loved it.

I loved when they started putting "landing gear" (and takeoff) on them wooden planes.

"Jacks." I can't picture any of today's kids playing that.

Believe it or not, my mom was the best with jacks. She was best I ever saw. I was amazed to watch her play. I think she "retired" undefeated. LOL.

Jacks was one of my favorites!!

Like Lou Costello, even I "played" (tried, all thumbs) jacks and ball, all over the place. Found the jacks fairly easy. Usually at the bottom of my feet. Ouch!

Jacks were awesome! Remember the first time you got "twelvsies?"

The metal (probably lead) jacks were the best because they had a bit of weight to them and stayed "put" when they landed. I loved jacks!

Loved Jacks and loved humazoos.

Yazoo!

Played w/Barbies for hours.

Matchbox & Hot Wheels car collections!! Great fun!!

Wow. Hot Wheels! The best and the Fastest.

Aurora HO slot cars!

Oh Yeah. Thanks Mark, I forgot about those. Loved 'em

Battleship via Walkie-Talkies late at night was a rip.

I loved my slot cars They were great

Brisk on the stoop.

Building models, Darts...at The Gaslight and Ryans...

Rockem Sockem Robots!

How about Pogo Sticks, are they still around? I used to love them.

400

Yo-Yos

Remembering Duncan yo-yos-'s

Tommy Smothers of the Smothers Brothers is a world champion yo-yo'er.

Boy do I remember them. Kinda went into a "relapse" when the new "High Tech" yo-yo's came out. Ball-bearings, adjustable tension, LED lights and sounds. High tech synthetic materials or aluminum, etc. Like Yomega, Da-Bomb, etc. You can literally spend over $100 for some. Crazy but true. Still love dem ol' Duncans. And tops too.

BY WHAMO!!" I had a Butterfly! & several Imperials I believe they were called!!

Yes, Imperial is right. I don't have any of the original Duncans, but I do have a Da'bomb,and a good supply of Yomega strings, bearings and oil. I still play with it once in a while. Lots of fun.

Yep butterfly.

Tried to get my kids interested in yo-yos once (didn't happen).

I loved them and all the tricks. Never quite mastered around the world.

Nah me either but I TRIED.

How about walkin' the Dog!!

Hah...tried that also. Remember it all well though!! Walking the tangle line was more like it.

I remember Duncan tops and Yo Yo's, Was good at both.

Tried and accomplished most of these tricks, seems like an innocent sport until you get knocked in the head with one! While you're taking a trip around the world, gone out of control...

<u>Tops</u>

Find a top and wind it up and all the day you'll have some fun, that is if you can first learn how to spin it...

Another lost toy.

Winding, winding, winding the string & Let em RIP!! LOL!! Thx !!

Remember the lazy boy's top....WIZZZER

"Lost" but not forgotten. I played so much with those things.

I was chipping little holes on the tile floor on the front patio, at our house. Never forget.

The best killer tops were the cheap ones with a sharp metal tip. You would throw that bad boy over hand deadly.

Betcha did!! LMAO!!

My brother wrecked both his front teeth with a top.

And then my other brother broke his two front teeth with a Yo Yo.

Let's play CRACK THE TOP.

I picked one of these tops up recently at a flea market. I was quite surprised when I spun it on the first throw!!! Not bad considering the last time I played with one...35 yrs ago?

We also had a few of the whistling tops...lol.

OH MAN, I forgot about these. I have to go buy one.

For hours and hours - then they had the bigger plastic ones and the little hard pointy ones would make them crack...great!!

I remember playing "war" with tops. Odds or Evens. You lose, you lay yours down and you try to hit and crack theirs.

I remember WAR!! Not tawkin the Group either!! LOL!!

The cheap tops with the point that looked like a nail were the best. Throw them overhand and kick the shit out of Duncan whistler which were like fat, slow ships.

Hey, I found one at a flea market and gave it a try, showed the kids a few tricks, fun. Now it's a decoration on the shelf and every time I look at it, I remember.

16 -Transportation

- 7th and 4th Ave. Trains
- Penny Gum Machine on Train
- Bus B77 B69 B63 B67
- First Car

7th And 4th Ave. Trains

This 9th St.-7th Ave.station always reminds me of a scene from the movie *Beat Street*!

Or *The Warriors*!

Shot a few movies & music videos there. A great spot to film something.

Yup, I walk through it every night on my way home from work.

I remember once in the early 80s, my friend and I were down there throwing light bulbs to hear the echo. We got caught by a cop who was hiding around the corner from the stairway that leads to 7th Ave. He took us home, and boy my mother didn't like that shit, LOL.

7th Ave.station. It reminds me of the Atlantic Ave., Nevins St. or Pacific St. stations downtown. When you got off Pacific St. you had to walk through all of these other stations to get to the Atlantic Ave. LIRR.

Ah yes, it's coming back to me now. Could you also enter the subway from 8th Ave.? Don't recall being able to do that.

We used to slide under the turnstiles when they were real close to the floor on 8th Ave.-9th Street. :)

The 7th Ave. station had a transit police station right there.

Remember it was the RR?

Double R, also the 4th Ave. local.

Yes, going back in time it was the RR. I took the RR to work every single day. Great time in my life.

Remember those days going to work, meeting at the 4th Ave. station for the RR?

I remember like it was yesterday! Only it was 40 years ago, ha.

As a kid I thought that was the "only" train. RR = railroad, LOL. Except when we went to Coney Island, confused? No, excited!! Who gave a damn?! Remember, there used to be multiple subway companies. IRT, BMT, IND, etc.

The B was the west end, the N train was the Sea Beach. I think the F was the 6th Ave. express. Remember the G train at Smith and 9th Street?

404

Yep, I remember falling asleep on the RR a few times and ending up @ the 95th Street station.

Good thing it wasn't the other "end of the line"...

The Rock and Roll to 95th...

Gotta love the RR underground on 4th Ave. and the B63 above-ground on 5th Ave.

That's an oldie but goodie...heard that many times.

The "Slow Boat to China"...LOL!

Yep..."The Slow boat to China."

It doesn't sound like a bad trip, lol.

There's no more RR?

Same train; just the "R" now...

Why'd they take one back...recession?

In May 1985, double letters on trains were eliminated in NYC.

Or falling asleep in Bay Ridge late on a Fri. or Sat. night, either waiting for the train or on it.

I've seen more train stations than I would like to remember.

RR and F were my trains. I remember when the F was once the D train. Anyone remember that far back? I also remember cane seats and open ceiling fan trains in the early 60s.

I remember the cane seats and fans! Man, I guess I'm getting old. The fare was a dime, but my mom always pushed me under the turnstile and said I was under 6 years old. We used to take the D train to Coney Island.

I also remember falling asleep on the RR when I got on at Union Street; when I woke up we were at Union Street again. Didn't realize I went to 95th Street and back until we got to Dekalb.

LOL, my mom used to push us kids under too—we used to take the D train from Prospect Park out to Coney Island and stay all day at the beach.

You know you're from Park Slope if you cut through the subway station to walk from Seventh Ave. to Eighth Ave. on Ninth Street to avoid the rain.

Remember when people would not tell you the actual train number or letter, but say take the IRT or IND, and you just knew which one was which?

No air conditioning? Back in the day, you were lucky the fans were working...LOL.

OMG!! Those were the days you WANTED to walk to Manhattan!!

I was little, and my mom would always dress me to go on a train trip. Snagged a few tights on those broken down cane seats.

I don't even remember the fans...

I remember that in the 80s they were still using those cars on the CC and GG lines. LOL.

I remember losing a layer or two of skin on my legs in the summer on the hot rattan seats. I remember the fans, and the hot, stinky air they swirled around. PUUUUUU. LOL.

Remember, these—probably circa '64—used to stick to ya if you were wearing shorts in summertime!! Probably lasted til the mid 60s on some lines!! They were probably comfy when they were new.

I remember some having red leather seats, too, nice and soft. You didn't get stuck with the straw seats.

406

My favorite ride was on the F train all the way to Coney Island.

Heat blew out from under the seats—in the summer!

Ever get stuck in the "old turnstile?"

I hated those things. They still have them at the 9th St. R station.

But how many times did you smush multiple friends into the outdoor one in Sheepshead Bay that was unmanned, on the way back from Manhattan Beach?!

Used to slide under the thing. We were all skinny brats.

Yes, I remember being able to slip under those things. I also remember getting stuck with a bunch of us, and asking some guy for help and he just shook his head and walked away.

Yup, got stuck on 7th & 9th. Four of us with coolers, umbrellas and chairs on our way to Coney Island. Cops had to push us thru. A train came at that moment and we ran!

Penny Gum Machine

Ahhhh...sweet memories...the vending machines were the best. I remember when I always looked forward to buying a bottle of Coke and a candy bar from the vending machines...oh, and the Chiclets, too.

Anyone remember the little sticks of gum from the machines in the subways?! I think they cost a penny (the silly things we remember!!).

Gum in the subway; gimme a penny.

I remember the vending machines; vandalism in the early seventies removed their profitability and forced their removal.

Mr. Dee Lish.

OMG, who could even guess how old that gum in there might have been!

I remember those, in the train station when my family would go out. I always had a penny.

I remember, too!

I remember the gum machines! Was always hesitant to buy them, since I didn't know how long they were in the machines.

I also remember some stations having a vending machine that dispensed ice cream. Does anyone else remember that?

I remember the soda & candy, too.

My dad always had these gums for me when he'd come home from work.

I think a lot of dads did. Especially those purple mints.

Loved the tutti frutti gum in the machine.

Loved Chiclets and Juicy Fruit (when I loved sugared gum).

I recall those machines. Lost some pennies in them as a child, it seemed like the worst thing to happen.

Every once in a while, I look for those machines on eBay. Never buy one, but enjoy seeing them.

How much do they go for?

VINTAGE ADAMS GUM CHICKLETS NYC SUBWAY ORIGINAL MILLS STAINLESS VENDING MACHINE, too much!

I loved Beeman's Pepsin Gum, and it's available here in VT!

OMG, I was just talking about this on the train ride home with my LIRR train friends.

Always bought the Dentyne...

Spearmint Chiclets...hated the taste of Dentyne.

And Chiclets, too...two in a small pack...I sooo loved them.

Little boxes with 2 Chiclets in them...

And Beech Nut gum.

It was Flavor-iffic...

I was always so happy when my mom gave me a penny to put in those machines. Ah, those were the days...simple pleasures!

Those machines were the only place I ever saw those little fat sticks of gum...

Although I remember those silver-colored machines more.

It was a circle with the raised part in the middle from top to bottom, and you gave it a good push to make it work.

I have a rare 1930s ADAMS 1 Penny Gum Vending Wall Mount Machine Subway Station.

They also had chocolates!

BMT Church Ave. Station was partially outdoors...lots of pigeons and penny machines filled with peanuts. My mother always let me feed the pigeons, and it never occurred to me that those peanuts could be eaten by people. Dopey kid! :)

I don't remember the silver machines so much...I do remember the red ones, tho (and the peanuts).

The little boxes with 2 Chiclets were my fave.

Yep...I remember the little peanuts, and other candies, too...

Yep & my first choice was always Juicy Fruit!

What happened to Chiclets? Now they have gum in a blister pack, which they think is new.

Yes, there were two Chiclets in a pack; what a great memory.

Turkish taffy is now being made again by Bonomo. I have not seen it, but it's out there.

None of the old-time candy that is still being produced is the same as it was when we were young. Different manufacturers, different ingredients. Cheap crap. Only the wrappers are the same to make you buy.

OMG, two Chiclets in the small boxes!

Does the Franklin Ave. IRT station still have them?

IDK? But not for a penny. :)

I haven't seen them in any stations anymore.

No vending machines on the subway stations anymore. Muggers used to hide behind them.

B77 Bus B69 B63

The Red Hook Express...only if the bridge ain't up!!

35 cents, I believe.

The change counters on those old buses were fascinating...Ka-Ching...

Yes, they were. With a see-through view, you basically saw the mechanics of the machine. Even when the coins went through, that machine would continue to cling & clang. It's funny that they now have those "donation" machines in numerous public places, where you can see your coins do cool stuff. Those bus machines were way better.

My bus, that ran down Union Street to Red Hook? It ran like every hour. So I knew when to be there.

Union St. House of Pizza and Calzone!

And Mazzola Bakery...best damn lard bread...

You could catch the 77 on 10th Street and 5th Avenue alongside of Kresges 5 & 10? It ran down 9th Street.

The 75 also ran on 9th Street, but split off down around Smith Street and headed toward Cobble Hill, Fulton Street.

That's the one I was thinking of; if you were below 5th Ave. & had to go all the way to Parkside, you had to be careful which bus you boarded, LOL.

Yes, and at Parkside you could catch the bus out to Coney Island...can't recall the bus # though.

The B-68...it was the bus to Grady HS, where I did 6 months...we used to smoke that bus up pretty good at 7 am!

It was the B-68, and it still runs to Coney Island.

Me either...time to check the MTA web site -- ugh that map is a bear to read. You know, back in May, I traveled through Port Authority & I tried to get subway & bus maps. They were nowhere to be found.

Thank you all!

First Cars

What was your first car?

I didn't drive when I lived in the Slope. I lived right around the corner from the F train, and like 3 bus lines!

For me, it was a 1970 Olds Toronado. 455 4 barrel 4500 pound two-door. Front wheel drive, no less.

1970 Buick Skylark 4dr. 350 V8. Gas was cheap then.

1972 new Volkswagen Super Beetle.

1961 Plymouth Fury, push-button transmission. Bought it for 100 bucks. The dashboard would fall on the passenger's lap when you hit a bump.

A 1973 Chevy Vega. The car got totally stripped overnight while parked next to the bar on 13th street and 6th Avenue.

I bought the best car I ever had. A 1978 Olds Cutlass Supreme, burgundy with a white vinyl top. Beautiful inside and out.

I spent many hours hanging out in satellite!! My first car was a Chevy Vega. It ended up in a store front on 15th Street and 7th Avenue. That's a long story.

You mean that I bought? Or that I stole?

I had a very good friend who had a Chevy Vega. It had a "two speed" tranny. I really feel for you, brother. LOL.

One of the problems with cars in NYC was the "where to park and when?" I'm happy that you found a parking spot in that store window. LOL.

Remember when you knew every make and model of cars?

Let's see...what did I have for breakfast?!

I think the Toronado was the first front-wheel drive car made in the US.

No hump; the front floorboard was flat across. Factory 8 track player that worked.

My first car was a 1970 blue Chevy Nova that my mom gave it to me in 1979.

A 1970 Nova, blue as well. Great, dependable car with a 250 In-Line six.

No, guys! Remember, the first front-wheel drive was the horse & carriage. LOL.

No hump, but a lot of bumps.

And I'm sure we all remember working on our cars in the streets of Brooklyn into the night hours.

MG! I freaking loved that little car. Mine was a Chevy Nova; I don't remember the year, but I have pictures. LOL.

Mine was Dad's '68 Plymouth Valiant—ran like a charm.

I remember when I was young, my parents always parked in front of our house (4th btwn 7th & 8th ave). By the time I had a car, you had to search for a spot. Now, you don't have a hope in hell. LOL.

Mine was a beautiful deep blue Ford Pinto. Paid 300 bucks for it in 1982.

1981 Pontiac Firebird, midnight blue gold-speckled paint.

1972 Pontiac Lemans.

Car? In Brooklyn? Alternate side of the street parking! YUCK! :)

Oh Lord--officially mine, and not a borrower from my dad--a '68 really ugly gold Rambler (only 5 years younger than me). It leaked when it rained, and I had to get the water off the floor with a turkey baster (not kidding). But hey, it got me where I needed to go and it was free!!

What about the fake white wall tires? Does anyone remember them? Had to glue them on, ha!

Yeah, for us guys that couldn't afford the real deal...

1984 midnight blue Honda Prelude...loved that car!!

Yes, my first car was an MG Midget. It was British, racing green with tan leather interior! I loved that car. What good memories!

Remember when caddy rims were in hot demand, what ya hadda do to get a set?

'74 silver Dodge Dart Swinger Slant 6—glove compartment popped open over any potholes. A great car.

The good old days...

1968 Chevy Caprice.

'69 Malibu, '73 Dodge Dart Swinger, 78 Mercury Monarch.

Plymouth Fury - it was actually my dad's car, but I drove it too.

Buick Riviera. It was beautiful and it was black.

'69 Ford Torino. Hubby taught me to drive on it on the good old streets of Bklyn.

My first car was a 1973 Maverick I bought new.

My parents never drove, so as a kid we had no car. My first car was a Toyota Corolla which my parents bought. So I spent a lot of time driving them around.

My first car was 1969 Bonnieville Convertible, yellow with a black hood. Then I had a Yellow Dodge Charger '68; after that I had a 1970 Cutlass Supreme White.

Wish I owned my dad's '57 Chevy now.

My first car was a used 1962 Fiat Millecento (1100) with suicide doors. Paid $300 - sold it for $150. Piece of "merde."

'69 Malibu.

Our first car was 1963 Chevy Impala, brand new...candy apple red.

I had a '48 Dodge sedan, and then a '61 Ford Galaxie. Late 60s.

I did not own a car until I left Brooklyn.

In 1969, I bought a baby blue 1962 Mercury Monterey.

'70 Plymouth Satellite V8 318...

'67 GTO Chery SS.

'69 Bonnieville Convertible, back in 1972 when I got out of the Navy...

A '74 Plymouth Valiant and an '82 Mazda 626.

1964 Chevy Nova.

1964 Rambler.

'56 Pontiac; '58 Chevy Impala. Best thing about it, you could buy a used car for 50 dollars and run it until it would not go anymore, and then go buy another used car for that price. Then, they went up to 100 dollars and you would do the same thing. Today, you can't get one tire for that price.

'68 Pontiac Tempest.

The Dodge Dart name is making a comeback.

Wow, really?

'76 Toyota Corolla. Still the best car I have ever owned.

1968 Coronet 440, 1976 Volare station wagon, 1987 Oldsmobile.

'63 T-Bird convertible, '66 Dodge Coronet straight six, '68 Olds 88, '72 Toyota Corolla, '73 Chevy Malibu. I had a lot of accidents!

'73 Chevy Vega.

'69 Camaro with a straight 6 and a power glide transmission.

Never owned a car in Brooklyn. Didn't need it.

'67 Road runner w 326 street hemi.

'66 Beetle and a '78 Chevy Nova.

'57 Chevy, '64 Impala, '67 Mustang.

I remember my brother's first car was a Volkswagen Bug. He had painted it metallic blue, then he grabbed my mother's flower-patterned curtain and laid it over the front of the car and spray painted it white; it was the coolest looking car—that is, until we had to push-start it in the winter months. We had to pop the clutch to get it running so he could give me a lift to I.S. 88. I still remember me and the guys, whoever was around at the time, trying to push it backwards down the street in the snow. '74? It was cold...what fun. Wish I could go back again.

Hope you had fun, and I'm sure we all wish we could go back again and relive some of these great memories that we all shared growing up in Park Slope, Brooklyn, NY in the 50s-80s

Some memories just stay forever...these are some of many... Adios to all my old South Brooklyn friends—yes, that's right; it was always called South Brooklyn in those days. Hats off to our parents, our families and the friends who set the foundation for Park Slope

THE END

Acknowledgments

This book was compiled with a little help from my friends, and with copyediting by Lauren Moccio. If you would like to join in the fun or just keep in touch with us—or to find some of your old friends from Park Slope, Brooklyn—social media is the way to do it. Please visit www.parkslopian.com for links to more memories and pictures of a Brooklyn long past, and the iconic things of yesteryear. I, for one, would love to hear from more of my old friends; how about you?

THEPARKSLOPIAN.COM

The Brooklyn Series

In which neighborhood in Brooklyn did you grow up? Do you
yearn for the good old days? This series of neighborhood books
is the closest you'll get to reliving the past—or, if you're not
from Brooklyn, experiencing the fun, the excitement and the
tragedies, right from the memories of the kids and the parents
who lived there during the fascinating middle of the twentieth
century. These books walk you through the various
neighborhoods in classic 1950s through 1980s Brooklyn,
detailing the iconic things of our time. From the doctors who
delivered us to the schools from which we graduated, from the
playgrounds and parks in which we played to the street games we
made up by ourselves, from all the great toys we had that have
since been replaced by sharper technology, our first bikes to our
first cars—we remember it all. Take a trip down memory lane
with these coffee table books, written in an enjoyable, accessible,
social media style. Revisit all the best places we ate; remember
all the silly slang and the nonsensical stuff we used to say. As
with every passing generation, we cling to the things that defined
our youth. However, we who grew up in the fifties through the
eighties experienced some of the most timeless pop culture in
history, and this extraordinary series will allow you to share that
with your children using a language they understand: social
media. Remember your youth and pass on your favorite
memories to your loved ones, one page at a time. Visit
www.parkslopian.com to be updated as to when the next book is
done. Will your neighborhood be next?